THEOSOPHICAL
ARTICLES AND NOTES

found that I believed in caste as a religious necessity no more than in the palm-tree yielding mangoes. I saw that, if it were not for this distinction, India would not have been so degraded, for this distinction engendered hatred among her sons. It made them hate and quarrel with one another. The peace of the land was disturbed. People could not unite with one another for good purposes. They waged war with one another, instead of devoting all their combined energies to the cause of ameliorating the condition of the country. The foundation of immorality was thus laid, until it has reached now so low a point that, unless this mischief is stopped, the tottering pillars of India will soon give way. I do not by this mean to blame my ancestors who originally instituted this system. To me their object seems to be quite a different one. It was based in my opinion on the qualities of every person. The caste was not then hereditary as it is now. This will be seen from the various ancient sacred books which are full of instances in which Kshatriyas and even Máhárs and Chámbhárs, who are considered the lowest of all, were not only made and regarded as Brahmins, but almost worshipped as demi-gods simply for their qualities. If such is the case, why should we still stick to that custom which we now find not only impracticable but injurious? I again saw that, if I were to observe outwardly what I did not really believe inwardly, I was practising hypocrisy. I found that I was thus making myself a slave, by not enjoying the freedom of conscience. I was thus acting immorally. But Theosophy had taught me that to enjoy peace of mind and self-respect, I must be honest, candid, peaceful and regard all men as equally my brothers, irrespective of caste, colour, race or creed. This, I see, is an essential part of religion. I must try to put these theoretical problems into practice. These are the convictions that finally hurried me out of my caste.

I would at the same time ask my fellow countrymen, who are of my opinion, to come out boldly for their country. I understand the apparent sacrifices one is required to make in adopting such a course, for I myself had to make them, but these are sacrifices only in the eyes of one who has regard for this world of matter. When a man has once extricated himself from this regard and when the sense of the duty he owes to his country and to himself reigns paramount in his heart, these are no sacrifices at all for him. Let us, therefore, leave off this distinction which separates us from one another, join in one common accord, and combine all our energies for the good of our country. Let us feel that we are Aryans, and prove ourselves worthy of our ancestors. I may be told that I am making a foolish and useless sacrifice; that I cut myself off from all social intercourse and even risk losing the decent disposal of my body by those upon whom our customs impose that duty; and that none but a visionary would imagine that he, even though chiefest among Brahmins, could restore his country's greatness and the enlightenment of a whole nation, so great as ours. But these are the arguments of selfishness and moral cowardice. Single men have saved nations before, and though my vanity does not make me even dream that so glorious a result is within my humble grasp, yet a good example is never valueless, and it can be set even by the most insignificant. Certain it is that, without examples and self-sacrifices, there can be no reform. The world, as I see it, imposes on me a duty, and I think the most powerful and the only permanent cause of happiness is the consciousness that I am trying to do that duty.

I wish it understood—in case what has preceded has not made this perfectly clear—that I have neither become a Materialist nor a Christian. I am an Aryan in religion as all else, follow the Ved, and believe it to be the parent of all religions among men. As Theosophy explains the secondary human religions, so does it make plain the meaning of the Ved. The teachings of the Rishis acquire a new splendour and majesty, and I revere them a hundred times more than ever before.

DAMODAR K. MAVALANKAR

Theosophist, May, 1880

ISBN 0-938998-29-3

FOREWORD

The articles in this volume come from a variety of sources. They are presented here for their intrinsic worth to students of Theosophy. They are grouped according to the place of first appearance —in the *Theosophist, Lucifer,* the *Path,* and other sources. Within these groupings they are arranged chronologically. Internal evidence strongly suggests that some of them have an "adept" origin, and they are so presented. One or two articles unintentionally omitted from *Theosophical Articles* by H.P.B. and W.Q.J. are included. Other contributions, not identified as to author, are of a quality which makes it appropriate to reprint them here. Thus there are articles, replies and notes which appeared in the *Theosophist* and *Lucifer,* also material by Damodar K. Mavalankar, and two articles signed "Murdhna Joti" from the *Path.* Cicero's "Vision of Scipio" is included by reason of H.P.B.'s briefly informative footnotes. Judge's "Notes on the Bhagavad Gita" is a *Path* article which was not a part of the book of that name. Finally, there is material taken from A.P. Sinnett's *The Occult World,* from the notes of Robert Bowen, a pupil of H.P.B., and also from notes found in the effects of Countess Wachtmeister, apparently taken down from dictation by H.P.B.

The value of the writings here presented will be self-evident to Theosophical students and readers.

The Editors

CASTES IN INDIA

NO man of sincerity and moral courage can read **Mr. G. C. Whitworth's** Profession of Faith, as reviewed in the April *Theosophist,* without feeling himself challenged to be worthy of the respect of one who professes such honourable sentiments. I, too, am called upon to make my statement of personal belief. It is due to my family and caste-fellows that they should know why I have deliberately abandoned my caste and other worldly considerations. If, henceforth, there is to be a chasm between them and myself, I owe it to myself to declare that this alienation is of my own choosing, and I am not cut off for bad conduct. I would be glad to take with me, if possible, into my new career, the affectionate good wishes of my kinsmen. But, if this cannot be done, I must bear their displeasure, as I may, for I am obeying a paramount conviction of duty.

I was born in the family of the Karháda Maháráshtra caste of Brahmins, as my surname will indicate. My father carefully educated me in the tenets of our religion, and, in addition, gave me every facility for acquiring an English education. From the age of ten until I was about fourteen, I was very much exercised in mind upon the subject of religion and devoted myself with great ardour to our orthodox religious practices. Then my ritualistic observances were crowded aside by my scholastic studies, but, until about nine months ago, my religious thoughts and aspirations were entirely unchanged. At this time, I had the inestimable good fortune to read "Isis Unveiled; a Key to the Mysteries of Ancient and Modern Religion and Science," and to join the Theosophical Society. It is no exaggeration to say that I have been a really living man only these few months; for between life as it appears to me now and life as I comprehended it before, there is an unfathomable abyss. I feel that now for the first time I have a glimpse of what man and life are—the nature and powers of the one, the possibilities, duties, and joys of the other. Before, though ardently ritualistic, I was not really enjoying happiness and peace of mind. I simply practised my religion without understanding it. The world bore just as hard upon me as upon others, and I could get no clear

FROM "THE PATH"

OTHER SOURCES

ARTICLES FROM "THE THEOSOPHIST"

CASTES IN INDIA

NO man of sincerity and moral courage can read Mr. G. C. Whitworth's Profession of Faith, as reviewed in the April *Theosophist,* without feeling himself challenged to be worthy of the respect of one who professes such honourable sentiments. I, too, am called upon to make my statement of personal belief. It is due to my family and caste-fellows that they should know why I have deliberately abandoned my caste and other worldly considerations. If, henceforth, there is to be a chasm between them and myself, I owe it to myself to declare that this alienation is of my own choosing, and I am not cut off for bad conduct. I would be glad to take with me, if possible, into my new career, the affectionate good wishes of my kinsmen. But, if this cannot be done, I must bear their displeasure, as I may, for I am obeying a paramount conviction of duty.

I was born in the family of the Karháda Maháráshtra caste of Brahmins, as my surname will indicate. My father carefully educated me in the tenets of our religion, and, in addition, gave me every facility for acquiring an English education. From the age of ten until I was about fourteen, I was very much exercised in mind upon the subject of religion and devoted myself with great ardour to our orthodox religious practices. Then my ritualistic observances were crowded aside by my scholastic studies, but, until about nine months ago, my religious thoughts and aspirations were entirely unchanged. At this time, I had the inestimable good fortune to read "Isis Unveiled; a Key to the Mysteries of Ancient and Modern Religion and Science," and to join the Theosophical Society. It is no exaggeration to say that I have been a really living man only these few months; for between life as it appears to me now and life as I comprehended it before, there is an unfathomable abyss. I feel that now for the first time I have a glimpse of what man and life are—the nature and powers of the one, the possibilities, duties, and joys of the other. Before, though ardently ritualistic, I was not really enjoying happiness and peace of mind. I simply practised my religion without understanding it. The world bore just as hard upon me as upon others, and I could get no clear view of the future. The only real thing to me seemed the day's routine; at best the horizon before me extended only to the rounding of a busy life with the burning of my body and the obsequial ceremonies rendered to me by friends. My aspirations were only for more Zamindáries, social position and the gratification of whims and appetites. But my later reading and thinking have shown me that all these are but the vapours of a dream and that he only is worthy of being called man, who has made caprice his slave and the perfection of his spiritual self a grand object of his efforts. As I could not enjoy these convictions and my freedom of action within my caste, I am stepping outside it.

In making this profession, let it be understood that I have taken this step, not because I am a Theosophist, but because in studying Theosophy I have learnt and heard of the ancient splendour and glory of my country—the highly esteemed land of Aryávarta. Joining the Theosophical Society does not interfere with the social, political, or religious relations of any person. All have an equal right in the Society to hold their opinions. So far from persuading me to do what I have, Mme. Blavatsky and Col. Olcott have strongly urged me to wait until some future time, when I might have had ampler time to reflect. But the glimpse I have got into the former greatness of my country makes me feel sadly for her degeneration. I feel it, therefore, my bounden duty to devote all my humble powers to her restoration. Besides, histories of various nations furnish to us many examples of young persons having given up everything for the sake of their country and having ultimately succeeded in gaining their aims. Without patriots, no country can rise. This feeling of patriotism by degrees grew so strong in me that it has now prepared my mind to stamp every personal consideration under my feet for the sake of my motherland. In this, I am neither a revolutionist nor a politician, but simply an advocate of good morals and principles as practised in ancient times. The study of Theosophy has thrown a light over me in regard to my country, my religion, my duty. I have become a better Aryan than I ever was. I have similarly heard my Parsi brothers say that they have been better Zoroastrians since they joined the Theosophical Society. I have also seen the Buddhists write often to the Society that the study of Theosophy has enabled them to appreciate their religion the more. And thus this study makes every man respect his religion the more. It furnishes to him a sight that can pierce through the dead letter and see clearly the spirit. He can read all his religious books between the lines. If we view all the religions in their popular sense, they appear strongly antagonistic to each other in various details. None agrees with the other. And yet representatives of those faiths say that the study of Theosophy explains to them all that has been said in their religion and makes them feel a greater respect for it. There must, therefore, be one common ground on which all the religious systems are built. And this ground, which lies at the bottom of all, is truth. There can be but one absolute truth, but different persons have different perceptions of that truth. And this truth is morality. If we separate the dogmas that cling to the principles set forth in any religion, we shall find that morality is preached in every one of them. By religion I do not mean all the minor sects that prevail to an innumerable extent all over the world, but the principal ones from which have sprung up these different sects. It is, therefore, proper for every person to abide by the principles of morality. And, according to them, I consider it every man's duty to do what he can to make the world better and happier. This can proceed from a love for humanity. But how can a man love the whole of humanity if he has no love for his country-men? Can he love the whole, who does not love a part? If I, there-fore, wish to place my humble services at the disposal of the world, I must first begin by working for my country. And this I could not do by remaining in my caste. I found that, instead of a love for his countrymen, the observance of caste distinction leads one to hate even his neighbour, because he happens to be of another caste. I could not bear this injustice. What fault is it of any one that he is born in a particular caste? I respect a man for his qualities and not for his birth. That is to say, that man is superior in my eyes, whose *inner* man has been developed or is in the state of development. This body, wealth, friends, relations and all other worldly enjoyments, that men hold near and dear to their hearts, are to pass away sooner or later. But the record of our actions is ever to remain to be handed down from generation to generation. Our actions must, therefore, be such as will make us worthy of our existence in this world, as long as we are here as well as after death. I could not do this by observing the customs of caste. It made me selfish and unmindful of the requirements of my fellow-brothers. I weighed all these circumstances in my mind, and found that I believed in caste as a religious necessity no more than in the palm-tree yielding mangoes. I saw that, if it were not for this distinction, India would not have been so degraded, for this distinction engendered hatred among her sons. It made them hate and quarrel with one another. The peace of the land was disturbed. People could not unite with one another for good purposes. They waged war with one another, instead of devoting all their combined energies to the cause of ameliorating the condition of the country. The foundation of immorality was thus laid, until it has reached now so low a point that, unless this mischief is stopped, the tottering pillars of India will soon give way. I do not by this mean to blame my ancestors who originally instituted this system. To me their object seems to be quite a different one. It was based in my opinion on the qualities of every person. The caste was not then hereditary as it is now. This will be seen from the various ancient sacred books which are full of instances in which Kshatriyas and even Máhárs and Chámbhárs, who are considered the lowest of all, were not only made and regarded as Brahmins, but almost worshipped as demi-gods simply for their qualities. If such is the case, why should we still stick to that custom which we now find not only impracticable but injurious? I again saw that, if I were to observe outwardly what I did not really believe inwardly, I was practising hypocrisy. I found that I was thus making myself a slave, by not enjoying the freedom of conscience. I was thus acting immorally. But Theosophy had taught me that to enjoy peace of mind and self-respect, I must be honest, candid, peaceful and regard all men as equally my brothers, irrespective of caste, colour, race or creed. This, I see, is an essential part of religion. I must try to put these theoretical problems into practice. These are the convictions that finally hurried me out of my caste.

I would at the same time ask my fellow countrymen, who are of my opinion, to come out boldly for their country. I understand the apparent sacrifices one is required to make in adopting such a course, for I myself had to make them, but these are sacrifices only in the eyes of one who has regard for this world of matter. When a man has once extricated himself from this regard and when the sense of the duty he owes to his country and to himself reigns paramount in his heart, these are no sacrifices at all for him. Let us, therefore, leave off this distinction which separates us from one another, join in one common accord, and combine all our energies for the good of our country. Let us feel that we are Aryans, and prove ourselves worthy of our ancestors. I may be told that I am making a foolish and useless sacrifice; that I cut myself off from all social intercourse and even risk losing the decent disposal of my body by those upon whom our customs impose that duty; and that none but a visionary would imagine that he, even though chiefest among Brahmins, could restore his country's greatness and the enlightenment of a whole nation, so great as ours. But these are the arguments of selfishness and moral cowardice. Single men have saved nations before, and though my vanity does not make me even dream that so glorious a result is within my humble grasp, yet a good example is never valueless, and it can be set even by the most insignificant. Certain it is that, without examples and self-sacrifices, there can be no reform. The world, as I see it, imposes on me a duty, and I think the most powerful and the only permanent cause of happiness is the consciousness that I am trying to do that duty.

I wish it understood—in case what has preceded has not made this perfectly clear—that I have neither become a Materialist nor a Christian. I am an Aryan in religion as all else, follow the Ved, and believe it to be the parent of all religions among men. As Theosophy explains the secondary human religions, so does it make plain the meaning of the Ved. The teachings of the Rishis acquire a new splendour and majesty, and I revere them a hundred times more than ever before.

Damodar K. Mavalankar

Theosophist, May, 1880

A REPLY TO OUR CRITICS
(Our final answer to several objections.)

IN the ordinary run of daily life speech may be silver, while "silence is gold." With the editors of periodicals devoted to some special object "silence" in certain cases amounts to cowardice and false pretences. Such shall not be our case.

We are perfectly aware of the fact that the simple presence of the word "Spiritualism" on the title-page of our journal, "causes it to lose in the eyes of materialist and sceptic 50 per cent of its value"—for we are repeatedly told so by many of our best friends, some of whom promise us more popularity, hence—an increase of subscribers, would we but take out the "contemptible" term and replace it by some other synonymous in meaning, but less obnoxious phonetically to the general public. That would be acting under *false pretences*. The undisturbed presence of the unpopular word will indicate our reply.

That we did not include "Spiritualism" among the other subjects to which our journal is devoted *"in the hopes that it should do us good service among the Spiritualists"* is proved by the following *fact*:—From the first issue of our *Prospectus* to the present day, subscribers from "Spiritual" quarters have not amounted to four per cent on our subscription list. Yet, to our merriment, we are repeatedly spoken of as "Spiritualists" by the press and—our opponents. Whether really ignorant of, or purposely ignoring our views, they tax us with *belief in Spirits*. Not that we would at all object to the appellation—too many far worthier and wiser persons than we, firmly believing in "Spirits"—but that would be acting under "false pretences" again. And so, we are called a "Spiritualist" by persons who foolishly regard the term as a "brand," while the orthodox Spiritualists, who are well aware that we attribute their phenomena to quite another agency than Spirits, resent our peculiar opinions as an insult to their belief, and in their turn ridicule and oppose us.

This fact alone ought to prove, if anything ever will, that our journal pursues an honest policy. That established for the one and

sole object, namely for the illumination of truth, however unpopular—it has remained throughout, true to its first principle—
that of absolute impartiality. And that as fully answers another
charge, viz., that of publishing views of our correspondents with
which we often do not concur ourselves. "Your journal teems
with articles upholding ridiculous superstitions and absurd ghost-
stories," is the complaint in one letter. "You neglect laying a sufficient stress in your editorials upon the necessity of discrimi-
nation between facts and *error,* and in the selection of the matter
furnished by your contributors," says another. A third one accuses
us of not sufficiently rising "from supposed facts, to principles,
which would prove to our readers in every case the former no
better than fictions." In other words—as we understand it—we
are accused of neglecting scientific *induction?* Our critics may be
right, but neither are we altogether wrong. In the face of the many
crucial and strictly scientific experiments made by our most eminent *savants* it would take a wiser sage than King Solomon
himself, to decide now between *fact* and *fiction.* The query: "What
is Truth?" is more difficult to answer in the nineteenth than in the
first century of our era. The appearance of his "evil genius" to
Brutus in the shape of a monstrous human form, which, entering
his tent in the darkness and silence of night promised to meet him
in the plains of Philippi—was a *fact* to the Roman tyrannicide;
it was but a dream—to his slaves who neither saw nor heard anything on that night. The existence of an antipodal continent and
the heliocentric system were *facts* to Columbus and Galileo years
before they could actually demonstrate them; yet the existence of
America as that of our present solar system was as fiercely denied
several centuries back as the phenomena of spiritualism are now.
Facts existed in the "pre-scientific past," and errors are as thick
as berries in our scientific present. With whom then, is the criterion
of truth to be left? Are we to abandon it to the mercy and judgment of a prejudiced society constantly caught trying to subvert
that which it does not understand; ever seeking to transform *sham*
and *hypocrisy* into synonyms of "propriety" and "respectability?"
Or shall we blindly leave it to modern *exact* Science so called? But
Science has neither said her last word, nor can her various branches
of knowledge rejoice in their qualification of *exact,* but so long as
the hypotheses of yesterday are not upset by the discoveries of
to-day. "Science is atheistic, phantasmagorical, and always in labor
with conjecture. It can never become knowledge *per se.* Not to

know is its climax," says Professor A. Wilder, our New York Vice-President, certainly more of a man of Science himself than many a scientist better known than he is to the world. Moreover, the learned representatives of the Royal Society have as many cherished hobbies, and are as little free of prejudice and preconception as any other mortals. It is perhaps, to religion and her handmaid theology, with her "seventy times seven" sects, each claiming and none proving its right to the claim of truth, that, in our search for it, we ought to humbly turn? One of our severe Christian Areopagites actually expresses the fear that "even some of the absurd stories of the *Puranas* have found favour with the *Theosophist.*" But let him tell us; has the Bible any less of "absurd ghost-stories" and *"ridiculous* miracles" in it than the Hindu *Puranas,* the Buddhist *Maha Jataka,* or even one of the most "shamefully superstitious publications" of the Spiritualists? (We quote from his letter). We are afraid in all and one it is but:

> "Faith, fanatic faith, once wedded fast
> To some dear falsehood, hugs it to the last . . ."

and—we decline accepting anything on faith. In common with most of the periodicals we remind our readers in every number of the THEOSOPHIST that its "Editors disclaim responsibility for opinions expressed by contributors" with some of which they (we) do not agree. And that is all we can do. We never started out in our paper as *Teachers* but rather as humble and faithful recorders of the innumerable beliefs, creeds, scientific *hypotheses,* and—even "superstitions" current in the past ages and now more than lingering yet in our own. Never having been a sectarian—*i.e.* an interested party—we maintain that in the face of the present situation, during that incessant warfare, in which old creeds and new doctrines, conflicting schools and *authorities,* revivals of blind faith and incessant scientific discoveries running a race as though for the survival of the fittest, swallow up and mutually destroy and annihilate each other—*daring, indeed, were that man* who would assume the task of deciding between them! Who, we ask, in the presence of those most wonderful and most unexpected achievements of our great physicists and chemists would risk to draw the line of demarcation between the *possible* and the *impossible?* Where is the *honest* man who conversant at all with the latest conclusions of archæology, philology, paleography, and especially Assyriology, would undertake to prove the superiority of the religious "superstitions" of the civilized Europeans over those of the "heathen," and even of the fetish-worshipping savages?

Having said so much, we have made clear, we hope, the reason why, believing no mortal man infallible, nor claiming that privilege for ourselves, we open our columns to the discussion of every view and opinion, provided it is not proved absolutely supernatural. Besides, whenever we make room to "unscientific" contributions it is when these treat upon subjects which lie entirely out of the province of physical science. Generally upon questions that the average and dogmatic scientist rejects *a priori* and without examination; but which, the real man of science finds not only *possible* but after investigation very often fearlessly proclaims the disputed question as an undeniable fact. In respect to most transcendental subjects the sceptic can no more disprove than the believer prove his point. FACT is the only tribunal we submit to and recognise it without appeal. And before that tribunal a Tyndall and an ignoramus stand on a perfect par. Alive to the truism that every path may eventually lead to the highway as every river to the ocean, we never reject a contribution simply because we do not believe in the subject it treats upon, or disagree with its conclusions. Contrast alone can enable us to appreciate things at their right value; and unless a judge compares notes and hears both sides he can hardly come to a correct decision. *Dum vitant stulti vitia in contraria*—is our motto; and we seek to prudently walk between the many ditches without rushing into either. For one man to demand from another that he shall believe like himself, whether in a question of religion or science is supremely unjust and despotic. Besides, it is absurd. For it amounts to exacting that the brains of the convert, his organs of perception, his whole organization, in short, be reconstructed precisely on the model of that of his teacher, and, that he shall have the same temperament and mental faculties as the other has. And why not his nose and eyes, in such a case? Mental slavery is the worst of all slaveries. It is a state over which brutal force having no real power, it always denotes either an abject cowardice or a great intellectual weakness. . . .

Among many other charges, we are accused of not sufficiently exercising our editorial right of selection. We beg to differ and contradict the imputation. As every other person blessed with brains instead of calf's feet-jelly in his head, we certainly have our opinions upon things in general, and things occult especially, to some of which we hold very firmly. But these being our *personal* views, and though we have as good a right to them as any, we have none whatever to force them for recognition upon others. *We* do not believe in the activity of "departed spirits"—*others* and among these, many of the Fellows of the Theosophical Society do—and we are bound to respect their opinions, so long as they respect ours. To follow every article from a contributor with an *Editor's Note* correcting "his erroneous ideas" would amount to turning our strictly impartial journal into a *sectarian* organ. We decline such an office of "Sir Oracle."

The THEOSOPHIST is a journal of our Society. Each of its Fellows being left absolutely untrammeled in his opinions, and the body representing collectively nearly every creed, nationality and school of philosophy, every member has a right to claim room in the organ of his Society for the defence of his own particular creed and views. Our Society being an absolute and an uncompromising *Republic of Conscience,* preconception and narrow-mindedness in science and philosophy have no room in it. They are as hateful and as much denounced by us as dogmatism and bigotry in theology; and this we have repeated *ad nauseam usque.*

Having explained our position, we will close with the following parting words to our sectarian friends and critics. The materialists and sceptics who upbraid us in the name of modern Science— the Dame who always shakes her head and finger in scorn at everything she has not yet fathomed—we would remind of the suggestive but too mild words of the great Arago: "He is a rash man, who outside of pure mathematics pronounces the word 'impossible'." And to theology, which under her many *orthodox* masks throws mud at us from behind every secure corner we retort by Victor Hugo's celebrated paradox: "In the name of RELIGION, we protest against all and every religion!"

Theosophist, July, 1881

MEDIUMS AND YOGEES

WHAT IS THE DIFFERENCE BETWEEN THE TWO?

BY * * *

A YOGEE is a man who has prepared himself by a long discipline of body and spirit, and is thereby rendered capable of dealing with phenomena, and receiving occult communications at will, the theory being that he, so to say, paralyzes his physical brain and reduces his mind to complete passivity by one of the numerous modes at his command, one of which is the magnetization of the second set of faculties pertaining to and exercised by the spiritual or inner man. The soul is inducted by the body, and, in its turn, is used to liberate the spirit, which is thus placed into direct rapport with the object desired. For example:—A telegraph line at stations A, B, C, D, E, in ordinary cases, sends messages from A to B, B to C and so on; but, when the several stations are connected, the message may be received direct at E from A without the intermediate stations being made aware of it. In the same manner, the nerves becoming passive, the "Yog" power controls the other faculties, and finally enables the spirit to receive a communication, which, in the other case, it cannot, because it must act through several mediums.

As the magnetic power is directed to any particular faculty, so that faculty at once forms a direct line of communication with the spirit,[1] which, receiving the impressions, conveys them back to the physical body.[2]

---

1 Sixth principle—*spiritual* soul.

2 In the normal or natural state, the sensations are transmitted from the lowest physical to the highest spiritual body, *i.e.*, from the first to the 6th principle (the 7th being no organized or conditioned body, but an infinite hence unconditioned principle or state), the faculties of each body having to awaken the faculties of the next higher one to transmit the message in succession, until they reach the last, when, having received the impression, the latter (the spiritual soul) sends it back in an inverse order to the body. Hence, the faculties of some of the "bodies" (we use this word for want of a better term) being less developed, they fail to transmit the message correctly to the highest principle, and thus also fail to produce the right impression upon the physical senses, as a telegram may have started, from the place of its destination, faultless and have been bungled up and misinterpreted by the telegraph operator at some intermediate station. This is why some people, otherwise endowed with great intellectual powers and perceptive faculties, are often utterly unable to appreciate—say, the beauties of nature, or some particular moral quality; as however perfect their physical intellect,—unless the original, material or rough physical impression conveyed has passed in a circuit through the sieve of every "principle"—(from 1, 2, 3, 4, 5, 6, up to 7, and down again from 7, 6, 5, 4, 3, 2, to No. 1)—and that every "sieve" is in good order,—the spiritual perception will always be imperfect. The Yogi, who, by a constant training and incessant watchfulness, keeps his septenary instrument in good tune and whose spirit has obtained a perfect control over all, can, at will, and by paralyzing the functions of the 4 intermediate principles, communicate from body to spirit and *vice versa*—direct.—*Ed. Theosophist.*

The spirit cannot grasp at the communications it desires to receive, unassisted by the physical organization, just as, in the case of a lunatic, the spirit is present, but the faculty of reason is lost, and, therefore, the spirit cannot make the man sane; or, as in the case of a blind man, the spirit and reasoning powers are sound, but the faculty of sight is destroyed; hence the soul of the blind man cannot realize the impressions which would be conveyed to it by the optic nerves and retina.

The spirit is an immortal ether (principle?) which cannot be impaired in any way, and, although it is, to a certain extent, subservient to the body and its faculties during the life-time of the body it is attached to, it can, through their agency, be so liberated in a higher or lesser degree as to be made to act independently of the other principles. This can be achieved by magnetic power or nerve power, if preferred, and thus the spiritual man be enabled to receive communications from other spirits, to traverse space and produce various phenomena, to assume any shape and appear in any form it desires.

The secret of the theory is this, that the Yogee, possessing the power of self-mesmerisation and having a perfect control over all his inner principles, sees whatever he desires to see, rejecting all elementary influences which tend to contaminate his purity.

The medium receives his communications differently. He *wishes* for "spirits"; they are attracted towards him, their magnetic influences controlling his faculties in proportion to the strength of their respective magnetic powers and the passivity of the subject; the nervous fluid conveys their impressions to the soul or spirit in the same manner, and often the same results are produced as in the case of the Yogee, with this important difference that they are not what the medium or spiritist wishes, but what the spirits (elementary influences) will produce; hence it is that sometimes (in spiritism) a question on one subject is asked, and a reply of a different nature received, irrelevant to the point and more or less after the "Elementary's" disposition. The spiritist cannot at desire produce a fixed result,—the Yogee can. The spiritist runs the risk of evil influences, which impair the faculties the soul has to command, and these faculties—being more prone to evil than good (as everything having a great percentage of impure matter in it)—are rapidly influenced. The Yogee overcomes this, and his faculties are entirely within his control, the soul acquiring a greater scope for working them and keeping them in check; for, although the soul is their ruler, yet it is subservient to them. I will give a familiar illustration:—A battery generates electricity, the wires convey the current, and the mechanism is put in motion. Just so, the soul is the generator or battery, the nerves the wires, and the faculties the mechanism made to work. The Yogee forms a direct connection between his spiritual soul and any faculty, and, by the power of his trained will, that is by magnetic influence, concentrates all his powers in the soul, which enables him to grasp the subject of his enquiry and convey it back to the physical organs, through the various channels of communication.[1]

If the Yogee desires to see a vision, his optic nerves receive the magnetic fluid; if an answer to a question is wanted, the faculties of thought and perception are charged by him; and so on. If he desires to traverse space in spirit, this is easily done by him by transferring the faculty of will,[2] and, as he may have acquired more or less power, so will he be able to produce greater or minor results.

The soul of the medium does not become the generator. It is not the battery. It is a Leyden jar, charged from the magnetic influence of the "spirits." The faculties are put in action just as the spirits so-called, make them work from the jar they have charged with their own currents. These currents, being magnetic, take after the invisibles' own good or evil disposition. The influence of a really good spirit is not left upon the earth after death, so that, in reality, there are *no* good spirits, although some may not be mischievous, while others may be full of real devilry. The question arises, how the influences of the bad ones are left behind, when the soul exists no more on earth after death? Well, just as light from the sun illumines an object, which reflects certain invisible active rays, and these, concentrated in a camera, produce a latent image on a photographic plate; in like manner the evil propensities of man are developed and form an atmosphere around him, which is so impregnated with his magnetic influence that this outer shell (as it were) retains the latent impressions of good or evil deeds. These, after death, are attached to certain localities, and travel as quick as thought wherever an attractive influence is exercised the stronger, they being less dangerous as less attracted to men in gen-

---

1 Or—direct, which is oftener the case, we believe.—*Ed. Theosophist.*

2 From the physical to the Spiritual body and concentrating it there, as we understand it.—*Ed. Theosophist.*

eral, but more to spiritists who attract them by the erratic power of their will, *i.e.,* their own ill-governed magnetic power. Have not many experienced coming across a man unknown to them, whose very appearance has been repulsive, and, at the sight of whom, feelings of distrust and dislike spring up in them spontaneously, although they knew nothing of or against him? On the other hand, how often do we meet a man who, at first sight seems to attract us to him, and we feel as if we could make a friend of him, and if, by chance, we become acquainted with that person, how much we appreciate his company. We seem lost in hearing him speak, and a certain sympathy is established between us for which we cannot account. What is this, but our own outer shell coming in contact with his and partaking of the magnetic influences of that shell or establishing a communication between each other.

The medium is also influenced by his own spirit sometimes, the reaction of his nerves magnetizing some faculties accidentally, while the elementary spirits are magnetizing the other senses; or a stray current reaches some faculty which their magnetism has not reached, and this leads to some of those incomprehensible messages, which are quite irrelevant to what is expected, and a frequent occurrence which has always been the great stumbling block at all séances.

Theosophist, May, 1882

WHENCE THE NAME "LUNATICS?"

IT is well known that the moon-beams have a very pernicious influence; and recently this question became the subject of a very
animated discussion among some men of science in Germany.
Physicians and physiologists begin to perceive at last, that the poets
had led them into a trap. They will soon find out, it is to be hoped,
that eastern Occultists had more real information about the genuine
character of our treacherous satellite than the Western astronomers with all their big telescopes. Indeed—"fair Diana," the
"Queen of Night," she, who in "clouded majesty"—

> ". . . unveils her peerless light,
> and o'er the dark her silver mantle throws . . ."

—is the worst—because secret—enemy of her Suzerain, and that
Suzerain's children, vegetable and animal as well as human. Without touching upon her occult and yet generally unknown attributes
and functions, we have but to enumerate those that are known to
science and even the profane.

The moon acts perniciously upon the mental and bodily constitution of men in more than one way. No experienced captain will
allow his men to sleep on deck during the full moon. Lately it was
proved beyond any doubt, by a long and careful series of experiments, that no person—even one with remarkably strong nerves—
could sit, lie or sleep for any length of time, in a room lit by moon-
light without injury to his health. Every observing housekeeper or
butler knows that provisions of any nature will decay and spoil far
more rapidly in moon-light than they would in entire darkness.
The theory that the cause of this does not lie in the specific per-
niciousness of the moon-beams but in the well-known fact that all
the refrangible and reflected rays will act injuriously—is an ex-
ploded one. This hypothesis cannot cover the ground in our case.
Thus, in the year 1693, on January 21, during the eclipse of the
moon, *thrice* as many sick people died on that day than on the preceding and following days. Lord Bacon used to fall down senseless at the beginning of every lunar eclipse and returned to consciousness but when it was over. Charles the VI, in 1399, became a

The spirit cannot grasp at the communications it desires to receive, unassisted by the physical organization, just as, in the case of a lunatic, the spirit is present, but the faculty of reason is lost, and, therefore, the spirit cannot make the man sane; or, as in the case of a blind man, the spirit and reasoning powers are sound, but the faculty of sight is destroyed; hence the soul of the blind man cannot realize the impressions which would be conveyed to it by the optic nerves and retina.

The spirit is an immortal ether (principle?) which cannot be impaired in any way, and, although it is, to a certain extent, subservient to the body and its faculties during the life-time of the body it is attached to, it can, through their agency, be so liberated in a higher or lesser degree as to be made to act independently of the other principles. This can be achieved by magnetic power or nerve power, if preferred, and thus the spiritual man be enabled to receive communications from other spirits, to traverse space and produce various phenomena, to assume any shape and appear in any form it desires.

The secret of the theory is this, that the Yogee, possessing the power of self-mesmerisation and having a perfect control over all his inner principles, sees whatever he desires to see, rejecting all elementary influences which tend to contaminate his purity.

The medium receives his communications differently. He *wishes* for "spirits"; they are attracted towards him, their magnetic influences controlling his faculties in proportion to the strength of their respective magnetic powers and the passivity of the subject; the nervous fluid conveys their impressions to the soul or spirit in the same manner, and often the same results are produced as in the case of the Yogee, with this important difference that they are not what the medium or spiritist wishes, but what the spirits (elementary influences) will produce; hence it is that sometimes (in spiritism) a question on one subject is asked, and a reply of a different nature received, irrelevant to the point and more or less after the "Elementary's" disposition. The spiritist cannot at desire produce a fixed result,—the Yogee can. The spiritist runs the risk of evil influences, which impair the faculties the soul has to command, and these faculties—being more prone to evil than good (as everything having a great percentage of impure matter in it)—are rapidly influenced. The Yogee overcomes this, and his faculties are entirely within his control, the soul acquiring a greater scope for working them and keeping them in check; for, although the soul is their ruler, yet it is subservient to them. I will give a familiar illustration:—A battery generates electricity, the wires convey the current, and the mechanism is put in motion. Just so, the soul is the generator or battery, the nerves the wires, and the faculties the mechanism made to work. The Yogee forms a direct connection between his spiritual soul and any faculty, and, by the power of his trained will, that is by magnetic influence, concentrates all his powers in the soul, which enables him to grasp the subject of his enquiry and convey it back to the physical organs, through the various channels of communication.[1]

If the Yogee desires to see a vision, his optic nerves receive the magnetic fluid; if an answer to a question is wanted, the faculties of thought and perception are charged by him; and so on. If he desires to traverse space in spirit, this is easily done by him by transferring the faculty of will,[2] and, as he may have acquired more or less power, so will he be able to produce greater or minor results.

The soul of the medium does not become the generator. It is not the battery. It is a Leyden jar, charged from the magnetic influence of the "spirits." The faculties are put in action just as the spirits so-called, make them work from the jar they have charged with their own currents. These currents, being magnetic, take after the invisibles' own good or evil disposition. The influence of a really good spirit is not left upon the earth after death, so that, in reality, there are *no* good spirits, although some may not be mischievous, while others may be full of real devilry. The question arises, how the influences of the bad ones are left behind, when the soul exists no more on earth after death? Well, just as light from the sun illumines an object, which reflects certain invisible active rays, and these, concentrated in a camera, produce a latent image on a photographic plate; in like manner the evil propensities of man are developed and form an atmosphere around him, which is so impregnated with his magnetic influence that this outer shell (as it were) retains the latent impressions of good or evil deeds. These, after death, are attached to certain localities, and travel as quick as thought wherever an attractive influence is exercised the stronger, they being less dangerous as less attracted to men in gen-

____

1 Or—direct, which is oftener the case, we believe.—*Ed. Theosophist.*

2 From the physical to the Spiritual body and concentrating it there, as we understand it.—*Ed. Theosophist.*

jective" in the living man's sensuous perceptions and the same as they appear to the psychic perceptions of a disembodied entity (Devachanee). It will not strengthen his case to put forth the objection that "the mode of the intercourse is not such as we can at present recognize from experience"; in other words, that until one becomes a "Devachanee" one cannot enter into sympathy with his feelings or perceptions. For, the disembodied individuality being identical in nature with the higher *triad* of the living man, when liberated as the result of *self* evolution effected by the full development of conscious and trained will, the adept can through this triad learn all that concerns the Devachanee; live for the time being his mental life, feel as he feels, and sharing thoroughly in his supersensuous perceptions, bring back with him on earth the memory of the same, unwarped by *mayavic* deceptions, hence—not to be gain-said. This, of course, assuming the existence of such *lusus naturæ* as an "adept," which may, perhaps, be conceded by the objectors for the sake of argument. And the further concession must be asked that no comparison shall be made to the adept's detriment between the perceptive powers of his triad, when so freed from the body, and those of the half liberated monad of the entranced somnambule or medium which is having its dazed glimpses into the "celestial arcana." Still less, is it allowable to gauge them by the reveries of an embodied mind, however cultured and metaphysical, which has no data to build upon, save the deductions and inductions which spring from its own normal activity.

However much European students may seem to have outgrown the crude beliefs of their earlier years, yet a special study of Asiatic mental tendencies is indispensable to qualify them to grasp the meaning of Asiatic expressions. In a word, they may have outgrown their hereditary ideas only far enough to qualify them as critics of the same; and not sufficiently to determine what is "inconsistent language" or consistent, of Eastern thinkers. Difference in the resources of language is also a most important factor to keep in mind. This is well illustrated in the alleged reply of an Oriental visiting Europe, when asked to contrast Christianity with Buddhism: "It requires an Index or glossary; for it (Christianity) has not the ideas for our words, nor the words for our ideas." Every attempt to explain the doctrines of Occultism in the meagre terminology of European science and metaphysics to students ignorant of our terms, is likely to result in disastrous misunderstandings despite good intentions on both sides. Unquestionably, such expressions as "life real in a dream" must appear inconsistent to a dualist who affirms the eternity of the individual soul, its independent existence, as distinct from the Supreme Soul or Paramatma, and maintains the *actuality* of (the personal) God's nature. What more natural than that the Western thinker, whose inferences are drawn from quite a different line of thought, should feel bewilderment when told that the Devachanic life is "reality"— though a dream, while earthly life is but "a flitting dream"— though imagined an actuality. It is certain that Prof. Balfour Stewart—great physicist though he be—would not comprehend the meaning of our Oriental philosophers, since his hypothesis of an unseen universe, with his premises and conclusions, is built upon the emphatic assumption of the actual existence of a personal God, the personal Creator, and personal moral Governor of the Universe. Nor would the Mussulman philosopher with his two eternities—*azl,* that eternity which has no beginning, and *abd,* that other eternity having a beginning but no end; nor the Christian who makes every man's eternity begin (!) at the moment when the personal God breathes a personal soul into the personal body— comprehend us. Neither of these three representatives of belief could, without the greatest difficulty, concur in the perfect reasonableness of the doctrine of Devachanic life.

When the word "subjective" is used in connection with the state of isolation of the Devachanee, it does not stand for the ultimate possible concept of subjectivity, but only for that degree of the same thinkable by the Western *non-Oriental* mind. To the latter everything is subjective without distinction which evades all sensuous perceptions. But the Occultist postulates an ascending scale of subjectivity which grows continually more real as it gets farther and farther from illusionary earthly objectivity: its ultimate, *Reality*—Parabrahm.

But Devachan being "but a dream," we should agree upon a definition of the phenomena of dreams. Has memory anything to do with them? We are told by some physiologists it has. That the dream-fancies being based upon dormant memory,[2] are determined and developed in most cases by the functional activity of some

---

[2] One of the paradoxes of modern physiology seems to be that "the more sure and perfect memory becomes, the more unconscious it becomes." (See *Body and Mind,* by H. Maudsley, M.D.)

know is its climax," says Professor A. Wilder, our New York Vice-President, certainly more of a man of Science himself than many a scientist better known than he is to the world. Moreover, the learned representatives of the Royal Society have as many cherished hobbies, and are as little free of prejudice and preconception as any other mortals. It is perhaps, to religion and her handmaid theology, with her "seventy times seven" sects, each claiming and none proving its right to the claim of truth, that, in our search for it, we ought to humbly turn? One of our severe Christian Areopagites actually expresses the fear that "even some of the absurd stories of the *Puranas* have found favour with the *Theosophist.*" But let him tell us; has the Bible any less of "absurd ghost-stories" and *"ridiculous* miracles" in it than the Hindu *Puranas,* the Buddhist *Maha Jataka,* or even one of the most "shamefully superstitious publications" of the Spiritualists? (We quote from his letter). We are afraid in all and one it is but:

> "Faith, fanatic faith, once wedded fast
> To some dear falsehood, hugs it to the last . . ."

and—we decline accepting anything on faith. In common with most of the periodicals we remind our readers in every number of the THEOSOPHIST that its "Editors disclaim responsibility for opinions expressed by contributors" with some of which they (we) do not agree. And that is all we can do. We never started out in our paper as *Teachers* but rather as humble and faithful recorders of the innumerable beliefs, creeds, scientific *hypotheses,* and—even "superstitions" current in the past ages and now more than lingering yet in our own. Never having been a sectarian—*i.e.* an interested party—we maintain that in the face of the present situation, during that incessant warfare, in which old creeds and new doctrines, conflicting schools and *authorities,* revivals of blind faith and incessant scientific discoveries running a race as though for the survival of the fittest, swallow up and mutually destroy and annihilate each other—*daring, indeed, were that man* who would assume the task of deciding between them! Who, we ask, in the presence of those most wonderful and most unexpected achievements of our great physicists and chemists would risk to draw the line of demarcation between the *possible* and the *impossible?* Where is the *honest* man who conversant at all with the latest conclusions of archæology, philology, paleography, and especially Assyriology, would undertake to prove the superiority of the religious "superstitions" of the civilized Europeans over those of the "heathen," and even of the fetish-worshipping savages?

Having said so much, we have made clear, we hope, the reason why, believing no mortal man infallible, nor claiming that privilege for ourselves, we open our columns to the discussion of every view and opinion, provided it is not proved absolutely supernatural. Besides, whenever we make room to "unscientific" contributions it is when these treat upon subjects which lie entirely out of the province of physical science. Generally upon questions that the average and dogmatic scientist rejects *a priori* and without examination; but which, the real man of science finds not only *possible* but after investigation very often fearlessly proclaims the disputed question as an undeniable fact. In respect to most transcendental subjects the sceptic can no more disprove than the believer prove his point. FACT is the only tribunal we submit to and recognise it without appeal. And before that tribunal a Tyndall and an ignoramus stand on a perfect par. Alive to the truism that every path may eventually lead to the highway as every river to the ocean, we never reject a contribution simply because we do not believe in the subject it treats upon, or disagree with its conclusions. Contrast alone can enable us to appreciate things at their right value; and unless a judge compares notes and hears both sides he can hardly come to a correct decision. *Dum vitant stulti vitia in contraria*—is our motto; and we seek to prudently walk between the many ditches without rushing into either. For one man to demand from another that he shall believe like himself, whether in a question of religion or science is supremely unjust and despotic. Besides, it is absurd. For it amounts to exacting that the brains of the convert, his organs of perception, his whole organization, in short, be reconstructed precisely on the model of that of his teacher, and, that he shall have the same temperament and mental faculties as the other has. And why not his nose and eyes, in such a case? Mental slavery is the worst of all slaveries. It is a state over which brutal force having no real power, it always denotes either an abject cowardice or a great intellectual weakness. . . .

Among many other charges, we are accused of not sufficiently exercising our editorial right of selection. We beg to differ and contradict the imputation. As every other person blessed with brains instead of calf's feet-jelly in his head, we certainly have of their personal *Egos*—that they have, in fact, *never separated from each other,* death itself being powerless to sever psychic association there, where pure spiritual love links the two. The "dream" was in this instance *the reality;* the latter a *maya,* a false appearance due to *avidya* (false notions). Thus it becomes more correct and proper to call the son's ignorance during his waking hours a "dream" and "a delusion," than to so characterize the *real* intercourse. For what has happened? A Spiritualist would say: "the spirit of the father *descended* upon earth to hold communion with his son's spirit, during the quiet hours of sleep." The Occultist replies; "Not so; neither the father's *spirit* descended, nor has the son's triad ascended (strictly and correctly speaking)." The centre of Devachanic activity cannot be localized: it is again *avidya.* Monads during that time even when connected with their five finite *Kosas* (sheaths or principles) know neither space nor time, but are diffused throughout the former, are omnipresent and ubiquitous. *Manas* in its higher aspect is *dravya* —an eternal "substance" as well as the *Buddhi,* the spiritual soul —when this aspect is developed; and united with the Soul *Manas* becomes spiritual *self*-consciousness, which is a *Vikara* (a production) of its original "producer" *Buddhi.*[4] Unless made utterly unfit, by its having become hopelessly mixed with, and linked to, its lower *Tanmatras,* to become one with Buddhi, it is inseparable from it. Thus the higher human triad, drawn by its affinity to those triads it loved most, with *Manas* in its highest aspect of self consciousness—(which is entirely disconnected with, and has no need as a channel of the internal organ of physical sense called *antah-karana*)[5]—helping, it is ever associated with, and enjoys the presence of all those it loves—in death, as much as it did in life. The intercourse is *real and genuine.*

The critic doubts whether such an intercourse can be called a "veritable one." He wants to know "whether the two disembodied entities are really and truly affected the one by the other," or, "is it merely that one *imagines* the presence of the other," such intercourse corresponding with no fact "of which the other person-

---

4 It is only when *Ego* becomes *Ego-ism* deluded into a notion of independent existence as the producer in its turn of the five *Tanmatras* that Manas is considered *Mahabhutic* and finite in the sense of being connected with *Ahancara,* the *personal* "I-creating" faculty. Hence *Manas* is both eternal and non-eternal: eternal in its atomic nature (*paramanu rupa*), finite (or *karya-rupa*) when linked as a duad—with *Kama* (*Volition*), a lower production.—*Ed.*

5 *Anta-karana* is the path of communication between soul and body, entirely disconnected with the former: existing with, belonging to, and dying with the body.—*Ed.*

ality (either embodied or disembodied) could take cognizance";
and while doubting, he denies that he is "postulating an incon-
gruity" in objecting that such an intercourse is *not* real, is a "mere
dream," for he says, "he *can* conceive a real intercourse—conscious
on both sides and truly acting and reacting which does *not* apply
only to the mutual relationship of physical existence." If he really
can, then where is the difficulty complained of? The real meaning
attached by the occultist to such words as dream, reality, and
unreality, having been explained, what further trouble is there to
comprehend this specific tenet? The critic may also be asked, how
he can conceive of a real conscious intercourse on both sides,
unless he understands the peculiar, and—to him as yet unknown
—intellectual reaction and inter-relation between the two. [This
sympathetic reaction is no fanciful hypothesis but a scientific fact
known and taught at initiations, though unknown to modern science and but hazily perceived by some metaphysicians—spiritualists.][6] Or is it that, alternatively, he anthropomorphises Spirit—in
the spiritualistic mistaken sense? Our critic has just told us that
"the mode of the intercourse is not such as we (he) can at present recognize from experience." What kind of intercourse is it
then that he *can* conceive of?

DREAM LIFE

REPLY II

The Appendix referred to in the *Fragments* No. VI, in the
Theosophist for March, is in no way inconsistent. When properly
understood in the light of our doctrines, App. C. (p. 136) gives
what it professes to explain and leaves nothing doubtful, while the
Fragments itself has perhaps a few expressions that may be misleading: though exclusively so to those who have not paid sufficient attention to that which preceded. For instance: "Love, the
creative force, has placed their (the associates') living image
before the personal soul which craves for their presence, and that
image will never fly away." It is incorrect to use the term "personal
soul" in connection with the monad. "The *personal* or animal
soul" is, as already said, the 5th principle, and cannot be in Deva-

---

6 It is demonstrated to Occultists by the fact that two adepts separated by hundreds
of miles, leaving their bodies at their respective habitations *and their astral bodies* (the
lower *manas* and volition *kama*) to watch over them, can still meet at some distant place
and hold converse and even perceive and sense each other for hours *as though* they were
both *personally* and bodily together, whereas, even their lower *mavavi-rupas* are absent.

chan, the highest state permitted to it on earth being *samadhi*. It is only its *essence* that has followed the monad into Devachan, to serve it there as its ground-tone, or as the background against which its future dream-life and developments will move; its entity, or the *reliquiæ* is the "shell," the dross that remains behind as an elementary to fade away and in time disappear. That which is in Devachan is no more the *personæ*—the mask, than the smell of a rose is the flower itself. The rose decays and becomes a pinch of dust: its aroma will never die, and may be recalled and resurrected ages thence. Correctly expressed, the sentence would have to read: ". . . the living image before the *Spiritual* Soul, which being now saturated with the essence of the personality, has thus ceased to be *Arupa* (formless or rather devoid of all substance) for its Devachanic duration, and craves for their presence, etc." The gestation period is over, it has won the day, been reborn as a new out of the old ego, and before it is ushered again into a new *personality,* it will reap the effects of the causes sown in its precedent birth in one of the Devachanic or Avitchian states, as the case may be, though the latter are found wide apart. *Avas'yam eva bhoktavyam kritam karma Shubhashubam.*[1] The Devachanic condition in *all its aspects* is no doubt similar to a dreamy state *when considered from the standpoint of our present objective consciousness when we are in our waking condition.* Nevertheless, it is real to the Devachanee himself as our waking state is to us. Therefore, when it is asked "Whether Devachan is a state corresponding to our waking life here or to our sleep with dreams,"—the answer given is that it is not similar to either of these conditions; but it is similar to the *dreamy condition* of a man who has no waking state at all, if such a being can be supposed to exist. A monad in Devachan has *but one state of consciousness,* and the contrast between a waking state and a dreamy state is never presented to it so long as it is in that condition. Another objection urged is, that if a Devachanee were to think of an object or person as if the object or person were present before him when they are not so (when judged from the common *ideas* of objective perception) then the Devachanee is "cheated by nature." If such is really the case, he is indeed always "cheated by nature," and the suggestion contained in the foregoing letter as to the possible mode of communication between a Devachanee and one living on earth will not save him from delusion. Leaving aside

---

[1] The fruit of the tree of action, whether good or bad, must unavoidably be eaten.

for a moment the nature of a Devachanee's communication with another monad either in or out of Devachan, let the nature of his ideas be examined so far as they are connected with objects; and then the truth of the above mentioned statement will be easily perceived. Suppose, for instance, Galileo in Devachan, subjectively engaged his favourite intellectual pursuit. It is natural to suppose that his telescope often comes within the range of his Devachanic consciousness, and that the Devachanee subjectively directs it towards some planet. It is quite clear that according to the general ideas of objectivity, Galileo has no telescope before him, and it cannot be contended that his train of ideas in any way actually affects the telescope which he left behind him in this world. If the objector's reasoning is correct, Galileo is "being cheated by nature," and the suggestion above referred to will in no way help him in this case.

Thus, the inference that it is neither correct nor philosophical to speak of a Devachanee as being "cheated by nature" becomes once more unavoidable. Such words as cheating, delusion, reality are always relative. It is only by contrast that a particular state of consciousness can be called real or illusionary; and these words cease to have any significance whatever, when the said state of consciousness cannot be compared with any other state. Supposing one is justified in looking upon Devachanic experience as delusion from his present stand-point as a human being living on this earth, what then? We fail to see how any one means to make use of this inference. Of course from the foregoing remarks the reader is not to suppose that a Devachanee's consciousness can never affect or influence the state of consciousness of another monad either in or out of Devachan. Whether such is the case or not, the reality or the unreality of devachanic experience, so far as a Devachanee is concerned, does not depend upon any such communicative influence.

In some cases it is evident that the state of consciousness of one monad whether in Devachan or yet on earth, may blend with, as it were, and influence the ideation of another monad also in Devachan. Such will be the case where there is strong, affectionate sympathy between the two *egos* arising from participation in the same higher feelings or emotions, or from similar intellectual pursuits of spiritual aspirations. Just as the thoughts of a mesmerizer standing at a distance are communicated to his subject by the emanation of a current of magnetic energy attracted readily towards the subject, the train of ideas of a Devachanee are communicated by a current of magnetic or electric force attracted towards another Devachanee by reason of the strong sympathy existing between the two monads, especially when the said ideas relate to things which are subjectively associated with the Devachanee in question. It is not to be inferred, however, that in other cases when there is no such action or reaction, a Devachanee becomes conscious of the fact that his subjective experience is a mere delusion, for it is not so. It was already shown that the question of reality or unreality does not depend upon any such communication or transmission of intellectual energy.

We are asked, "if some of those (the Devachanee loved) are not themselves fit for Devachan, how then?" We answer: "Even in the case of a man still living on earth, or even of one suffering in Avitchi, the ideation of a monad in Devachan may still affect his monad if there is strong sympathy between the two as indicated above,[2] Yet the Devachanee will remain ignorant of the mental suffering of the other."

If this generous provision of nature that never punishes the innocent outside this our world of delusion, be still called "a cheating of nature," and objected to, on the ground that it is not an "honest symbol" of the other personality's presence, then the most reasonable course would be to leave the occult doctrines and Devachan alone. The noble truths, the grandest goal in soul-life, will remain for ever a closed book to such minds. Devachan instead of appearing what it is—a blissful rest, a heavenly oasis during the laborious journey of the Monad toward a higher evolution, will indeed present itself as the culmination, the very essence of death itself. One has to sense intuitionally its logical necessity; to perceive in it, untaught and unguided, the outcome and perpetuation of that strictest justice absolutely consonant with the harmony of the universal law, if one would not lose time over its deep significance. We do not mean it in any unkind spirit, yet with such an opposition to the very exposition (since no one is pressed for its acceptance) of our doctrine by some western minds, we feel bound to remind our opponents that they have the freedom of choice. Among the later great world philosophies there

---

2 The reader is reminded in this connection that neither Devachan nor Avitchi is a locality, but a *state* which affects directly the being in it and all others only by *reaction.—Ed.*

are two,—the more modern the outgrowth of the older,—whose "after states" are clearly and plainly defined, and the acceptance of either of which, moreover, would be welcomed: one—by millions of spiritualists, the other—by the most respectable portion of humanity, viz., civilized Western society. Nothing equivocal, or like cheating of nature in the latter: her Devachanees, the faithful and the true, are plainly and charitably promised the ineffable rapture of seeing during an eternity those whom they may have loved best on earth suffering the tortures of the damned in the depths of Gehenna. We are, and do feel willing to give out some of our *facts*. Only occult philosophy and Buddhism having both failed as yet to produce a Tertullian to strike for us the key-note of an orthodox hell,[3] we cannot undertake to furnish fictions to suit every taste and fancy.

There is no such place of torture for the innocent, no such state in which under the plea of reward and a necessity for "honest symbols," the guileless should be made witness to, or even aware of, the sufferings of those they loved. Were it otherwise, the active bliss of the Dhyan Chohans themselves would turn into a shoreless ocean of gall at such a sight. And He who *willed*— "Let all the sins and evils flowing from the corruption of *Kaliyug,* this degenerate age of ours fall upon me, but let the world be redeemed"—would have so willed in vain, and might have given preference to the awes of the visible to those of the invisible world. To suppose that a "Soul" escaping from this evil-girdled planet where the innocent weep while the wicked rejoice, should have a like fate in store for it even within the peaceful haven of Devachan, would be the most maddening, the dreadful thought of all! But we say, it is *not* so. The bliss of a Devachanee is complete, and nature secures it even at the risk of being accused of *cheating* by the pessimists of this world unable to distinguish between *Vastu*— the one reality and *Vishaya*—the "mayas" of our senses. It is fetching rather too far the presumption that our *objective* and *subjective* shall be the true standards for the realities and unrealities of the rest of the universe; that *our* criterion of truth and honesty is to stand as the only universal land-mark of the same. Had

---

3 Reference is probably made here to the soul-inspiring monologue that is found in Tertullian's *Despectæ,* Chapter XXX. Falling into a wild ecstasy of joy over the bare prospect of seeing some day all the philosophers "who have persecuted the name of Christ burn in a most cruel fire in hell. . . ." this saintly Patristic character, a Father of the Christian Church, exclaims: "Oh what shall be the magnitude of that scene. How I shall laugh! How I shall rejoice! How I shall triumph" etc.—*Ed.*

we to proceed upon such principles, we would have to accuse nature of cheating incessantly not only her human but also her animal offspring. Who, of our objectors, when treating of facts of natural history and the phenomena of vision and colour, would ever hazard the remark that because ants are utterly unable to see and distinguish colours as human beings do, (the red, for instance, having no existence for them) therefore, are they also "cheated by nature." Neither *personality* nor *objectivity* as known to us, have any being in the conceptions of a monad; and could, by any miracle, any living human creature come within the range of the Devachanic vision, it would be as little perceived by the Devachanee as the elementals that throng the air around us are perceived with our natural eyes.

One more error of the critic. He seems to be labouring under the impression that if one has some conception of Devachanic state of subjective consciousness while in this life, he will know that such experience is illusionary when he is actually there; and then Devachanic beatitudes will have lost all their reality so far as he is concerned. There is no reason to apprehend any such catastrophe. It is not very difficult to perceive the fallacy that underlies this argument. Suppose, for instance, A, now living at Lahore, knows that his friend B is at Calcutta. He dreams that they are both at Bombay engaged in various transactions. Does he know *at the time he is dreaming* that the whole dream is illusionary? How can the consciousness that his friend is really at Calcutta, which is only realized when he is in his waking condition, help him in ascertaining the delusive nature of his dream *when he is actually dreaming?* Even after experiencing dreams several times during his life and knowing that dreams are generally illusionary, A will not know that he is dreaming when he is actually in that condition.

Similarly, a man may experience the devachanic condition while yet alive, and call it delusion, if he pleases, when he comes back to his ordinary state of objective consciousness and compares it to the said condition. Nevertheless, he will not know that it is a dream either when he experiences it a second time (for the time being) while still living, or when he dies and goes to Devachan.

The above is sufficient to cover the case were even the state under discussion indeed "a dream" in the sense our opponents hold it in. But it is neither a "dream" nor in any way "cheating." It may be so from the stand-point of Johnson's dictionary; from that of *fact* independent of all human definition, and the stand-point of him who knows something of the laws that govern the worlds invisible, the intercourse between the monads is real, mutual, and as *actual* in the world of subjectivity, as it is in this our world of deceptive reality. It is the old story of Zöllner's man from the two-dimensional region disputing the reality of the phenomena taking place in the three-dimensional world.

THE VARIOUS STATES OF DEVACHAN

REPLY III

The foremost question that presents itself to the mind of the occultist of Asiatic birth, upon seeing the multifarious difficulties which beset the European students of Esotericism, as regards Devachan: how to account for their weird fancies with regard to the after states! It is natural for one to measure other persons' intellectual operations by his own; not without an effort can he put himself in his neighbour's place and try to see things from his stand-point. As regards Devachan, for example, nothing would apparently be clearer than the esoteric doctrine, incompletely as it may have been expressed by "Lay Chela"; yet it is evidently not comprehended, and the fact must be ascribed, I think, rather to the habitual differences in our respective ways of looking at things than to the mechanical defects in the vehicle of expression. It would be very hard for an Asiatic Occultist to even conjure up such a fancy as that of Swedenborg, who makes the angels our *post-mortem* "inquisitors," obliged to estimate a soul's accumulated merits and demerits by physical inspection of its body, beginning at the tips of the fingers and toes and tracing thence to centres! Equally baffling would be the attempt to bring ourselves to the point of seriously tracing a denizen of the American Summer-Land of Spirits through the nurseries, debating clubs, and legislative assemblies of that optimistic Arcadian Eden. A warp of anthropomorphism seems to run through the entire woof of European metaphysics. The heavy hand of a *personal* deity and his personal ministers seems to compress the brain of almost every Western thinker. If the influence does not show itself in one form, it does in another. Is it a question about God? A metaphysical slide is inserted, and the stereopticon flashes before us a picture of a gold-paved, pearly-doored New Jerusalem, with its Durbar Hall, peacock throne, Maharajah, Dewans, courtiers, trumpeters, scribes, and general train. Is the intercourse between disembodied spirits under discussion? The Western constitutional bias of mind can conceive of no such intercourse without some degree of mutual consciousness of an objective presence of the corporeal kind: a sort of psychic chit-chat. I hope I do not wrong our Western correspondents, but it is impossible, for myself at least, to draw any other conclusions from the whole tenor of the British Theosophist's memorandum. Vapoury and etherealized as his concept may be it is yet materialistic at the core. As we would say, the germ-point of metaphysical evolution is of Biblical derivation: and through its opalescent vapour sparkle the turrets of the "New Jerusalem."

There is much fanciful exotericism to be sure, in Asiatic systems. Quite as much and more perhaps than in the Western; and our philosophies have many a harlequin cloak. But we are not concerned now with externals: our critic comes upon metaphysical ground and deals with esotericism. His difficulty is to reconcile "isolation," as he understands it, with "intercourse" as we understand it. Though the monad is not like a seed dropped from a tree, but in its nature is ubiquitous, all-pervading, omnipresent; though in the subjective state time, space and locality are not factors in its experiences; though, in short, all mundane conditions are reversed; and the now thinkable becomes the then unthinkable and *vice-versâ*—yet the London friend goes on to reason as though all this were not so. . . .

Now, Buddhistically speaking, there are states and states and degrees upon degrees in Devachan, in all of which, notwithstanding the (to us) objective isolation of the principal hero, he is surrounded by a host of actors in conjunction with whom he had during his last earth-life created and worked out the causes of those effects that are produced first on the field of *Devachanic* or *Avitchean* subjectivity, then used to strengthen the Karma to follow on the objective (?) plane of the subsequent rebirth. Earth-life is, so to say, the *Prologue* of the drama, (or we should, perhaps, call it *mystery*) that is enacted in the *rupa* and *arupa* lokas. Now were we to say that nature, with every due regard to personality and the laws of objectivity as understood in exotericism, "constitutes a veritable intercourse" between the devachanic heroes and actors; and instead of *dissociating* the monads not only

as regards "personal corporeal" but even *astral* "association"—
establishes "actual companionship" between them, as on the
earth-plane, we might, perhaps, avoid the strange accusation of
"nature cheating" in Devachan. On the other hand, after thus
pandering to emotional objections, we could hardly help placing
our European Chelas in a far more inextricable dilemma. They
would be made to face a problem of personal *post-mortem* ubiquity, throwing that of the Western deity far in to the background
of illogical absurdity. Suppose for one moment a Devachanic
father, twice wedded, and loving both his wives as he does his
children, while the step-mother loves neither his progeny nor
their mother, the coolest indifference if not actual aversion reigning between the two. "Actual companionship," and "real *personal*
intercourse" (the latter applied even to their astral bodies) implies
here bliss for the father and irritation for the two wives and
children, all equally worthy of Devachanic bliss. Now imagine
again the real mother attracting by her intense love the children
within her devachanic state, and thus depriving the father of *his*
legitimate share of bliss. It has been said before, that the devachanic mind is capable only of the highest spiritual ideation;
that neither objects of the grosser senses nor any thing provocative
of displeasure could ever be apprehended by it—for otherwise,
Devachan would be merging into *Avitchi,* and the feeling of unalloyed bliss destroyed for ever. How can nature reconcile in the
above case the problem without either sacrificing her duty to our
terrestrial sense of *objectivity* and *reality,* or without compromising
her status before *our* criterion of truth and honest dealing? On one
hand, the children would have to double and treble themselves
ad infinitum—as they too may have disembodied, devachanic objects of spiritual attachment clamouring elsewhere for their presence—which process of ubiquity would hardly be consistent with
our notions of personal, actual presence, at one and the same time
and at several different places; or, there would always be somebody, somewhere "cheated by nature." To place the *monads*
promiscuously together, like one happy family—would be fatal to
truth and fact: each man, however insignificant he may have been
on earth, is yet mentally and morally *sui generis* in his own distinct
conceptions of bliss and desires, and has, therefore, a right to,
and an absolute necessity for, a specific, personal, "isolated"
devachan.

The speculations of the Western mind have hitherto scarcely ever depicted any higher future life than that of the *Kama* and *Rupa lokas,* or the lower, intra-terrestrial "spirit-worlds." In Appendix D. many states and spheres are hinted at. According even to exoteric Buddhistic philosophy disincarnate beings are divided into three classes of—(1) *Kamawâchera,* or those who are still under the dominion of the passions in *Kamaloka;* (2) *Rupawâchera,* or those who have progressed to a higher stage, but still retain vestiges of their old form in *Rupa* loka; and (3) *Arupawâchera,* or those who are become formless entities in the *Arupa lokas* of the highest Devachan. All depends on the degree of the monad's spirituality and aspirations. The astral body of the 4th principle—called *Kama,* because inseparable from *Kama loka,* —is always within the attraction of terrestrial magnetism; and the monad has to work itself free of the still finer yet equally potent attractions of its *Manas* before it ever reaches in its series of Devachanic states, the upper-*Arupa* regions. Therefore, there are various degrees of Devachanees. In those of the *Arupa lokas* the entities are as *subjective* and truly "not even as material as that ethereal body-shadow—the Mayavirupa." And yet even there, we affirm there is still "actual companionship." But only very few reach there skipping the lower degrees. There are those Devachanees, men of the highest moral calibre and goodness when on earth, who, owing to their sympathy *for old intellectual researches and especially for unfinished mental work,* are for centuries in the Rupa-lokas in a strict Devachanic isolation—literally so, since men and loved relatives have all vanished out of sight before this intense and purely spiritual passion for intellectual pursuit. For an example of the study-bound (pardon the new word for the sake of its expressiveness) condition, take the mental state of the dying Berzelius, whose last thought was one of despair that his work should be interrupted by death. This is *Tanha* (Hindu *Trishna*) or an unsatisfied yearning which must exhaust itself before the entity can move on to the purely *a-rupa* condition. A provision is made for every case, and in each case it is created by the dying man's last, uppermost desire. The scholar who had mainly lived under the influence of *manas,* and for the pleasure of developing his highest physical intelligence, kept absorbed in the mysteries of the material universe, will still be magnetically held by his mental attractions to scholars and their work, influencing and being influenced by them *subjectively*—(though in a manner quite different from that known in seance-rooms and by mediums,) until the energy exhausts itself and *Buddhi* becomes the only regnant influence. The same rule applies to all the activities, whether of passion or sentiment, which entangle the travelling monad (the Individuality) in the relationships of any given birth. The disincarnate must consecutively mount each ring of the ladder of being upward from the earthly subjective to the *absolutely* subjective. And when this limited Nirvanic state of Devachan is attained, the entity enjoys it and its vivid though spiritual realities until that phase of Karma is satisfied and the physical attraction to the next earth-life asserts itself. In Devachan, therefore, the entity is affected by and reciprocally affects the psychic state of any other entity whose relationship is so close with it as to survive, as was above remarked, the purgatorial evolution of the lower post-mortem spheres. Their intercourse will be sensed spiritually, and still, so far as any relationship until now postulated by Western thinkers goes, each will be "dissociated from the other." If the questioner can formulate to himself the condition of the monad as pure spirit, the most subjective entity conceivable, without form, color, or weight, even so great as an atom; an entity whose recollections of the last personality (or earth-birth) are derived from the late union of the *Manas* with the lower five principles—he may then find himself able to answer his own interrogatory. According to Esoteric Doctrine this evolution is not viewed as the extinguishment of individual consciousness but its infinite expansion. The entity is not obliterated, but united with the universal entity, and its consciousness becomes able not merely to recall the scenes of one of its earth-evolved Personalities, but of each of the entire series around the Kalpa, and then those of every other Personality. In short from being finite it becomes infinite consciousness. But this comes only at the end of all the births at the great day of the absolute Resurrection. Yet, as the monad moves on from birth to birth and passes its lower and devachanic spheres after each fresh earthly existence, the mutual ties created in each birth must weaken and at last grow inert, before it can be reborn. The record of those relationships imperishably endures in the Akasa, and they can always be reviewed when, in any birth, the being evolves his latent spiritual powers to the "fourth stage of Dhyana"; but their hold upon the being gradually relaxes. This is accomplished in each inter-natal Devachan; and when the personal links— magnetic or psychic, as one may prefer to call them—binding the Devachanee to other entities of that next previous life, whether relatives, friends, or family, are worn out, he is free to move on in his cyclic path. Were this obliteration of personal ties not a fact, each being would be travelling around the Kalpa entangled in the meshes of his past relationships with his myriad fathers, mothers, sisters, brothers, wives &c., &c., of his numberless births: a jumble, indeed! It was the ignorant delusion of the geocentric hypothesis which begot all the exoteric theologies, with their absurd dogmas. So, likewise, it is the ignorant theory of monogenesis, or but one earth life for each being, which makes it so hard for European metaphysicians to read the riddle of our existence and comprehend the difference between the monad's individuality, and its physical appearance in a series of earth-lives as so many different, totally distinct personalities. Europe knows much about atomic weights and chemical symbols, but has little idea of Devachan.

Theosophist, August, 1883

PROJECTION OF THE DOUBLE

IN one of the daily issues of the *N. Y. World*—an influential
journal of the great American metropolis—for the year 1878,
appeared a description of the events of an evening at the then
Head-quarters of our Society, in the city of New York. The
writer was one of the Editorial Staff, and among other wonders
related was the following: Some lady or gentleman among the
visitors had doubted the possibility of an Adept to leave his physical body in a torpid state in the Himalayas, and come in his astral
body (*Mayavi-rupa*) across land and seas to the other side of the
world. Three or four of the company sat so as to face the two
large windows of the room which gave upon the Avenue—then
brilliantly lighted with the gas of the shops and street-lamps. The
doubting surmise was barely uttered when these persons simultaneously started in surprise and pointed towards the left-hand
window. All looking there, saw deliberately and slowly passing
on the outside, from left to right, first one, then another figure of
Asiatic men, with *fehtas* on their heads and clad in one of the long
white garments of the East. Passing by the window and out of
sight, they presently returned, and repassing the window, were
seen no more. Two of the witnesses (Col. Olcott and the Editor
of this journal) recognized them, from personal acquaintance, as a
certain Mahatma and one of his pupils. The window was nearly
twenty feet from the ground and, there being no verandah or
other roof for a crow to walk upon—the figures had been moving
through the air. Thus, upon the instant and most unexpectedly,
the doubter had been silenced and the truth of the Aryan Esoteric
Science vindicated. Since we came to India a number of perfectly
credible witnesses, Native and European, have been favoured with
a sight of similar apparitions of the Blessed Ones, and usually
under the most convincing circumstances. Only a few weeks ago
at our Madras Head-quarters, one appeared suddenly in full light,
in an upstairs room and approached within two feet of certain
Hindu members of our society, retained the perfectly visible and
solid form for about one minute, and then receding half a dozen

paces—disappeared upon the spot. At Bombay, the astral *sarira* of Mahatma K. H. was seen repeatedly two years ago—by over twenty members in all—some of whom had been very sceptical as to such a possibility before, proclaiming it after the occurrence as "the most glorious, solemn of sights." Three times, during one evening the "form," perfectly recognizable, and seemingly solid to a hair of the moustache and beard—glided through the air from a cluster of bushes to the verandah, in brilliant moon-light . . . and then faded out. Again, the case of Mr. Ramaswamier, B. A., affords proof of the most cumulative kind ever recorded in the history of this branch of Esoteric Science: he first saw a Mahatma's portrait; then saw him in the "double"; and finally met him in the flesh in a lonely pass in Sikkim, conversed with him for above two hours in his (Mr. R.'s) own vernacular—a foreign tongue to the Mahatma—had explained to him many facts relating to the Theosophical Society, and was charged with messages to Colonel Olcott about certain confidential matters which none but himself and this particular Mahatma knew about. The existence of the Mahatmas, their power to travel in the inner, or astral body at will, to preserve full command of all their intelligence, and to condense their "phantom" form into visibility or dissolve it into invisibility at their own pleasure, are now facts too well established to permit us to regard it as an open question.

Objectors to the above propositions are found only among the inexperienced, as objectors to every other new thing have been. There must be a particular moment in every case when doubt and disbelief vanish, to give place to knowledge and certainty. Few, comparatively, of any generation have ever or in the nature of things could ever see the splendid phenomenon of a Mahatma's astral apparition; for merely the magneto-psychic law of attraction and repulsion keeps Adepts and the reeking stew of social corruption far apart. Sometimes, under very favourable conditions they may approach an individual devoted to occult research, but this happens rarely; for even he, pure though he be, is wallowing in the world's corrupt *akasa* or magnetic aura and contaminated by it. To his inner self it is as stifling and deadly as the heavy vapour of carbonic oxide to his physical lungs. And, remember, it is by the inner, not the outer, self that we come into relations with Adepts and their advanced Chelas. One would not expect to hold improving conversation with a besotted inebriate, lying in a state of swine-like stupefaction after a debauch; yet it is quite as impracticable for the spiritualised Mahatma to exchange thoughts with a man of society, living daily in a state of *psychic intoxication* among the magnetic fumes of its carnality, materialism, and spiritual atrophy.

But other living persons than the Eastern Adepts can project their doubles so as to appear at a distance from their bodies. The literature of Western mysticism—not to mention the voluminous records of the Orient—contain many instances of the kind; notably the works of Glanvil, Ennemoser, Crowe, Owen, Howitt, Des Mousseaux and many other Roman Catholic writers, and a host beside. Sometimes the figures talk, but usually not; sometimes they wander while the subject's outer body sleeps, sometimes while awake; often the apparition is the forerunner of death, but occasionally it seems to have come from its distant body for the mere pleasure of seeing a friend, or because the desire to reach a familiar place outran the physical power of the body to hurry there soon enough. Miss C. Crowe tells (*Night Side of Nature*) of a German Professor whose case was of the latter kind. Returning to his house one day, he saw the double of himself pass there before him, knock at the door, and enter when the servant maid opened it. He hastened his pace, knocked in his turn, and when the maid came and saw him, she started back in terror saying, "Why, Sir, I have just let you in!" (or words to that effect.) Mounting the stairs to his library, he saw himself seated in his own arm-chair as was his custom. As he approached, the phantom melted away into air. Another example of a similar nature is the following, of which the circumstances are as satisfactorily established, as could be desired.

The story is told of one—Emilie Sagèe, governess in a ladies' school at Riga, in Livonia. Here the body and its double were observed simultaneously, in broad day, and by many persons. "One day all the school, forty-two in number, were in a room on the ground-floor, glass doors leading into the garden. They saw Emilie gathering flowers in the garden, when suddenly her figure appeared on a vacant sofa. Looking instantly into the garden, they still saw Emilie there; but they observed that she moved languidly and as if exhausted or drowsy. Two of the bolder approached the double, and offered to touch it; they felt a slight resistance which they compared to that of muslin or crepe. One of them passed through part of the figure; the apparation remained some moments longer, then disappeared, but gradually. This phenomenon occurred, in different ways, as long as Emilie remained at the school, for about a year and a half in 1845 and 1846, with intermittent periods from one to several weeks. It was remarked that the more distinct and material the double appeared, the more uneasy, languid, and suffering was the real person; when, on the contrary, the double became feeble, the patient recovered strength. Emilie had no consciousness of her double, nor did she ever see it."

Theosophist, October, 1883

CONTEMPLATION

A GENERAL misunderstanding of this term seems to prevail. The popular idea appears to be to confine oneself for half an hour—or at the utmost two hours—in a private room, and passively gaze at one's nose, a spot on the wall, or, perhaps, a crystal. This is supposed to be the true form of contemplation enjoined by *Raj Yoga*. It fails to realize that true occultism requires "physical, mental, moral and spiritual" development to run on parallel lines. Were the narrow conception extended to all these lines, the necessity for the present article would not have been so urgently felt. This paper is specially meant for the benefit of those who seem to have failed to grasp the real meaning of Dhyan, and by their erroneous practices to have brought, and to be bringing, pain and misery upon themselves. A few instances may be mentioned here with advantage, as a warning to our too zealous students.

At Bareilly the writer met a certain Theosophist from Farrukhabad, who narrated his experiences and shed bitter tears of repentance for his past follies—as he termed them. It would appear from his account that the gentleman, having read *Bhagavat-Gita* about fifteen or twenty years ago and not comprehending the esoteric meaning of the contemplation therein enjoined, undertook nevertheless the practice and carried it on for several years. At first he experienced a sense of pleasure, but simultaneously he found he was gradually losing self-control; until after a few years he discovered, to his great bewilderment and sorrow, that *he was no longer his own master*. He felt his heart actually growing heavy, as though a load had been placed on it. He had no control over his sensations; in fact the communication between the brain and the heart had become as though interrupted. As matters grew worse, in disgust he discontinued his "contemplation." This happened as long as seven years ago; and, although since then he has not felt worse, yet he could never regain his original normal and healthy state of mind and body.

Note.—This article by Damodar, published in the *Theosophist* drew correspondence and two further replies by him.—Eds.

Another case came under the writer's observation at Jubbulpore. The gentleman concerned, after reading Patanjali and such other works, began to sit for "contemplation." After a short time he commenced seeing abnormal sights and hearing musical bells, but neither over these phenomena nor over his own sensations could he exercise any control. He could not produce these results at will, nor could he stop them when they were occurring. Numerous such examples may be multiplied. While penning these lines, the writer has on his table two letters upon this subject, one from Moradabad and the other from Trichinopoly. In short, all this mischief is due to a misunderstanding of the significance of contemplation as enjoined upon students by all the schools of Occult Philosophy. With a view to afford a glimpse of the Reality through the dense veil that enshrouds the mysteries of this Science of Sciences, an article, the "Elixir of Life," was written. Unfortunately, in too many instances, the seed seems to have fallen upon barren ground. Some of its readers only catch hold of the following clause in the said paper:

> Reasoning from the known to the unknown, meditation, must be practised and encouraged.

But, alas! their preconceptions have prevented them from comprehending what is meant by meditation. They forget that it "is the inexpressible yearning of the inner Man to 'go out towards the infinite,' which in the olden time was the real meaning of adoration"—as the next sentence shows. A good deal of light will be thrown upon this subject if the reader were to turn to the preceding portion of the same paper, and peruse attentively the following paragraphs on page 141 of the *Theosophist* for March, 1883 (Vol. III, No. 6):[1]

> So, then, we have arrived at the point where we have determined—literally, *not* metaphorically—to crack the outer shell known as the mortal coil, or body, and hatch out of it, clothed in our next. This "next" is not a spiritual, but only a more ethereal form. Having by a long training and preparation adapted it for a life in this atmosphere, during which time we have gradually made the outward shell to die off through a certain process . . . we have to prepare for this physiological transformation.
>
> How are we to do it? In the first place we have the actual, visible, material body—man, so called, though, in fact, but his

---

1 From "The 'Elixir of Life'," reprinted in *Five Years of Theosophy.—Eds.*

outer shell—to deal with. Let us bear in mind that science teaches us that in about every seven years we *change skin* as effectually as any serpent; and this so gradually and imperceptibly that, had not science after years of unremitting study and observation assured us of it, no one would have had the slightest suspicion of the fact. . . . Hence, if a man partially flayed alive, may sometimes survive and be covered with a new skin,—so our astral, vital body . . . . may be made to harden its particles to the atmospheric changes. The whole secret is to succeed in evolving it out, and separating it from the visible; and while its generally invisible atoms proceed to concrete themselves into a compact mass, to gradually get rid of the old particles of our visible frame so as to make them die and disappear before the new set has had time to evolve and replace them. . . . We can say no more.

A correct comprehension of the above scientific process will give a clue to the esoteric meaning of meditation or contemplation. Science teaches us that man changes his physical body continually, and this change is so gradual that it is almost imperceptible. Why then should the case be otherwise with the *inner man?* The latter too is constantly developing and changing atoms at every moment. And the attraction of these new sets of atoms depends upon the Law of Affinity—the desires of the man drawing to their bodily tenement only such particles as are *en rapport* with them or rather giving them their own tendency and coloring.

> For Science shows that thought is dynamic, and the thought-force evolved by nervous action expanding itself outwardly, must affect the molecular relations of the physical man. The *inner* men, however sublimated their organism may be, are still composed of actual, *not hypothetical* particles, and are still subject to the law that an "action" has a tendency to repeat itself; a tendency to set up analogous action in the grosser "shell" they are in contact with and concealed within. ("The Elixir of Life.")

What is it the aspirant of *Yog Vidya* strives after if not to gain *Mukti* by transferring himself gradually from the grosser to the next more ethereal body, until all the veils of *Maya* being successively removed his *Atma* becomes one with *Paramatma?* Does he suppose that this grand result can be achieved by a two or four hours' contemplation? For the remaining twenty or twenty-two hours that the devotee does not shut himself up in his room for meditation—is the process of the emission of atoms and their replacement by others stopped? If not, then how does he mean to attract all this time,—only those suited to his end? From the above remarks it is evident that just as the physical body requires incessant attention to prevent the entrance of a disease, so also the *inner man* requires an unremitting watch, so that no conscious or unconscious thought may attract atoms unsuited to its progress. This is the real meaning of contemplation. The prime factor in the guidance of the thought is WILL.

> Without that, all else is useless. And, to be efficient for the purpose, it must be, not only a passing resolution of the moment, a single fierce desire of short duration, but *a settled and continued strain, as nearly as can be continued and concentrated without one single moment's remission.*

The student would do well to take note of the italicized clause in the above quotation. He should also have it indelibly impressed upon his mind that

> It is no use to fast *as long as one requires* food. . . . To get rid of the inward desire is the essential thing, and to mimic the real thing without it is barefaced hypocrisy and useless slavery.

Without realizing the significance of this most important fact, any one who for a moment finds cause of disagreement with any one of his family, or has his vanity wounded, or for a sentimental flash of the moment, or for a selfish desire to utilize the divine power for gross purposes—at once rushes in for contemplation and dashes himself to pieces on the rock dividing the known from the unknown. Wallowing in the mire of exotericism, he knows not what it is to live in the world and yet be not of the world; in other words to guard *self* against *self* is an incomprehensible axiom for nearly every profane. The Hindu ought at least to realize it by remembering the life of Janaka, who, although a reigning monarch, was yet styled *Rajarshi* and is said to have attained *Nirvana*. Hearing of his widespread fame, a few sectarian bigots went to his Court to test his *Yoga*-power. As soon as they entered the courtroom, the king having read their thought—a power which every *chela* attains at a certain stage—gave secret instructions to his officials to have a particular street in the city lined on both sides by dancing girls who were ordered to sing the most voluptuous songs. He then had some *gharas* (pots) filled with water up to the brim so that the least shake would be likely to spill their contents. The wiseacres, each with a full *ghara* (pot) on his head, were ordered to pass along the street, surrounded by soldiers with drawn swords to be used against them if even so much as a drop of water were allowed to run over.

The poor fellows having returned to the palace after successfully passing the test, were asked by the King-Adept what they had met with in the street they were made to go through. With great indignation they replied that the threat of being cut to pieces had so much worked upon their minds that they thought of nothing but the water on their heads, and the intensity of their attention did not permit them to take cognizance of what was going on around them. Then Janaka told them that on the same principle they could easily understand that, although being outwardly engaged in managing the affairs of his state, he could at the same time be an Occultist. He, too, while *in* the world, was not *of* the world. In other words, his inward aspirations had been leading him on continually to the goal in which his whole inner self was concentrated.

Raj Yoga encourages no sham, requires no physical postures. It has to deal with the inner man whose sphere lies in the world of thought. To have the highest ideal placed before oneself and strive incessantly to rise up to it, is the only true concentration recognized by Esoteric Philosophy which deals with the inner world of *noumena,* not the outer shell of *phenomena.*

The first requisite for it is thorough purity of heart. Well might the student of Occultism say, with Zoroaster, that purity of thought, purity of word, and purity of deed,—these are the essentials of one who would rise above the ordinary level and join the "gods." A cultivation of the feeling of unselfish philanthropy is the path which has to be traversed for that purpose. For it is that alone which will lead to Universal Love, the realization of which constitutes the progress towards deliverance from the chains forged by Maya around the Ego. No student will attain this at once, but as our VENERATED MAHATMA says in the *Occult World*:

> The greater the progress towards deliverance, the less this will be the case, until, to crown all, human and purely individual personal feelings, blood-ties and friendship, patriotism and race predilection, will all give way to become blended into one universal feeling, the only true and holy, the only unselfish and eternal one, Love, an Immense Love for Humanity as a whole.

In short, the individual is blended with the ALL.

Of course, contemplation, as usually understood, is not without its minor advantages. It develops one set of physical faculties as gymnastics does the muscles. For the purposes of physical mesmerism, it is good enough; but it can in no way help the development of the psychological faculties, as the thoughtful reader will perceive. At the same time, even for ordinary purposes, the practice can never be too well guarded. If, as some suppose, they have to be entirely passive and lose themselves in the object before them, they should remember that by thus encouraging passivity, they, in fact, allow the development of mediumistic faculties in themselves. As was repeatedly stated—the Adept and the Medium are the two Poles; while the former is intensely active and thus able to control the elemental forces, the latter is intensely passive, and thus incurs the risk of falling a prey to the caprice and malice of mischievous embryos of human beings, and—the Elementaries.

DAMODAR K. MAVALANKAR

CORRESPONDENCE ON "CONTEMPLATION"

I

I regret the whole article is totally misunderstood. All I meant to say was that temporary estrangement, from family or friends, does not constitute an essential qualification for advancement in occultism. This ought to be plain to one who weighs carefully my illustration of Janaka. Although *in* the world, to be not *of* it. Failing to realize the meaning of this important teaching, many people rush in from a sentimental disgust of worldliness, arising probably out of some worldly disappointment—and begin practising what they consider to be a true form of *contemplation*. The very fact that the *motive* which leads them to go in for this practice, is as described . . . —this fact is a sufficient indication that the candidate does not know the "contemplation" of a *Raja Yogi*. It is thus impossible in the nature of things that he can follow the right method; and the physical practice, which he necessarily undertakes, leads him to the disastrous results adverted to in the article.

Any reader, who has intuition enough to be a practical student of occultism, will at once see that to work up to perfection is the highest ideal that a man can have before him. That is not the work of a day nor of a few years. "The Adept *becomes;* he is NOT MADE" —is a teaching which the student must first realize. The aspirant works up to his goal through a series of lives. Col. Olcott says in his *Buddhist Catechism*:—". . . Countless generations are required to develop man into a Buddha, and *the iron will to become one runs throughout all the successive births.*"

That *"iron will"* to become *perfect* must be *incessantly* operating, without a single moment's relaxation, as will be apparent to one who reads *carefully the article as a whole*. When it is distinctly said that during the time that this contemplation is not practiced, *i.e.,* the iron will is not exerting, the process of the emission and attraction of atoms is not stopped, and that the desires, instinctive or otherwise, must be so regulated as to attract only such atoms as may be suited to his progress—I cannot understand my correspondent when he asks me what he should do at a particular hour in the morning. He should cultivate only such thoughts as would not be incompatible with the highest ideal he has to work up to.

By perfection, which should be his highest ideal, (I must add) I mean that *divine* manhood which the Occult Philosophy contemplates the seventh race of the seventh Round will attain to. This, as every tyro knows, depends largely upon a cultivation of the feeling of Universal Love, and hence an earnest desire to do some practical philanthropic work is the first requisite. Even this state, I admit, is not *absolute perfection*: but that maximum limit of ultimate Spiritual perfection is beyond our comprehension at present. That condition can only be intellectually realized as a practical ideal by those *divine men*—Dhyan-Chohans. To be identified with THE ALL, we must live in and feel through it. How can this be done without the realization of the feeling of Universal Love? Of course Adeptship is not within the easy reach of all. On the other hand, occultism does not fix any unpleasant place or locality for those who do not accept its dogmas. It only recognizes higher and higher evolution according to the chain of causation working under the impulse of Nature's immutable law. The article on "Occult Study" in the last number[2] gives the necessary explanation on this point.

It is painful for me to find that the very thing I attempted to point out in that article to be mischievous in its results, is again put forward as a desirable attribute or adjunct of true contemplation. I would ask my correspondent to read again the same article, with these additional remarks, before thinking of the necessity of

---

2 *The Theosophist,* March, 1884, pp. 131-3.—Eds.

any peculiar or particular posture for the purpose of *contemplation*. I, at any rate, am unable to prescribe any specific posture for the kind of *incessant contemplation* that I recommend.

II

Notwithstanding the article on the above subject in the February *Theosophist,* many of its readers still seem to imagine that "contemplation" is a particular form of gazing or staring at something, which process, when undergone a set number of hours every day, will give psychological powers. This misunderstanding is apparently due to the fact that the main point discussed has been lost sight of. Instead of realizing that there is but one chief idea meant to be conveyed by that article by arguing it through many of its phases, it seems to be imagined that almost every sentence expresses quite a distinct idea. It may not therefore be uninteresting or unprofitable to revert to the subject and put forward the same idea from another stand-point and, if possible, in a clearer light. It must first be borne in mind that the writer of the article did not at all mean to imply the act of gazing by the word "contemplation." The former word would have been made use of, were that the idea. *The Imperial Dictionary of the English Language* (1883)—defines the word contemplation thus:—

(1) The act of the mind in considering with attention; meditation; study; continued attention of the mind to a particular subject. Specifically—(2) Holy meditation; attention to sacred things.

Webster's dictionary thoroughly revised—also gives the same meaning.

Thus we find that contemplation is the "continued attention of the mind to a particular subject," and, religiously, it is the "attention to sacred things." It is therefore difficult to imagine how the idea of gazing or staring came to be associated with the word contemplation, unless it be due to the fact that generally it so happens that when any one is deeply absorbed in thought, he apparently seems to be gazing or staring at something in blank space. But this gazing is the effect of the act of contemplation. And, as usually happens, here too the effect seems to be confounded with the cause. Because the gazing attitude follows the act of contemplation, it is at once assumed the gazing is the cause which produces contemplation! Bearing this well in mind, let us now see what kind of contemplation (or meditation) the *Elixir of*

Life recommends for the aspirants after occult knowledge. It says:
—"Reasoning from the known to the unknown, meditation must
be practised and encouraged."

That is to say, a *chela's* meditation should constitute the "reasoning from the known to the unknown." The "known" is the phenomenal world, cognizable by our five senses. And all that we see in
this manifested world are the effects, the causes of which are to
be sought after in the noumenal, the unmanifested, the "unknown
world:" this is to be accomplished by meditation, *i.e.,* continued
attention to the subject. Occultism does not depend upon one
method, but employs both the deductive and inductive. The student must first learn the general axioms. For the time being, he
will of course have to take them as assumptions, if he prefers to
call them so. Or as the *Elixir of Life* puts it:—

"All we have to say is that if you are anxious to drink of the
Elixir of Life and live a thousand years or so, you must take our
word for the matter, at present, and proceed on the assumption.
For esoteric science does not give the faintest possible hope that
the desired end will ever be attained by any other way; while
modern, or the so-called exact science laughs at it."

These axioms have sufficiently been laid out in the articles on
the *Elixir of Life* and various others treating on occultism, in the
different numbers of the *Theosophist*. What the student has first
to do is to *comprehend* these axioms and, by employing the deductive method, to proceed from universals to particulars. He has
then to reason from the "known to the unknown," and see if the
inductive method of proceeding from particulars to universals sup-
ports those axioms. This process forms the primary stage of true
contemplation. The student must first grasp the subject intellectually before he can hope to realize his aspirations. When this is
accomplished, then comes the next stage of meditation which is
"the inexpressible yearning of the inner man to 'go out towards the
infinite'." Before any such yearning can be properly directed, the
goal, to which it is to be its aim to run, must be determined by the
preliminary stages. The higher stage, in fact, consists in realizing
practically what the first steps have placed within one's comprehension. In short, contemplation, in its true sense, is to recognize
the truth of Eliphas Levi's saying:—"To believe without knowing
is weakness; to believe because one knows, is power."

Or, in other words, to see that "KNOWLEDGE IS POWER." The

Elixir of Life not only gives the preliminary steps in the ladder of *contemplation* but also tells the reader how to *realize* the higher conceptions. It traces, by the process of contemplation as it were, the relation of man, "the known," the manifested, the phenomenon, to "the unknown," the unmanifested, the noumenon. It shows to the student what ideal he should contemplate and how to rise up to it. It places before him the nature of the inner capacities of man and how to develop them. To a superficial reader, this may, perhaps, appear as the acme of selfishness. Reflection or contemplation will, however, show the contrary to be the case. For it teaches the student that to comprehend the noumenal, he must identify himself with Nature. Instead of looking upon himself as an isolated being, he must learn to look upon himself as a part of the INTEGRAL WHOLE. For, in the unmanifested world, it can be clearly perceived that all is controlled by the "Law of Affinity," the attraction of one to the other. There, all is Infinite Love, understood in its true sense.

It may now be not out of place to recapitulate what has already been said. The first thing to be done is to study the axioms of Occultism and work upon them by the deductive and the inductive methods, which is real contemplation. To turn this to a useful purpose, what is theoretically comprehended must be practically realized. It is to be hoped that this explanation may make the meaning of the former article on this subject clearer.

—D.K.M.

Theosophist, February, April, and August, 1884

THE METAPHYSICAL BASIS OF
"ESOTERIC BUDDHISM"

THE pamphlet of Mr. C. C. Massey, an F. T. S., of the London Lodge of the Theosophical Society, is a valuable contribution of the discussion now being raised by the publication of Mr. Sinnett's *Esoteric Buddhism*. It is a trite axiom that truth exists independent of human error, and he who would know the truth, must rise up to its level and not try the ridiculous task of dragging it down to his own standard. Every metaphysician knows that Absolute Truth is the eternal Reality which survives all the transient phenomena. The preface to *Isis Unveiled* expresses the idea very clearly when it says:—"Men and parties, sects and creeds, are the mere ephemera of the world's day, while Truth, high seated on its rock of Adamant, is alone eternal and supreme." Language belongs to the world of relativity, while Truth is the Absolute Reality. It is therefore vain to suppose that any language, however ancient or sublime, can express Abstract Truth. The latter exists in the world of ideas, and the ideal can be perceived by the sense belonging to that world. Words can merely clothe the ideas, but no number of words can convey an idea to one who is incapable of perceiving it. Every one of us has within him the latent capacity or a sense dormant in us which can take cognisance of Abstract Truth, although the development of that sense or, more correctly speaking, the assimilation of our intellect with that higher sense, may vary in different persons, according to circumstances, education and discipline. That higher sense which is the potential capacity of every human being is in eternal contact with Reality, and every one of us has experienced moments when, being for the time *en rapport* with that higher sense, we realise the eternal verities. The sole question is how to focalise ourselves entirely in that higher sense. Directly we realise this truth, we are brought face to face with occultism. Occultism teaches its votaries what sort of training will bring on such a development. It never dogmatises, but only recommends certain methods which the experience of ages has proved to be the best suited to the purpose. But just as the harmony of nature consists in symphonious discord, so also the harmony of occult training (in other words, individual human progress) consists in discord of details. The scope of Occultism being a study of Nature, both in its phenomenal and noumenal aspects, its organisation is in exact harmony with the plan of Nature. Different constitutions require different details in training, and different men can better grasp the idea clothed in different expressions. This necessity has given rise to different schools of Occultism, whose scope and ideal is the same, but whose modes of expression and methods of procedure differ. Nay, even the students of the same school have not necessarily a uniformity of training. This will show why it is that until a certain stage is reached, the *Chela* is generally left to himself, and why he is never given verbal or written instructions regarding the truths of Nature. It will also suggest the meaning of the Neophyte being made to undergo a particular kind of sleep for a certain period before each initiation. And his success or failure depends upon his capacity for the assimilation of the Abstract Truth his higher sense perceives. However, just as unity is the ultimate possibility of Nature, so there is a certain school of Occultism which deals only with the synthetic process, and to which all the other schools, dealing with analytical methods wherein alone can diversity exist, owe their allegiance. A careful reader will thus perceive the absurdity of a dogmatism which claims for its methods a universal application. What is therefore meant by the Adwaitee Philosophy being identical with the Arhat Doctrine, is that the final goal or the ultimate possibility of both is the same. The synthetical process is one, for it deals only with eternal verities, the Abstract Truth, the noumenal. And these two philosophies are put forth together, for in their analytical methods they proceed on parallel lines, one proceeding from the subjective and the other from the objective stand-point, to meet ultimately or rather converge together in one point or centre. As such, each is the complement of the other and neither can be said to be complete in itself. It should be distinctly remembered here that the Adwaitee Doctrine does not date from Sankaracharya, nor does the Arhat Philosophy owe its origin to Gautama Buddha. They were but the latest expounders of these two systems which have existed from time immemorial as they must. Some natures can better comprehend the truth from a subjective stand-point, while others must proceed from the objective. These two systems are therefore as old as Occultism itself, while the later phases of the Esoteric Doctrine are but another aspect of either of these two, the details being modified according to the comprehensive faculties of the people addressed, as also the other surrounding circumstances. Attempts at a revival of the knowledge of this Truth have been numberless, and therefore to suggest that the present is the first attempt in the world's history, is an error which those whose sense has just been awakened to the glorious Reality are apt to commit. It has already been stated that the diffusion of knowledge is not limited to one process. The possessors of it have never jealously guarded it from any personal or selfish motives. In fact such a frame of mind precludes the possibility of the attainment of knowledge. They have at every opportunity tried all available means to give its benefit to humanity. Times there were undoubtedly when they had to rest content with giving it only to a few chosen pupils, who, it should be remembered, differ from ordinary humanity only in one essential particular, and that is, that by abnormal training they bring on a process of self-evolution in a comparatively very short period, which ordinary humanity may require numberless ages to reach during the ordinary course of evolution. Those who are acquainted with the history of Count St. Germain and the works of the late Lord Lytton, need not be told that even during the past hundred years constant efforts have been made to awaken the present races to a sense of the knowledge which will assist their progress and ensure future happiness. It should not be, moreover, forgotten that to spread a knowledge of philosophical truths forms but a small fraction of the important work the occultists are engaged in. Whenever circumstances compel them to be shut out from the world's view, they are most actively engaged in so arranging and guiding the current of events, sometimes by influencing people's minds, at others by bringing about, as far as practicable, such combinations of forces as would give rise to a higher form of evolution and such other important work on a spiritual plane. They have to do and are doing that work now. Little therefore do the public know what in reality it is that they ask for when they apply for *Chelaship*. They have to thus pledge themselves to assist the MAHATMAS in that spiritual work by the process of self-evolution, for, the energy expended by them in the act of self-purification, has a dynamic effect and produces grand results on a spiritual plane. Moreover, they gradually fit themselves to take an active share in the grand work. It may perhaps be now apparent why "THE ADEPT BECOMES; HE IS NOT MADE," and why he is the "rare efflorescence of the age." The foregoing considerations should never be lost sight of by the reader of *Esoteric Buddhism*.

The great difficulty which an ordinarily philosophic mind has to contend against, is the idea that consciousness and intelligence proceed out of non-consciousness and non-intelligence. Although an abstruse metaphysical intellect can comprehend or rather perceive the point subjectively, the present undeveloped state of humanity, at any rate, can conceive the higher truths only from an objective stand-point. Just as, therefore, we are obliged to talk of the setting of the sun, in common parlance, although we know that it is not the movement of the sun that we really refer to, and just as in the geocentric system we have to speak as though the earth were a fixed point in the centre of the universe so that the unripe mind of the student may understand our teachings, so in the same manner the Abstract Truth has to be presented from an objective point of view, so that it may be more easily comprehended by minds with not a very keen metaphysical intellect. Thus one may say that Buddhism is rational Vedantism, while Vedantism is transcendental Buddhism. Keeping this difference in view, an explanation of the difficulty above put forth may be given from the Buddhist stand-point. If the reader will here recall the answer of the MAHATMAS to Question V of "An English F. T. S.," published in the *Theosophist* for September 1883,* he will remember the explanation concerning "the mineral monad." The one Life permeates ALL. Here it may be added that consciousness and intelligence also permeate ALL. These three are inherent potentially everywhere. But we do not talk of the life of a mineral, nor of its consciousness or intelligence. These exist in it only potentially. The differentiation which results in individualisation is not yet complete. A piece of gold, silver, copper or any other metal, or a piece of rock, &c., has no sense of separate existence, because the mineral monad is not individualised. It is only in the animal kingdom that a sense of personality begins to be formed. But for all that, an occultist will not say that life, consciousness or intelligence, do not potentially exist in the minerals. Thus it will be seen that although consciousness and intelligence exist everywhere, all objects are not conscious or intelligent. The latent potentiality when developed to the stage of individualisation by the Law of

---

* See *Five Years of Theosophy—Eds.*

Cosmic Evolution, separates the subject from the object, or rather the subject falls into *Upadhi,* and a state of personal consciousness or intelligence is realized. But the absolute consciousness and intelligence which has no *Upadhi* cannot be conscious or intelligent, for there is no duality, nothing to wake intelligence or to be conscious of. Hence the *Upanishads* say that *Parabrahm* has no consciousness, no intelligence, for these states can be cognised by us only on account of our individualisation, while we can have, from our differentiated and personal state, no conception of the undifferentiated, non-dualistic consciousness or intelligence. If there were no consciousness or intelligence in Nature, it were absurd to talk of the Law of Karma or every cause producing its corresponding effect. The MAHATMA, in one of the letters published in the *Occult World,* says that matter is indestructible, but enquires whether the modern Scientist can tell why it is that Nature *consciously* prefers that matter should remain indestructible under organic rather than inorganic form. This is a very suggestive idea in regard to the subject under notice. At the beginning of our studies we are apt to be misled by the supposition that our earth, or the planetary chain, or the solar system, constitutes infinity and that eternity can be measured by numbers. Often and often have the MAHATMAS warned us against this error, and yet we do, now and then, try to limit the infinity to our standard instead of endeavouring to expand ourselves to its conception. This has led some naturally to a sense of isolation, and to forget that the same Law of Cosmic Evolution which has brought us to our present stage of individual differentiation, is tending to lead us gradually to the original undifferentiated condition. Such allow themselves to be imbued so much with a sense of personality that they try to rebel against the idea of Absolute Unity. Forcing themselves thus in a state of isolation, they endeavour to ride the Cosmic Law which must have its course: and the natural result is annihilation through the throes of disintegration. This it is which constitutes the bridge, the dangerous point in evolution referred to by Mr. Sinnett in his *Esoteric Buddhism.* And this is why selfishness, which is the result of a strong sense of "personality, is detrimental to spiritual progress. This it is that constitutes the difference between white and black magic. And it is this tendency to which reference is made when talking of the end of a Race. At this period, the whole humanity splits up into two classes, the Adepts of the good Law and the Sorcerers (or *Dugpas*). To that period we are fast rushing; and to save humanity from a cataclysm which must overtake those who go against the purposes of Nature, the MAHATMAS, who are working with her, are endeavouring to spread knowledge in a manner to prevent its abuse as far as possible. We should therefore constantly remember that the present is not the apex of evolution, and that if we would not be annihilated, we must not allow ourselves to be influenced by a sense of personal isolation and consequent worldly vanities and shows. This world does not constitute infinity, nor does our solar system, nor does the immeasurable expanse our physical senses can take cognisance of. All these and more are but an infinitesimal atom of the Absolute Infinity. The idea of personality is limited to our physical senses which, belonging as they do to the *Rupa Loka* (world of forms), must perish, since we see no permanent form anywhere. All is liable to change, and the more we live in transient personality, the more we incur the danger of final death, or total annihilation. It is only the seventh principle, the *Adi Buddha,* that is the Absolute Reality. The objective stand-point, however, adds further that *Dharma,* the vehicle of the seventh principle or its Upadhi, is co-existent with its Lord and Master, the *Adi Buddha*; because it says nothing can come out of nothing. A more correct form of expressing the idea would be that in the state of *Pralaya* the sixth principle exists in the seventh as an eternal potentiality to be manifested during the period of cosmic activity. Viewed in this light both the seventh and the sixth principles are Eternal Realities, although it would be more correct to say that the seventh principle is the only Reality, since it remains immutable both during cosmic activity as also during cosmic rest, while the sixth principle, the Upadhi, although absorbed into the seventh during *Pralaya,* is changing during Manvantara, first differentiating to return to its undifferentiated condition as the time for *Pralaya* approaches. It was from this standpoint that Mr. Subba Row was arguing in his article on "A Personal and an Impersonal God,"* which was meant as a reply to Mr. Hume, who was then talking of the Arhat Philosophy.

Now the Vedantin doctrine says that *Parabrahm* is the *Absolute Reality* which never changes and is thus identical with the *Adi Buddha* of the Arhats. While *Mulaprakriti* is that aspect of Para-

---

* This article appeared in *The Theosophist,* Feb. and March, 1883, as a Reply to an article by H. X. (A. O. Hume), *The Theosophist,* Dec., 1882.—*Eds.*

brahm, which at the time of *Manvantara* emanates from itself *Purush* and *Prakriti,* and which thus undergoes change during the period of cosmic activity. As *Purush* is force, which remains immutable throughout, it is that aspect of *Mulaprakriti* which is identical with *Parabrahm.* Hence it is that *Purush* is said to be the same as *Parabrahm,* or the *Absolute Reality.* While *Prakriti,* the differentiated cosmic matter, constantly undergoes change, and is thus impermanent, forming the basis of phenomenal evolution. This is a purely subjective stand-point from which Mr. Subba Row was arguing with the late Swami of Almora who professed to be an Adwaitee. A careful reader will thus perceive that there is no contradiction involved in Mr. Subba Row's statements, when he says from the objective standpoint that *Mulaprakriti and Purush* are eternal, and when again from a subjective standpoint he says tnat *Purush* is the only eternal Reality. His critic has unconsciously mixed up the two stand-points by culling extracts from two different articles written from two different points of view and imagines that Mr. Subba Row has made an error.

Attention must now be turned to the idea of the *Dhyan Chohans.* It has been already stated above that the sixth and the seventh principles are the same in all, and this idea will be clear to every one who reads carefully the foregoing remarks. It has also been added that the sixth principle, being a differentiation of *Mulaprakriti,* is personal, however exalted and ubiquitous that personality may be. In the Adwaitee Philosophy the *Dhyan Chohans* correspond to *Iswara,* the Demiurgus. There is no *conscious Iswara outside* of the 7th principle of Menu as vulgarly understood. This was the idea Mr. Subba Row meant to convey when he said:— "expressions implying the existence of a conscious Iswar which are to be found here and there in the *Upanishads,* are not to be literally construed." Mr. Subba Row's statement is therefore neither "perfectly inexplicable," nor "audacious," as it is consistent with the teaching of *Sankaracharya.* The *Dhyan Chohans,* who represent the aggregate cosmic intelligence, are the immediate artificers of the worlds, and are thus identical with *Iswara* or the Demiurgic Mind. But their consciousness and intelligence, pertaining as they do to the sixth and the seventh states of matter, are as such as we cannot cognise, so long as we prefer to remain in our isolation and do not transfer our individuality to the sixth and the seventh principles. As artificers of the worlds, they are the primary principle of the Universe, although they are at the same time the *result* of Cosmic Evolution. It is an incorrect understanding of the consciousness of *Dhyan Chohans* that has given rise to the current vulgar notion of God. Little do the dogmatic theists realise that it is within their power to become *Dhyan Chohans* or *Iswara,* or at least they have the latent potentiality in them to rise to that spiritual eminence if they will but work *with* Nature. They know not themselves, and thus allow themselves to be carried away and buried under a sense of personal isolation, looking upon Nature as something apart from themselves. They thus isolate themselves from the *spirit* of Nature, which is the only eternal Absolute Reality and hurry towards their own disintegration.

The reader will now perceive that *Esoteric Buddhism* is not a system of materialism. It is, as Mr. Sinnett calls it, "transcendental Materialism" which is non-materialism just as the absolute consciousness is non-consciousness and the absolute personality, of which Mr. Massey talks, is non-personality.

Mr. Massey's description of evolution from the idealist standpoint, with which his pamphlet closes, no occultist will disagree with. The book shows such various phases of thought that different portions must evidently have been written at different times. It is undoubtedly a valuable addition to the existing literature on the subject and will be read with extreme interest by the students of "The metaphysical basis of *Esoteric Buddhism.*"

DAMODAR K. MAVALANKAR

Theosophist, May, 1884

ASTROLOGY

THE popular idea seems to be that the planets and the stars exercise a certain influence upon the destiny of man, which the science of Astrology can determine; and that there are means within the reach of that science which can be used to propitiate "the evil stars." This crude notion, not philosophically understood, leads to two unscientific fallacies. On the one hand it gives rise to a belief in the doctrine of fatality, which says that man has no free-will inasmuch as everything is predetermined, and on the other it leads one to suppose that the laws of Nature are not immutable, since certain propitiatory rites may change the ordinary course of events. These two extreme views induce the "rationalist" to reject "Astrology" as a remnant of the uncivilized condition of our ancestors, since as a matter-of-fact student he refuses to recognize the importance of the saying, "Real philosophy seeks rather to solve than to deny." It is an axiom of the philosophic student that truth generally lies between the extremes. If one therefore proceeds in this spirit, he will find that there is yet not an unreasonable or unscientific hypothesis which can reconcile all these different views, and which, not unlikely, was what the ancients meant by Astrology.

Although a study of this science may enable one to determine what the course of events will be, it cannot necessarily be inferred therefrom that the planets exercise any influence over that course. The clock indicates, it does not influence, the time. And a distant traveller has often to put right his clock so that it may indicate correctly the time of the place he visits. Thus, though the planets may have no hand in changing the destiny of the man, still their position may indicate what that destiny is likely to be. This hypothesis leads us to the question, "What is destiny?" As understood by the Occultist, it is merely the chain of causation producing its correspondential series of effects. One who has carefully followed the teachings of Occultism, as recently given out, concerning *Devachan* and future re-births, knows that every individual is his own creator or his own father, *i.e.,* our future personality will be the result of our pres-

---

Note.—This article appeared in the *Theosophist* as a commentary on another writer's review of an "elementary work on Astrology."—Eds.

ent mode of living. In the same manner our present birth, with all its conditions, is the tree grown out of the germ sown in our past incarnations. Our physical and spiritual conditions are the effects of our actions produced on those two planes in previous existences. Now it is a well-known principle of Occultism that the ONE LIFE which pervades ALL connects all the bodies in space. All heavenly bodies have this mutual relation, which is blended with man's existence, since he is but a microcosm in the macrocosm. Every thought, as much as action, is dynamic and is impressed in the imperishable Book of Nature—the *Akasa,* the objective aspect of the UNMANIFESTED LIFE. All our thoughts and actions thus produce the vibrations in space, which mould our future career. And astrology is a science which, having determined the nature of the laws that govern these vibrations, is able to state precisely a particular or a series of results, the causes of which have already been produced by the individual in his previous life.

Since the present incarnation is the child of the previous one, and since there is but that ONE SELF which holds together all the planets of the Solar system, the position of those planets at the time of the birth of an individual—which event is the aggregate result of the causes already produced—gives to the true Astrologer the data upon which to base his predictions. It should be well remembered at the same time that just as the "astronomer who catalogues the stars cannot add one atom to the universe," so also can no astrologer, no more than the planet, *influence* the human destiny. Perhaps the following beautiful passage from the exquisite work of Bulwer Lytton's *Zanoni,* may help to make the meaning clearer:

> For the accomplishment of whatever is great and lofty, the clear perception of truths is the first requisite—truths adapted to the object desired. The warrior thus reduces the chances of battle to combinations almost of mathematics. He can predict a result, if he can but depend upon the materials he is forced to employ.

This necessitates a consideration of the element of clairvoyance necessary to constitute a true astrologer.

The ancient *Rishis,* to condemn whose books without a hearing was till recently a general practice, had by observation, experiment and deep occult knowledge, taken account of all conceivable combinations of various causes and determined with mathematical precision, almost to an infinitesimal point their effects. But yet, since the cosmos is infinite, no finite being can ever take cognisance of *all* the possibilities of Nature; at any rate they cannot be committed to writing, since as *Isis Unveiled* says: "to express divine ideas, divine language is necessary." Recognizing the truth of this most important but unfortunately often neglected axiom, they laid down as the first condition to success in astrology a pure life, physically, morally and spiritually. This was intended to develop the psychic capacities of the astrologer who could thus see in *Akasa* the combinations, not alluded to in the written works, and predict their results in the manner beautifully illustrated in the above extract from *Zanoni*.

In short, true Astrology is a mathematical science, which teaches us what particular causes will produce what particular combinations, and thus, understood in its real significance, gives us the means of obtaining the knowledge how to guide our future births. True, [of] such astrologers there are but few: but are we justified in condemning the science of electricity because there may be very few real electricians? We must not at the same time lose sight of the fact that although there are numberless combinations which must be determined by the psychic vision of the astrologer, there are yet a very large number of them which have been determined and put on record by the ancient sages. It is these cases which baffle us when we find that some astrological calculations prove correct while others are quite beside the mark.

Theosophist, June, 1884

INITIATION

AS every one knows, in all the great religions of old time, there were certain grades among the devotees, and the successive steps by which these grades were attained were marked off by initiation into the mysteries.

Such initiations still exist among the votaries of the Wisdom-Religion and, being by their very nature involved in the most profound mystery, much curiosity has been awakened as to their precise character. There are many who seem to look upon initiation as a purely mechanical process which depends solely upon the will of the initiator, and some seem inclined to blame the stewards of the mysteries for not publishing whatever knowledge they may possess as widely as possible, so that it may be within the reach of any individual of an enquiring turn of mind.

The really important part of initiation is however the fitness of the candidate himself. Just as it is said in the Bible that new wine put into old bottles is liable to burst those bottles, so, in like manner, if esoteric knowledge is imparted too far in advance of the progress already made, the mental balance of the candidate will be upset and madness is liable to supervene.

Hence the attitude we should adopt is not so much one of an intense desire for initiation—often but a form of ambition, the wish to be wiser than our fellows—as an intense determination to do everything in our power to fit ourselves for reception as initiates.

If it is true that "the whole universe is an aggregate of states of consciousness," it would seem to follow that the real difference between one who is an initiate and one who is not lies in the fact that the former looks at all things from a totally different standpoint to the majority of men. It is not that he has acquired certain items of knowledge that others do not possess, such as the way to manipulate the hidden forces of nature, but that he is on a higher plane of consciousness altogether. If such a higher plane has been attained, it will follow that his whole range of ideas will differ from that of others and he will be sensible of the operation of causes of a more far-reaching character than those cognized by others. He will be as it were in the possession of higher and superior information and so will be able to form juster conclusions and this fact alone will give him enormous power.

The action of the entire universe is but a detailed manifestation and example of the action of mind on matter, governed at the highest point by the action of the universal mind. Between the finite human mind of the ordinary uninitiated individual and this universal mind lie an infinite number of gradually ascending degrees, and the higher the plane of consciousness the nearer is the approach to the universal mind which is, as it were, the mainspring of the whole. Although there are no hard and fast lines in nature yet these various grades may be marked off into great main divisions; and it is the successive attainment of these, one after the other that is represented by the degrees of initiation. When one plane of experience has been exhausted, there is needed, as it were, a fresh impulse to enable us to go on higher and this it is that is supplied at the time of initiation.

ALPHA

Theosophist, June, 1886

LE PHARE DE L'INCONNU

VII

[Unfortunately, this concluding installment of H.P.B.'s article, "Le Phare de l'Inconnu," which first appeared in *La Revue Theosophique,* was omitted from the first volume of H.P.B.'s periodical writings. Since it will doubtless be years before another edition of her *Theosophical Articles* will be required, we reprint here Part VII of "Le Phare," in partial correction of the mistake.—Eds.]

WE hope that we have by this time sufficiently refuted in these pages several grave misconceptions of our doctrine and beliefs; that amongst others which insists in regarding Theosophists,—those, at least, who have founded the Society,—as polytheists or atheists. We are neither one or other, any more than certain Gnostics were, who, while believing in the existence of planetary, solar and lunar gods, offered no prayers to them nor dedicated any altars. Not believing in a personal god, *outside of man who is the temple thereof* according to Paul and other Initiates, we believe in an impersonal and absolute Principle,* so far beyond human conception, that we see nothing less than a blasphemer and presumptuous madman in anyone who tries to define that great universal Mystery. All that has been taught us about this eternal and unique spirit, is that, it is not spirit, nor matter, nor substance, nor thought, but is the *container of all those things, the absolute container.* In a word, it is the "God nothing" of Basilides, so little understood even by the learned and ingenious annalists of the Musée Guimet (Vol. XIV), who define the term somewhat satirically when they speak of this "god nothing, who has ordained and foreseen everything, although he has neither reason nor will."

Yes, truly, and this "god nothing," being identical with the Parabrahm of the Vedantins—the grandest as well as the most philosophical of conceptions—is identical also with the AIN-SOPH of the

---

* This belief only concerns those who think as I do. Every Fellow has the right to believe what he likes, and how he likes. As we have said elsewhere, the Theosophical Society is "the Republic of Conscience."

Jewish Kabalists. The latter is also "the god who is not," "Ain" signifying *non-being* or the Absolute, the *nothing* or Τὸ οὐδέν ἕν of Basilides: that is to say, the human intelligence being limited on this material plane, cannot conceive anything that *is,* which does not exist under any form. The idea of a *being* being limited to *something* which exists, either in substance,—actual or potential, —or in the nature of things, or only in our ideas; that which cannot be perceived by the senses, or conceived by our intellect that conditions everything, does not exist for us.

"Where, then, do you locate Nirvana, Oh great Arhat?" asked a king of a venerable Buddhist ascetic whom he was questioning about the Good Law.

"Nowhere, Oh great king," was the reply.
"Nirvana, then, does not exist?" said the king.
"Nirvana *is,* but it does not exist," answered the ascetic.

The same is true of the God "who is not," a faulty *literal* translation, for one ought to read esoterically *"the god who does not exist but who is."* For the root of οὐδέν is οὐδ-εἰς and means "and not somebody," which signifies that which is spoken of is not a *person* or *any thing,* but the negative of both (οὐδέν, neuter, is employed as an adverb; "in nothing"). Therefore the *to ouden en* of Basilides is absolutely identical with the *En* or *"Ain-Soph"* of the Kabalists. In the religious metaphysics of the Hebrews, the Absolute is an abstraction, "without form or existence," "without any likeness to anything else." (Franck, *Le Kabbale,* p. 153, 596.) "God therefore is NOTHING, nameless, and without qualities; that is why it is called AIN-SOPH, for the word AIN signifies *nothing."* (Franck, *Le Kabbale,* p. 153, 196.)

It is not from this immutable and absolute principle, which is only *in posse,** that the gods, or active principles of the manifested universe, emanate. The Absolute neither having, nor being able to have, any relation with the conditioned or the limited, that from which the emanations proceed is the "God that speaks" of Basilides: that is to say, the *Logos,* which Philo calls "the second God," and the creator of forms. "The second God is the Wisdom of God ONE." (*Quræst. et salut.*) "But is this *Logos,* the 'Wisdom,' always an emanation?" it will be asked, "for to make *something* emanate from NOTHING is an absurdity." Not in the least. In the first

---

* "Qui n'est qu'en puissance d'être."

place, this "nothing," is a *nothing,* because it is the *Absolute,* and consequently the WHOLE. In the next place, this "second God" is no more an emanation than the shadow that our body casts upon a white wall is an emanation of that body. At all events this God is not the effect of a cause or an act that is reasoned, or of conscious and deliberate will. It is the periodical effect† of an eternal and immutable law, independent of time and space, and of which the *Logos* or creative intelligence is the *shadow* or the *reflection.*

"But that idea is ridiculous!" We fancy we hear the believers in a personal and anthropomorphic God declare, "Of the two—man and his shadow—it is the latter which is *nothing,* an optical illusion; and the man who projects it is the intelligence, although passive in this case!"

Quite so; but that is true only upon our plane, where all is but illusion; where everything is reversed, like things seen in a mirror. For, since the domain of the real is for us, whose perceptions are falsified by matter, the unreal; and, since, from the point of view of the Absolute Reality, the universe with all its conscious and intelligent inhabitants is but a poor phantasmagoria, it follows that it is the shadow of the Real, upon the plane of this latter, that is endowed with intelligence and attributes; while the Absolute, from our point of view, is deprived of all conditioned qualities, *by the very fact that it is the absolute.* One need not be versed in Oriental metaphysics to understand all that; and it is not necessary to be a distinguished palæographer or palæologist to see that the system of Basilides is that of the Vedantins, however twisted and disfigured it may be by the author of *Philosophumena.* That it is so is conclusively proved even by the fragmentary resumé of the Gnostic systems which that work gives us. It is only the esoteric doctrine that can explain what is incomprehensible and chaotic in the little understood system of Basilides, such as it has been transmitted to us by the Fathers of the Church, those executioners of *Heresies.* The *Pater innatus* or God not begotten, the great *Archon* (’Αρχων), and the two Demiurgoi, even the three hundred and sixty-five heavens, the number contained in the name of Abraxas their ruler,—all that was derived from the Indian systems. But this is denied by our pessimistic century, in which everything goes by

---

† For him at least who believes in an uninterrupted succession of "creations," which we call "the days and nights of Brahmâ," or the *Manvantaras,* and Pralayas (dissolutions).

steam, even human life; in which nothing that is abstract,—which only is eternal,—interests anyone except a handful of *eccentrics;* and in which man dies, without having lived for one moment in the presence of his own soul,—swept away as he is by the whirlwind of egoistic and mundane affairs.

Apart from metaphysics, however, each person who enters the Theosophical Society can find therein a science and an occupation to his taste. An astronomer could make more scientific discoveries by studying the allegories and symbols relating to each star,* in the old Sanscrit books, than he could ever make by the aid only of Academies. A doctor who had intuition would learn more from the works of Charaka,† translated into Arabic in the 8th century, or in the dusty manuscripts to be found in the Adyar Library,— not understood like all the rest,—than in modern works on physiology. Theosophists interested in medicine, or *the art of healing,* might do worse than consult the legends and symbols revealed and explained through Asclepios or Æsculapius. For, just as Hypocrates consulted the votive tablets at the temple of Epidaurus, (surnamed the Tholos) at Cos,‡ so could they find therein prescriptions for compounding remedies unknown to the modern pharmacœpia.§ From thenceforth they might perhaps cure, instead of killing.

Let us repeat for the hundredth time: The Truth is one! but the moment it is presented, not under all its aspects, but according to the thousand and one opinions which its servants form about it, it is no longer the divine TRUTH, but the confused echo of human voices. Where can one look for it as a whole, even approximately? Is it among the Christian Kabalists, or the modern European Occultists? Or among the Spiritists of to-day, or the early spiritualists?

A friend said to us one day, "In France there are as many systems as there are Kabalists. Here they all pretend to be Christ-

---

* Every god or goddess of the 333,000,000, that compose the Hindu Pantheon, is represented by a star. As the number of the stars and constellations known to astronomers hardly reach that figure, one might suspect that the ancient Hindus knew more stars than the moderns.

† Charaka was a physician of the Vedic period. A legend represents him as the incarnation of the Serpent of Vishnu, under the name of Secha, who reigned in Patala (the infernal regions).

‡ Strabo, XIV, 2, 19. See also Pausan, II, 27.

§ It is known that those who were cured in the *Asclepieia* left pious memorials in the temples; that they had the names of their maladies and of the medicines that cured them engraved upon plates. A number of these tablets have lately been dug up in the Acropolis. See *L'Asclepieion d'Athens* M. P. Girard, Paris, Thorin, 1881.

ians. There are some of them who are all for the Pope, to the point of dreaming about a universal crown for him,—that of a Pontif-Cæsar. Others are against the papacy, but in favour of a Christ, not indeed the historical Christ, but one created by their imagination, an *intriguing* ("politiquant") and anti-Cæsarian Christ, and so forth. Every Kabalist believes that he has redis-covered the lost Truth. It is always his own science that is the eternal Truth, and every other nothing but a mirage; and he is always ready to support or defend it with the point of his pen."

"But the Jewish Kabalists," I asked, "are they also in favour of Christ?"

"Well, they have their own Messiah. It is only a question of dates."

There can, indeed, be no anachronisms in Eternity. The only thing is, that since all these variations of terms and systems, all these contradictory teachings, cannot contain the true Truth, I do not see how our friends, the French Kabalists, can pretend to a knowledge of the Occult Sciences. They have the Kabala of Moses de Leon,* compiled in the 13th century; but his *Zohar,* compared with the "Book of Numbers" of the Chaldeans, repre-sents the work of the Rabbi Simeon Ben Iochai, about as much as the *Pimander* of the Greek Christians represents the true Egyp-tian Book of Thoth. The ease with which the Kabala of Rosenroth and its mediæval Latin manuscripts, when read by the *system* of *Notarion,* transform themselves into Christian and Trinitarian texts, is like an effect in a fairy scene. Between the Marquis de Mirville and his friend the Chevalier Drach, a converted Rabbi, the "good Kabala" has become a Catechism of the Church of Rome. The Kabalists may be satisfied therewith if they like; we prefer to stick to the Kabala of the Chaldeans, the "Book of Numbers."

Whoever is satisfied with the dead letter, may wrap himself up in the mantle of the Tanaim (the ancient initiates of Israel); in the eyes of the experienced occultist he will never be anything but the wolf disguised in the nightcap of Little Red Riding Hood's grand-mother. But the wolf will not gobble up occultism as he does

---

* The same who compiled the *Zohar* of Simeon ben Iochai, the originals dating from the first centuries having been lost. He has been falsely accused of inventing what he has written. He collated all he could find, but he supplemented from his own resources where passages were wanting, with the help of the Christian Gnostics of Chaldea and Syria.

Little Red Riding Hood, symbol of the profane outsider athirst after mysticism. It is the "wolf" more likely who will perish, by falling into his own trap.

Like the Bible, the Kabalistic books have their dead letter, the exoteric sense, and their true or esoteric meaning. The key to the true symbolism, which is that also of the Hindu systems, is hidden to-day beyond the gigantic peaks of the Himalayas. No other key can open the sepulchres where, interred thousands of years ago, lie the intellectual treasures which were deposited there by the primitive interpreters of the divine Wisdom. But the great cycle, the first of the Kali Yuga, is at its end; the day of resurrection for all these dead cannot be far away. The great Swedish seer, Emmanuel Swedenborg, said: "Look for the lost word among the hierophants of Great Tartary and Tibet."

However much appearances may be against the Theosophical Society, however unpopular it may be among those who hold all *innovation* in horror, one thing is certain. *That which our enemies look upon as an invention of the 19th century, is as old as the world.* Our Society is the tree of Brotherhood sprung from a seed planted in the world by the angel of Charity and of Justice, on the day when the first Cain killed the first Abel. During the long centuries of the slavery of woman and the misery of the poor, this seed was watered by all the bitter tears shed by the weak and the oppressed. Blessed hands have replanted this seed in one corner of the earth and another, and in different climes, and at epochs far apart. "Do not to another the thing thou wouldst not he should do to thee," said Confucius to his disciples. "Love one another, and love every living creature," preached the Lord Buddha to his Arhats. "Love one another," was repeated like a faithful echo in the streets of Jerusalem. To the Christian nation belongs the honour of having obeyed this supreme commandment of their master, in a particularly paradoxical fashion! Caligula, the *pagan,* wished that mankind had only one head that he might cut it off with a single blow. The *Christian* powers have improved upon this idea, which remained only in theory, by seeking for, and at last finding a means to put it in practice. Let them make ready to cut each other's throats; let them continue to exterminate in one day in their wars more men than the Cæsars killed in a year; let them depopulate whole countries and provinces in the name of their paradoxical religions, and let those who kill with the sword perish by the sword themselves. What have we to do with all that?

Theosophists are powerless to stop them. Be it so. But it is their business to save as many of the survivors as possible. Nucleus of a true Brotherhood, it depends upon them to make their Society a bridge destined in the near future to carry the humanity of the new cycle beyond the muddy waters of the deluge of hopeless materialism. These waters rise continuously, and at this moment are inundating all civilized countries. Shall we leave the good to perish with bad, terrified by the clamours and mocking cries of the latter, whether against the Theosophical Society or ourselves? Shall we watch them perish one after the other,—this one of lassitude, that one unable to obtain a ray of the sun that shines for every one,— without stretching to them a plank of safety?—Never!

It may be that the beautiful Utopia, the dream of the philanthropist who sees as in a vision the accomplishment of the triple desire of the Theosophical Society, may be far off. Full and entire liberty of conscience allowed to all, fraternity reigning between the rich and the poor, equality recognized in theory and practice between the aristocrat and the plebeian,—are still so many castles in the air and for a good reason. All this must come about naturally and voluntarily on both sides, but the time has not yet arrived for the lion and the lamb to lie down together. The great reform must take place without any social shocks, without a drop of blood being spilled; which can happen in no other way than by the recognition and the axiomatic truth of Oriental Philosophy, which teaches us that the great diversity of fortune, of social rank and of intellect, is due but to the personal Karma of each human being. We reap only what we have sown. If the *personality* of each physical man differs from that of every other, the immortal *individuality,* or immaterial being in him, emanates from the same divine essence, as does that of his neighbours. He who is thoroughly impressed with the philosophic truth that every Ego begins and ends by being the indivisible WHOLE, cannot love his neighbor less than he does himself. But, until this becomes a religious truth, no such reform can take place. The egoistical proverb: "Charity begins at home," or that other one: "Everyone for himself and God for us all," will always impel "superior" and *Christian* races to oppose the practical realization of this beautiful pagan saying: "The poor man is the son of the rich one," and still more that which tells us, "Give to eat first to him that is hungry, and take that which remains for thyself."

But the time is coming when this "barbarian" wisdom of the "inferior" races will be better appreciated. What we must try to do in the meantime is to bring a little peace into the world, in the hearts of those who suffer, by raising for them a corner of the veil which hides the divine truth. Let those who are strongest show the road to those who are weaker, and help them to climb the steep hill of life; and let them teach these to fix their eyes on the Beacon which shines on the horizon like a new star of Bethlehem beyond the mysterious and unknown sea of the Theosophical Sciences,—and let the disinherited ones of life recover hope.

H. P. BLAVATSKY

(The end.)

(Translated from "Le Revue Theosophique.")

Theosophist, October, 1889

NOTES FROM "THE THEOSOPHIST"

NOTES FROM "THE THEOSOPHIST"

[During the years when H.P.B. was editor of the *Theosophist*, she often appended notes of comment, criticism, and elaboration to statements made by other writers. The frequency of these notes makes it possible to select and arrange many of them in sequence, as collations on various subjects, thus making their valuable content available to students.—Eds.]

The Theosophists *not* having as yet studied all these Bhasyas [scholarly commentaries mentioned by a contributor] have no intention to uphold any particular sectarian school. They leave this to the pandits, for whose especial benefit, among others, this journal was founded. A great American quarterly—the *North American Review*—adopts the plan of submitting some famous contributor's manuscript to one or more equally famous writers of very antagonistic views, and then printing all of the criticisms together. By this wise device, the reader of the magazine is able to see what can be said of a given subject from every point of view. We will do likewise. . . . [I, 88.]

We hold *no views at all* on anything "beyond mortal ken." Claiming the possession of our full senses, we can neither prove nor disprove that which is *beyond* the knowledge of mortal man, leaving all speculations and theories thereon to emotional enthusiasts endowed with *blind faith* that creates self-delusion and hallucinations. [IV, 186 fn.]

In our humble opinion, since there cannot be but one and only Truth, the thousand and one interpretations by different sectarians of the same and one thing are simply the outward and evanescent appearances or aspects of that which is too dazzling (or perchance too dark and too profound) for mortal eye to correctly distinguish and describe. As already remarked by us in *Isis Unveiled* the multitudinous creeds and faiths have all been derived from one primitive source. TRUTH standing as the one white ray of light, it is decomposed by the prism into various and eye-deceiving colours of the solar spectrum. Combined, the aggregate of all those endless human interpretations—shoots and offshoots—represent one eternal truth; separate, they are but shades of human error and the signs of human blindness and imperfection. However, all such publications are useful, since they fill the arena of discussion with new combatants and that truth can be reached at but after the explosion of innumerable errors. [IV, 197.]

Few have identical beliefs, and every religionist of whatever faith is firmly impressed with the truth and superiority of his own creed, with no regard whatever for the truths possibly contained in that of his brother—the result is, that sectarianism is kept ever alive, with no chance in it for mutual toleration—least of all, feelings of Brotherhood. [IV, 274 fn.] Each of them [Theosophist] believes in whatever he likes, and there is no one to interfere with his private beliefs. The Theosophical Society is no school of sectarianism and holds to no special dogmas. . . . [V, 29 fn.]

When challenged to give out our views, we do so, adding every time that they are our own *personal views*: and as such—since we do not believe ourselves infallible—are not to be taken as final truths. Instead of preaching our own religion, we implore every one to first study his own and remain in it, whatever it is. Besides which, theosophy is compatible with every religion, the world over. There were thaumaturgists in every creed, and mysticism has as much room in idolatrous as in monotheistic systems. Theosophy is the culmination and the practical demonstration of the *truths* underlying every creed. It requires but sincerity and a firm will in the application to the Essentials of any of them—whether they be Theism or Adwaitism or even Atheism. Theosophy is simply the informing life of creed and of every religion and goes to prove their *raison d'etre,* instead of their negation. [IV, 274 fn.]

The inaugural addresses of the respective presiding officers of the Ionian and Bombay Branches of the Theosophical Society, so well illustrate its policy of mutual tolerance and confraternity. Here we see the Italian thinker moved by the same lofty aspirations for individual perfection and the happiness and enlightenment of mankind, as the Parsi thinker of Bombay. And though the one conceives of the First Cause, or Deity, quite differently from the other, whose ancestors from time immemorial have worshipped the Sun as a visible type of Hormazd, yet a common religious feeling moves the heart of each, and a common instinct makes him see the way upward towards the truth brighter and clearer by the light of Theosophy. Ours is not an atheistical society, though it does contain atheists; nor is it a Christian one, even though our brother Dr. Wyld, President of the British Theosophical Society, would have us accept Jesus as the most divine personage that ever appeared among men. Our Fellows are of the most varied opinions; and each has a right to claim respect for his ideas as he is bound to respect those of his brothers. We have presidents who are severally Christian, Deist, Buddhist, Hindu and Atheist; none dogmatizers, none claiming to be wiser or more infallible than the other, yet each taking the other by the hand, calling him brother, and helping him and being helped in the divine quest after knowledge. Nor are all, or even a large minority, students of occult sciences, for rarely is the true mystic born. Few, alas! have they ever been, who so yearned after the discovery of Nature's secrets as to be willing to pursue that hard and unselfish course of study: and our own century can show fewer than any of its predecessors. As to the secrets of the Theosophical Society, when we mention the masonic-like signs of recognition, and the privacy secured for the handful who do make their experiments in psychological science, all has been said. The Parent Society is, in one word, a Republic of Conscience, a brotherhood of men in search of the Absolute Truth. As was sufficiently explained in our opening October number, every one of us professes to be ready to help the other, whatever the branch of science or religion to which his personal predilections may lead him. [I, 298.]

———•———

The Theosophical Society requires no oaths, as it deems no pledge more binding than the word of honour. [I, 35 fn.]

The comprehension of what occult science really is, has spread in Europe so very imperfectly as yet, that we must not be impatient. . . . European mystics, when further advanced in the tedious study of unintelligible books, will often be hardest to persuade that they must go back some distance on the paths they have travelled, before they can strike into those which lead to the fully illuminated regions of Eastern knowledge. They are naturally loath to confess that much time has been wasted; they try to make the fragments of esoteric Eastern philosophy they may pick up here and there, fit into the vacant places in the scheme of things they have painfully constructed for themselves, and when the fragments will not fit, they are apt to think the corners want paring down here and there, and the hollows, filling up. The situation which the European mystic does not realise is this:—The Eastern occult philosophy is the great block of solid truth from which the quaint, exoteric mysticism of the outer world has been casually thrown off from time to time, in veiled and symbolical shapes. These hints and suggestions of mystic philosophy may be likened to the grains of gold in rivers, which early explorers used to think betokened somewhere in the mountains from which the rivers sprang, vast beds of the precious metal. The occult philosophy with which some people in India are privileged to be in contact, may be likened to the parent deposits. Students will be altogether on a wrong track as long as they check the statements of Eastern philosophy by reference to the teachings and conceptions of any other systems. In saying this we are not imitating the various religionists who claim that salvation can only be had within the pale of their own small church. We are not saying that Eastern philosophy is right and everybody else is wrong, but that Eastern philosophy is the main stream of knowledge concerning things spiritual and eternal, which has come down in an unbroken flood through all the life of the world. That is the demonstrable position which we, occultists of the Theosophical Society, have firmly taken up, and all archaeological and literary research in matters connected with the earliest religions and philosophies of historical ages helps to fortify it. The casual growths of mystic knowledge in this or that country and period, may or may not be *faithful* reflections of the actual, central doctrines; but, whenever they seem to bear some resemblance to these, it may be safely conjectured that at least they are reflections, which owe what merit they possess to the original light from which they derive their own. [III, 81.]

. . . Since beginning our Indian work, we have never publicly preached our private religious views. It would be well, if this fact were never lost sight of. Colonel Olcott, in addressing audiences of various religious faiths, has always tried to put himself, for the moment in the mental attitude of believer in that faith which his audience represented, and to bring prominently before their minds the highest standard of morals and attainable wisdom which it contains. Thus, he has, to the Parsis, shown the magnificence of ancient Mazdianism; to the Hindus, the splendours of Aryan philosophy, &c. And this, not from a poor desire to indiscriminately please, but from the deep conviction, shared by us both, that there is truth in every religion, and that every sincere devotee of any faith should be respected in that devotion, and helped to see whatever of good his faith contains. [III, 237.] Our journal is *absolutely* unsectarian and equally open to every sincere and honest defender and advocate of his own faith—whatever the latter may be. We are devoted admirers of the *Vedas,* holding it in veneration as the oldest, and, as we believe, the wisest book of the world, although its mystical and allegorical language needs the interpretation of one who thoroughly understands its Spirit. As we do not feel competent to decide which of the various and many interpreters is the right one, we try to be impartial to all and let every sect (with the exception of the "Maharaja sect," of course) advocate its own cause before the public . . .

The *Rules* of our Society strictly forbid its Founders and the Presidents of its many Branches to advocate either in our journal, or at mixed and general *meetings,* any one religion in preference to any other. We are all upon neutral ground, and even our own personal religious leanings or preferences have nothing to do and must not interfere with the general work. We preach and advocate an incessant and untiring search for TRUTH, and are ever ready to receive and accept it from whatever quarter. We are all enquirers and never offered ourselves as teachers, except in so far as to teach mutual tolerance, kindness and reciprocal enlightenment and a firm resistance to bigotry and arrogant conceit whether in RELIGION OR SCIENCE [III, Supplement, October, p. 4].

To say that offering knowledge or discoveries of any sort to the Masters of Occult philosophy is carrying coals to Newcastle, is to say nothing. There may be some small details of modern science which occult philosophy has not anticipated (centuries ago), but if so, that can only be because the genius of occult philosophy leads it to deal with the main lines of principle and to care as a rule very little for details—as little as for the material advantage or comfort they may be designed to subserve. Such broad conceptions as the theory of evolution, for example, have not only been long ago known to Eastern occultists, but as developed in Europe, are now recognized by them as the first faltering step of modern science in the direction of certain grand principles with which they have been familiar,—we will not venture to say since when. . . . If the European scientists whose fancy has for the first time been caught, within these last few years, by the crude outlines of an evolutionary theory, were less blankly ignorant of all that appertains to the mysteries of life, they would not be misled by some bits of knowledge concerning the evolution of the body, into entirely absurd conclusions concerning the other principles which enter into the constitution of Man.

But we are on the threshold of a far mightier subject than any reader in Europe who has not made considerable progress in real occult study, is likely to estimate in all its appalling magnitude. Will any one who has perused with only some of the attention it really deserves the article we published but two months ago [*Theosophist,* October, 1881] under the title "Fragments of Occult Truth" make an effort to account, in his own mind, even in the most shadowy and indistinct way, for the history of the six higher principles in any human creature, during the time when his body was being gradually perfected, so to speak, in the matrix of evolution. Where, and what were his higher spiritual principles when the body had worked into no more dignified shape than that of a baboon? Of course, the question is put with a full recognition of the collateral errors implied in the treatment of a single human being as the apex of a series of forms, but even supposing that physical evolution were as simple a matter as that how to account for the final presence in the perfected human body of a spiritual soul?— or to go a step back in the process, how to account for the presence of the animal soul in the first creature with independent volition that emerges from the half vegetable condition of the earlier forms? Is it not obvious, if the blind materialist is not to be accepted as a sufficient guide to the mysteries of the universe,—if there really are these higher principles in Man of which we speak, that there must be some vast process of spiritual evolution going on in the universe *pari passu* with the physical evolution? . . . [III, 81.]

No more than any given material form is destined to infinite perpetuation can the finer organisms which constitute the higher principles of living creatures be doomed to unchangeability. What has become of the particles of matter which composed the physical bodies of "man's predecessors on the earth"? They have long ago been ground over in the laboratory of Nature, and have entered into the composition of other forms. And the idea or design of the earlier forms has risen into superior idea or design which has impressed itself on later forms. So also, though the analogy may give us no more than a cloudy conception of the course of events, it is manifest that the higher principles, once united with the earlier forms, must have developed in their turn also. Along what infinite spirals of gradual ascent the spiritual evolution has been accomplished, we will not stop now to consider. Enough to point out the direction in which thought should proceed, and some few considerations which may operate to check European thinkers from too readily regarding the realms of spirit as a mere phantasmagorical cemetery, where shades of the Earth's buried inhabitants doze for ever in an aimless trance. [III, 82.]

For the present we merely throw out hints and endeavour to provoke thought and enquiry; to attempt in this casual manner, a complete exposition of the conclusions of Eastern philosophy . . . would be like starting on a journey to the South Pole *apropos* to a passing enquiry whether one thought there was land there or not. [III, 81-2.]

———•———

To the Editor of the *Theosophist*
Madame,
    On the last page of No. 4 of "Psychic Notes," a correspondent is made to state that he, together with a few friends *"out of mere curiosity and for the fun of the thing,"* arranged a series of *séances*. The first was unsuccessful, but the remaining ones were productive of *"proofs innumerable."* And yet none of the parties present was a "conjuror, mesmerist, medium or spiritualist!"
    Is this possible? I always thought that the presence of a medium at *séances* was a necessary condition of manifestations. Or can it be that some one at the *séances* in question was—if that were possible—an *unconscious* medium?
    Your opinion will be highly valued by

Yours obediently,

H.

The possible explanation of such manifestations can be found only in one of the following three hypotheses:

(1) The presence of a medium—either conscious or unconscious.

(2) The presence of an adept, or his influence; although no adept would trouble himself with such—(what to him are)—trifles. Or—which is the most probable—

(3) The combined result of the magnetic aura of the persons present, forming a strong battery. This would be very likely to produce such manifestations, whether there were a medium present or not. [III, 162-63.]

Many and varied are the psychic phenomena in life, which unintentionally or otherwise are either attributed to the agency of disembodied "spirits" or entirely and intentionally *ignore*d. By saying this we do not intend at all depriving the spiritual theory of its *raison d'être*. But beside that theory there exist other manifestations of the same psychic force in man's daily life, generally disregarded or erroneously looked upon as a result of simple chance or coincidence, for the only reason that we are unable to forthwith assign for it a logical and comprehensive cause though the manifestations undoubtedly bear the impress of a scientific character, evidently belonging, as they do, to that class of psycho-physiological phenomena which, even men of great scientific attainments and such specialists as Dr. Carpenter are now busying themselves with. The cause for this particular phenomenon is to be sought in the occult (yet no less undeniable for it) influence exercised by the active will of one man over the will of another man, whenever the will of the latter is surprised in a moment of rest or a state of passiveness. We speak now of *presentiments*. Were every person to pay close attention—in an experimental and scientific spirit of course—to his daily action and watch his thoughts, conversation and resultant acts, and carefully analyze these, omitting no details trifling as they might appear to him, then would he find for the most of these actions and thoughts coinciding *reasons* based upon mutual psychic influence between the embodied intelligences.

Several instances, more or less familiar to every one through *personal* experience, might be here adduced. We will give but two. Two friends or even simple acquaintances are separated for years. Suddenly one of them—he who remained at home and who may have never thought of the absent person for years, thinks of that individual. He remembers him without any possible cause or reason, and the long-forgotten image sweeping through the silent corridors of MEMORY brings it before his eyes as vividly as if he were there. A few minutes after that, an hour perhaps, that absent person *pays the other an unexpected visit.* Another instance —A lends to B a book. B having read and laid it aside thinks no more of it, though A requested him to return the work immediately after perusal. Days, perhaps months after that, B's thought occupied with important business, suddenly reverts to the book, and he remembers his neglect. Mechanically he leaves his place and stepping to his library gets it out, thinking to send it back without fail this once. At the same moment, the door opens, A enters, telling that he had come purposely to fetch his book, as he needed it. Coincidence? Not at all. In the first case it was the thought of the traveller, which, as he had decided upon visiting an old friend or acquaintance, *was concentrated upon the other man,* and that thought by its very activity proved energetic enough to overpower the *then passive* thought of the other.

The same explanation stands good in the case of A and B. But Mr. Constantine [a correspondent] may argue, "my late friend's thought could not influence mine since he was already dead, when I was being irresistibly drawn to Agra." Our answer is ready. Did not the warmest friendship exist between the writer and the deceased? Had not the latter promised to be with him in "thought and spirit?" And that leads to the positive inference that his thought was strongly pre-occupied before his death, with him whom he had unintentionally disappointed. Sudden as may have been that death, thought is instantaneous and more rapid still. Nay, it surely was a hundredfold intensified at the moment of death. Thought is the last thing that dies or rather fades out in the human brain of a dying person, and thought, as demonstrated by science, is material, since it is but a mode of energy, which itself changes form but is eternal. Hence, that thought whose strength and power are always proportionate to its intensity, became, so to say, concrete and palpable, and with the help of the strong affinity between the two, it enveloped and overpowered the whole sentient and thinking principle in Mr. Constantine subjecting it entirely, and forcing the will of the latter to act in accordance with his desire. The thinking agent was dead, and the instrument lay shattered for ever. But its last sound lived, and could not have completely died out, in the waves of ether.

Science says, the vibration of one single note of music will linger on in motion through the corridors of all eternity; and theosophy, the last thought of the dying man changes into the man himself; it becomes his *eidolon*. Mr. Constantine would not have surprised us, nor would he have indeed deserved being accused by the skeptical of either superstition or of having labored under a hallucination had he even seen the *image,* or the so-called "ghost" of his deceased friend before him. For that "ghost" would have been neither the conscious spirit nor the soul of the dead man; but simply his short—for one instant—*materialized* thought projected unconsciously and by the sole power of its own intensity in the direction of him who occupied that THOUGHT. [II, 188.]

———————•———————

[The following are replies to questions by two correspondents. Since the questions are sometimes long, argumentative, and of small interest, H.P.B.'s answers and comments have been extracted so that they may be read as independent statements of the philosophy.—Eds.]

We fear our correspondent is labouring under various misconceptions. . . . But we will briefly answer his numbered questions at the close of the letter.

1. Spirit got itself entangled with gross matter for the same reason that *life* gets entangled with the *foetus* matter. It followed a law, and therefore could not help the entanglement to occur.

2. We know of no eastern philosophy that teaches that "matter originated out of Spirit." Matter is as eternal and indestructible as Spirit and one cannot be made cognizant to our senses without the other—even to our, the highest, spiritual sense. Spirit *per se* is a *non-entity* and *non-existence*. It is the *negation* of every affirmation and of all that is.

3. No one ever held—as far as we know—that *Spirit* could be *annihilated* under whatever circumstances. Spirit can get divorced of its manifested matter, its personality, in which case, it is the latter that is annihilated. Nor do we believe that "Spirit breathed out Matter"; but that, on the contrary, it is *Matter which manifests Spirit*. Otherwise, it would be a *puzzle* indeed. [IV, 89-90].

To our utter amazement, we are called upon to prove that matter is indestructible; at any rate, that "matter is as eternal and indestructible as spirit!" Though the question and proofs as to the eternity and indestructibility of matter alone, might be safely left to the Royal Society to answer, yet we are fully prepared to satisfy our learned correspondent, and, with his permission, will answer all his queries.

We are asked to bear in mind that the *entities* in question are "matter and spirit beyond the present developed form, or in the stage of perfect *Laya*."

We are unable to understand what is really meant by "spirit beyond the present developed form." The sentence presents no sense to our mind, trained as it has been by our great masters to think of "Spirit" as of something formless and entirely beyond the ken of our sensual perceptions, and, therefore, not to be considered apart from, or independently of, corporeal existence. Universal Intelligence and the One Life as we call it, conceived of, apart from any physical organization, becomes vital essence, an energy or force; and none of these we believe can be considered as a distinct entity, a substance, or, as having a being or even a form separate from matter. Locke's definition, that "Spirit is a *substance,* in which thinking, knowing, doubting and a power of moving do subsist"—would hardly be accepted by the average Vedantee, and would find itself absolutely rejected by every true Adwaitee and Eastern Occultist. The latter would answer that "matter alone is a substance, in which thinking, knowing, doubting, and a power of moving, are *inherent* whether as a latent or active potentiality—and whether that matter is in a differentiated, or an undifferentiated state."

Thus, in our humble opinion, the something, or rather the *nothing*, called Spirit, has by itself no form or forms in either progressive or stationary "states of development"; and we say again that the expression is perfectly unintelligible to every real Adwaitee. Even supposing that the qualifying clause refers only to matter, the meaning conveyed by the expression "matter and spirit beyond the present developed form" is the same as conveyed by that of—"matter and spirit in the stage of perfect *Laya*." We fail to see the point made, or even any sense in such a sentence as "matter and spirit in the stage of perfect *Laya*," implying as it does the possibility of spirit, a pure abstraction, being dissolved and annihilated—we will not say—as matter—since the latter in its primordial, cosmic state can be no more annihilated or even dissolved than spirit—but as a *thing* of matter having substance and form. Can a *void* be annihilated? And what is pure, *absolute* spirit but the "void" of the ancient Greek philosophers? Well says Lucretius: "there can be no third thing besides body and void; for if it be to the smallest extent tangible—it is *body;* if not— it is void." And let it not be urged, on the strentgh of this quotation, that, because we quote the words of a great "Atheist," a *materialist,* as an authority, we are therefore a materialist and an atheist (in the usual sense of both terms) ourself. We object to the very term "materialism" if it is to be made identical with, or a synonym of "corporealism," that is to say, an antithesis of, "Spiritualism." In the light we, Occultists, regard matter, we are all materialists. But it does not at all stand to reason that because of that, we should be, at the same time, "corporealists" denying in any sense or way the reality of the so-called spiritual existence, or of any being or beings, living on another plane of life, in higher and far more perfect worlds than ours, or having their being in *states* of which no untrained mind can have the smallest conception. Hence our objection to the idea and possibility of "matter and spirit, in the stage of perfect *Laya"* unless it can be shown that we have misunderstood the latter word. According to the doctrines of the Arhat philosophy there are *seven* states of matter, the 7th state being the sum total, the condition or aspect of *Mula-prakriti!*[1]

Consequently the state of cosmic matter beyond its "present developed form" may mean any of the other six states in which it exists: and hence it cannot necessarily mean "matter in a stage of perfect Laya." In what sense then, does the learned querist want us to interpret the words "matter" and "spirit?" For, though we are aware that there exist, even in the present age of science and enlightenment, persons who, under the pretext of religion teach the ignorant masses that there was a time when matter *did not exist* (since it was *created*) implying thus that there will come a moment when it will be annihilated, we have never yet met any one, whether atheist or deist, materialist or spiritualist, who would presume to say that spirit—whether we call it "void" or "divine breath"—can ever be *annihilated;* and if the word *Laya*

---

1 Undifferentiated cosmic matter.

means *annihilation,* the very expression used by the respected Swami involves an assumption that "spirit" can be destroyed in course of time. In such a case, we are evidently called upon to demonstrate that matter and spirit are eternal on the supposition that both have a period of *"Laya."* If we are to avoid this extremely—*awkward* conclusion, what is the purport of the Swami's questions? . . .

Our "assertion" then means the following: undifferentiated cosmic matter or *Mulaprakriti,* as it is called in Hindu books, is *uncreated* and eternal. It would be impossible to prove this assertion from *a priori* reasons, but its truth can be tested by the ordinary inductive method. In every objective phenomenon perceived, either in the present plane of consciousness or in any other plane requiring the exercise of spiritual faculties, there is but change of cosmic matter from one form to another. There is not a single instance, or the remotest suspicion of the annihilation of an atom of matter even brought to light either by Eastern adepts or Western scientists. When the common experience of generations of adepts in their own spiritual or psychic field of observation, and of the ordinary people in theirs—(*i.e.,* in the domain of physical science) points to the conclusion that there never has been the utter annihilation of a single material particle, we are justified, we believe, in saying that matter is indestructible, though it may change its forms and properties and appear in various degrees of differentiation. Hindu and Buddhist philosophers have ages ago recognised the fact that *Purush* and *Prakriti* are eternal, co-existent, and not only correlative and interdependent but positively one and the same thing for him who can read between the lines. Every system of evolution commences with postulating the existence of *Mulaprakriti* or *Tamas* (primeval darkness). . . . . All those great philosophers of India who have added the ancient wisdom-religion of Agasthya, Thoorwasa and other Rishis to the pure Adwaita philosophy of Vasishta, Vyasa and Suka, have recognized this fact. Goodapatha and Sankaracharya have given expression to their views on the subject in their works, and those views are in perfect accordance with the doctrines of the Arhat philosophy. The authority of the latter two great philosophers will, we believe, be sufficient to show to the learned Swami, since he is an Adwaitee, that our statement is correct. And Primeval cosmic matter, whether called Asath or Tamas, or Prakriti or Sakti, is ever the same, and held to be eternal by both Hindu and Arhat philosophers, while *Purusha* is inconceivable, hence non-existent, save when manifesting through Prakriti. In its undifferentiated condition, some Adwaitees refuse to recognise it as matter, properly so called. Nevertheless this entity is their PARABRAHMAM, with its dual aspect of Purush and Prakriti. In their opinion it can be called neither; hence in some passages of the *Upanishads* we find the expression "PRAKRITI-*layam*" mentioned; but in all such passages the word "Prakriti" means, as we can prove—*matter in a state of differentiation,* while *undifferentiated* cosmic matter in conjunction with, or rather in its aspect of, *latent* spirit is always referred to as "MAH-ISWARA," "Purusha" and "Parampada." . . .

In reference to the real meaning of *"Satta Samanya* and *Parampada*[2] of the Aryan adepts, Nirvana of the Buddhas and the Philosopher's stone," their meanings are identical in both the Aryan and Arhat secret doctrines. *Satta Samanya* sometimes means *latent spirit*. It also means "Guna *Samyapadhi,"* or the undifferentiated condition of SATWAGUNA, RAJAGUNA AND TAMAGUNA.[3] As to *Parampada* and Nirvana, both mean the same thing. From an objective point of view it is the condition of Purush-Prakriti as above described; from the subjective—it is a state of perfect unconsciousness resulting as bare *Chidakasam.* [IV, 128-29.]

Spirit is not "sublimated matter" in our opinion. Matter or manifested *prakriti,* however sublimated or refined, is but an emanation from Parabrahmam. The 7th principle of evoluted matter, as it is now technically called in theosophical phraseology, has of course its *latent* existence (which, when closely examined, amounts merely to a permanent possibility of its evolution) in this principle eternally. If the term matter is however used to mean what is technically called Mulaprakriti, this principle may be described as material. But in our opinion this will be misleading. This principle is no doubt in one sense the remote *Upadana Karanam* of the Universe. Every object in the Universe is constructed out of the elements that emanated from it. But there is no entity in the Universe of which it is *immediately* the *Upadana Karanam.* [V, 300.]

The term "Master Atom" is not applicable to the 7th principle,

---

2 Literally—*the most sacred place;* means Nirvana or the condition of *Moksha.*

3 *Satwaguna*—the quality of passivity, or absence of any cause or disturbance: *Rajaguna*—the quality of activity, or that which induces to action; *Tamaguna*—the quality of ignorance, inactivity of mental and spiritual faculties arising from that ignorance.

though it can be very properly used in reference to the 6th, the vehicle of spirit, or spiritual soul. The views of the occultists upon *spirit* and soul may be said to adopt the middle ground between the theories of Boscovich and Helmholtz, on the intimate nature of matter. The 7th principle, or rather its essence, belongs to the *seventh* state of matter, *i.e.,* a state which may be viewed in our mundane conceptions as pure spirit; while the nature of the *sixth* principle is not a *center of force* like its spirit, a centre in which the idea of all substance disappears altogether, but a fluidic or rather ethereal "atom." The former is undifferentiated, the latter—differentiated matter, though in its highest and purest state. One—the life that animates the atom, the other the vehicle that contains it. [IV, 244 fn.]

The *Maha-Pralaya* of the Universal Dissolution occurring at the end of every "Day of Brahma" is followed by a Universal *Rebirth* at the end of the "Night of Brahma" which corresponds in length of period to the "Day." It is the beginning of such a rebirth that is considered by the vulgar minds as the "creation" of the world, whereas it is but one of the number of successive existences in an infinite series of *re*-evolutions in the Eternity. Therefore, as Spirit and Matter are one and eternal, the one being thrown into objectivity by the other, and none capable of asserting itself *per se* to our sensual perceptions unless linked together, these "Entities" have "always" existed. [II, 253.]

No Planetary Spirit (and each human "Soul"—rather *Spirit* at the beginning of every new *Pralaya* or the periodical resurrection to objective and subjective life of *our* universe,—limited, of course, to our planetary System—is a planetary pure and formless Spirit) can avoid the "Cycle of Necessity." Descending from, and re-ascending to the first starting-point, that junction in the Infinity where Spirit or *Purusha* first falls into *Prakriti* (plastic matter) or that primordial and yet formless cosmic matter which is the first out-breathing of the Infinite and Changeless Universal Soul (the *Parabrahm* of the Vedantins), the Planetary Spirit has to take shape and form and live successively in each of the spheres—our own earth included—which compose the great *Maha Yug*, or the Circle of Existences, before he can lead a *conscious* Ego-life. Alone the "Elementals"—those half-blind Forces of Nature—say the Kabalists—which are the coruscations of matter and of the rudimentary minds of the descending "spirits" who have failed on their downward way—have not yet lived but will live some day on earth. The esoteric philosophies of both the eastern and western initiates, whether Greek or Hindu, Egyptian or Hebrew, agree on the whole." Whenever they seem to clash, it will be always found due rather to the difference of terms and mode of expression than to any essential difference in the systems themselves. [II, 252.]

Buddhism and Adwaitism are as much religions as any theistic system. A "religion" does not necessarily imply the doctrine of a personal God or any kind of God in it. Religion, as every dictionary can show, comes from the Latin word *relegere,* to "bind" or collect together. Thus whether people pursue a common idea with, or without, a deity in it, if they are bound together by the same and one belief in something, that belief is a *religion.* Theology without the vital warmth of Theosophy is a corpse without life, a dry stick without sap. Theosophy blesses the world; Theology is its curse. Our whole endeavour is to test Theology by the theosophical *experimentum crucis.* The affliction of India is, that it lost theosophy when the persecuted adepts had to fly beyond the mountains. And true religious living can never be again prevalent until their help is invoked to illumine the *Shastras.* Our Brother has had many years' experience of the hopelessness of converting India to even the benign form of theism which his *Adi Brahmo* Samaj teaches. The saintly characters of Ram Mohun Roy, Debendro Nath Tagore, and a few others of his colleagues, have not won the Hindus from their exoteric worship—we think, because neither of them has had the Yogi power to prove *practically* the fact of there being a spiritual side to nature. If we hold so strongly to esoteric Buddhism and Adwaitism, it is exactly because no religion can stand save on the foundation of philosophy and science. No religion can prove by *practical,* scientific demonstration that there is such a thing as one *personal* God; while the esoteric philosophy, or rather *theosophy* of Guatama Buddha and Sankaracharya *prove* and give means to every man to ascertain the undeniable presence of a living God in man himself—whether one believes in or calls his divine indweller Avalokiteswara, Buddha, Brahma, Krishna, Jehovah, Bhagwan, Ahura-mazda, Christ, or by whatever name—there is no such God outside of himself. The former—the one ideal outsider—*can never be demonstrated* —the latter, under whatever appellation, may always be found present if a man does not extinguish within himself the capacity to perceive this Divine presence, and hear the "voice" of that only manifested deity, the murmurings of the Eternal *Vach,* called by the Northern and Chinese Buddhist Avalokiteswara and Kwan-shen-yi and by the Christians—*Logos.* [IV, 275.]

For us there is no *over-soul* or under-soul; but only ONE—*substance*: the last word being used in the sense Spinoza attaches to it; calling it the ONE *Existence,* we cannot limit its significance and dwarf it to the qualification "over"; but we apply it to the universal, ubiquitous Presence, rejecting the word "Being," and replacing it with *"All*-Being." Our Deity as the "God" of Spinoza and of the true Adwaitee—neither *thinks,* nor *creates,* for it is *All-thought* and *All-creation.* We say with Spinoza—who repeated in another key but what the Esoteric doctrine of the Upanishads teaches: 'Extension is visible Thought; Thought is invisible Extension.' For Theosophists of our school the Deity is a UNITY in which all other units in their infinite variety merge and from which they are indistinguishable—except in the prism of theistic *Maya.* The individual drops of the curling waves of the universal Ocean have no independent existence. In short, while the Theist proclaims his God a gigantic universal BEING, the Theosophist declares with Heraclitus, as quoted by a modern author, that the ONE Absolute is not Being—but *becoming*: the ever-developing, cyclic evolution, the Perpetual Motion of Nature visible and invisible—moving, and breathing even during its long Pralayic Sleep. . . .

We do not maintain that Parabrahm is absolutely without *any guna,* for *Presence* itself is a *guna,* but that it is beyond the three *gunas*—*Satva, Rajas* and *Tamas.*

When the term Logos, Verbum, Vach, the mystic *divine voice* of every nation and philosophy comes to be better understood, then only will come the first glimmering of the Dawn of one Universal Religion. *Logos* was never *human* reason with us. [V, 75.]

For the benefit of those of our readers in India, who, although excellent Vedantic scholars, may have never heard of Arthur Schopenhauer and his philosophy, it will be useful to say a few words regarding this German Metaphysician, who is ranked by many among the world's great philosophers. . . . A student of the Göttingen and Berlin Universities, a friend of Goethe and his disciple initiated by him into the mysteries of colour (See A. Schopenhauer's Essay *Ueber Sehen and Farben,* 1816), he evoluted, so to say, into a profoundly original thinker without any seeming transaction, and brought his philosophical views into a full system before he was thirty. Possessed of a large private fortune, which enabled him to pursue and develop his ideas uninterruptedly, he remained an independent thinker and soon won for himself, on account of his strangely pessimistic view of the world, the name of the "misanthropic sage." The idea that the present world is radically evil, is the only important point in his system that differs from the teachings of the Vedanta. According to his philosophical doctrines, the only thing truly real, original, metaphysical and absolute, is WILL. The world of objects consists simply of appearances; of *Maya* or illusion—as the Vedantins have it. It lies entirely in, and depends on, our representation. Will is the "thing in itself" of the Kantian philosophy, "the substratum of all appearances and of nature herself. It is totally different from, and wholly independent of, cognition, can exist and manifest itself without it, and actually does so in all nature from animal beings downward."

Not only the voluntary actions of animated beings, but also the organic frame of their bodies, its form and quality, the vegetation of plants, and in the inorganic kingdom of nature, crystallization and every other original power which manifests itself in physical and chemical phenomena, as well as gravity, are something outside of appearance and identical with, what we find in ourselves and call—WILL. An intuitive recognition of the identity of will in all the phenomena separated by individuation is the source of justice, benevolence, and love; while from a non-recognition of its identity spring egotism, malice, evil and ignorance. This is the doctrine of the Vedantic *avida* (ignorance) that makes of *Self* an object distinct from Parabrahm, or Universal Will. Individual soul, physical self, are only imagined by ignorance and have no more reality and existence than the objects seen in a dream. With Schopenhauer it also results from this original identity of will in all its phenomena, that the reward of the good and the punishment of the bad are not reserved to a future heaven or a future hell, but are ever present (the doctrine of *Karma,* when philosophically considered and from its esoteric aspect). Of course the philosophy of Schopenhauer was radically at variance with the systems of Schelling, Hegel, Herbert and other contemporaries, and even with that of Fichte, for a time his master, and whose philosophical system while studying under him, he openly treated with the greatest contempt. But this detracts in nothing from his own original and profoundly philosophical though often too pessimistic views. His doctrines are mostly interesting when compared with those of the Vedanta of "Sankaracharya's" school, inasmuch as they show the great identity of thought arriving at the same conclusions between men of two quite different epochs, and with over two milleniums between them.

When some of the mightiest and most puzzling problems of being are thus approximately solved at different ages and by men entirely independent of one another, and that the most philosophically profound propositions, premises and conclusions arrived at by our best modern thinkers are found on comparison nearly, and very often entirely, identical with those of older philosophers as enunciated by them thousands of years back, we may be justified in regarding "the heathen" systems as the primal and most pure sources of every subsequent philosophical development of thought. [IV, 210.]

Let it not be understood that we here speak of the "Magi" in general, whether we view them as one of the Medean tribes(?) as some Orientalists (Darmesteter for one), relying upon a vague statement of Herodotus believe, or a sacerdotal caste like the Brahmans—as we maintain. We refer but to their initiates. The origin of the Brahmans and Magi in the night of time—is one, the secret doctrine teaches us. First, they were a hierarchy of adepts, of men profoundly versed in physical and spiritual sciences and occult knowledge, of various nationalities, all celibates, and enlarging their numbers by the transmission of their knowledge to voluntary neophytes. Then when their numbers became too large to be contained in the "Airyânâm vaejô," the adepts scattered far and wide, and we can trace them establishing other hierarchies on the model of the first in every part of the globe, each hierarchy increasing, and finally becoming so large, as to have to restrict admission; the "half adepts" going back to the world, marrying and laying the first foundation of the "left-hand" science or sorcery, the misuse of the Holy Knowledge. In the third stage— the members of the *True ones* become with every age more limited and secret, the admissions being beset now with new difficulties. We begin to see the origin of the Temple Mysteries. The hierarchy divides into two parts. The chosen few, the hierophants —the *imperium in imperio*—remaining celibates, the *exoteric* priests make of marriage a law, an attempt to perpetuate adepts by hereditary descent, and fail sadly in it. Thus we find Brahmans and Magi, Egyptian priests and Roman hierarchs and Augurs enjoining married life and inventing religious clauses to prove its necessity. No need repeating and reminding the reader of that which is left to his own knowledge of history, and his intuitions. In our day we find the descendants, the heirs to the old wisdom scattered all over the globe in small isolated and unknown communities, whose objects are misunderstood, and whose origin has been forgotten; and only two religions, the result of the teaching of those priests and hierophants of old. The latter are found in the sorry remains called respectively—Brahmans and Dasturs or Mobeds. But there is still the nucleus left, albeit it be so strenuously denied, of the heirs of the primitive Magi, of the Vedic *Magha* and the Greek *Magos*—the priests and gods of old, the last of whom manifested openly and defiantly during the Christian era in the person of Apollonius of Tyana. [IV, 225, fn.]

Although the Himalayan Brothers admit the esoteric meaning of the Vedas and the Upanishads, they refuse to recognize as Gods, the powers and other spiritual entities mentioned in the Vedas. The language used in the Vedas is allegorical and this fact has been fully recognized by some of the greatest Indian Philosophers.

There are Mahatmas among the Himalayan Brothers who are Hindus—*i.e.,* born of Hindu and Brahmin parents and who recognize the *esoteric* meaning of the Vedas and the Upanishads. They agree with Krishna, Buddha, Vyasa, Suka, Goudapatha and Sankaracharya in considering that the *Karma kanda* of the Vedas is of no importance whatsoever so far as man's spiritual progress is concerned. Remember in this connection Krishna's celebrated advice to Arjuna. "The subject matter of the Vedas is related to the three Gunas; oh Arjuna, divest thyself of these gunas." Sankaracharya's uncompromising attitude towards Purwamimansa is too well known to require any special mention here. [IV, 146.]

Funeral Rites among Savage Races

In your note to the letter on "The Efficacy of Funeral Ceremonies" (see *Theosophist,* June, 1883, p. 221), you remark "that very few among the so-called savage primitive races, had or have any funeral rites or ceremonies."

Allow me to point out that the aborigines of the Chota Nagpur plateau have a very ancient custom of erecting large blocks of unhewn stone in memory of their "departed dead."

These pillars vary in height from 5 to 15 feet.

I append hereto a rough copy of some at a village called Pokuria, 4 miles south of Chaibassa, the highest of which is 8 feet 4 inches above ground. Vide Col. Dalton's "Ethnology of Bengal," p. 203.

W.D.

We are sorry to be unable to reproduce the sketch of the said pillars. But we would observe to our amiable correspondent, that in saying that "very few among the savage primitive races had or have any funeral ceremonies," we were not thinking of the monoliths, and memorial stones placed on their tombs. The latter cannot be classed with either "rites," or "ceremonies," but belong to the various modes of disposing of the dead, and preserving the memory of the seat where they were buried. They entail none of that extravagant expenditure lavished by the Hindus and Parsees as well as by the Roman Catholic and Greeks upon obsequial ceremonies in which human variety forces them to outvie each other in the eyes of their indifferent neighbours, and to satisfy the lucre of their Brahmins and priests, under the alleged penalty of offending their dead—a superstition worthy of, and pardonable in, savages, but wholly unworthy and as unpardonable in the XIXth century, and among civilized nations. [IV, 281.]

In every country, as among all the peoples of the world from the beginning of history, we see that some kind of burial is performed —but that very few among the so-called savage primitive races had or have any funeral rites or ceremonies. The well-meaning tenderness felt by us for the dead bodies of those whom we loved or respected, may have suggested, apart from the expression of natural grief, some additional marks of family respect for them who had left us for ever. But rites and ceremonies as prescribed by our respective Churches and their theologians, are an afterthought of the priest, an outgrowth of theological and clerical ambition, seeking to impress upon the laity a superstition, a well-paying awe and dread of a punishment of which the priest himself knows nothing beyond mere speculative and often very illogical hypotheses. The Brahmin, the Mobed, the Augur, the Rabbi, the Moollah and the Priest, impressed with the fact that their physical welfare depended far more upon his parishioners, whether dead or alive, than the spiritual welfare of the latter on his alleged mediatorship between men and God, found the device expedient and good, and ever since worked on this line. Funeral rites have originated among the theocratically governed nations, such as the ancient Egyptians, Aryans, and Jews. Interwoven with, and consecrated by the ceremonies of theology, these rites have been adopted by the respective religions of nearly all the nations, and are preserved by them to this day; for while religions differ considerably among themselves, the rites often surviving the people as the religion to which they owed their origin have passed from one people to another. Thus, for instance, the threefold sprinkling with earth with which the christian is consigned to the tomb, is handed down to the westerns from the Pagan, Greeks and Romans; and modern Parseeism owes a considerable portion of its prescribed funeral rites, we believe, to the Hindus, much in their present mode of worship being due to grafts of Hinduism. Abraham and other Patriarchs were buried without any rites, and even in Leviticus (Chap. xix. v. 28) the Israelites are forbidden to "make any cuttings in the flesh, for the dead, nor print any marks" upon themselves. In the same manner the oldest Zoroastrian books, the old and the new *Desatir,* with the exception of a few acts of charity (to the poor, not to the Mobeds) and the reading of sacred books, prescribe no special ceremonies. We find in the Book of the Prophet Abad (*Desatir*) simply the following:

"154. A corpse you may place in a vase of aqua-fortis, or consign it to the fire, or to the earth, (when cleansed of its *Nasu* or dead matter)."

And again:

"At the birth of a child or the death of a relative, read the

Nosk, and give something in the road of Mazdam (for Ormuzd's sake, or in charity.)"

That's all, and nowhere will one find in the oldest books the injunction of the ceremonies now in use, least of all that of spending large sums of money which often entails ruin upon the survivors . . . [IV, 221-22.]

A ceremony to furnish the shell "with an armour" against terrestrial attraction need not be repeated "a number of years" to become efficacious, could it but be performed by a person versed in the knowledge of the Magi of old. One such ceremony on the night of death would suffice. But where is the *Mobed* or priest capable of performing it *now?* It requires a true occultist—and these are not found at every street corner. Hence—it becomes useless to add ruin to the *living,* since the *dead* cannot be helped.

Nor, from the occult stand-point, do such rites benefit in the least the departed soul. The correct comprehension of the law of Karma is entirely opposed to the idea. As no person's karma can be either lightened or overburdened with the good or bad actions of the next of kin of the departed one, every man having his Karma independent and distinct from that of his neighbour—no more can the departed soul be made responsible for the doings of those it left behind. As some make the credulous believe that the four principles may be made to suffer from colics, if the survivors ate immoderately of some fruit. Zoroastrianism and Hinduism have wise laws—far wiser than those of the Christians—for the disposal of their dead, but their superstitions are still very great. For while the idea that the presence of the dead brings pollution to the living is no better than a superstition, unworthy of the enlightened age we live in, the real cause of the religious prohibition to handle too closely the dead and to bury them without first subjecting the bodies to the disinfectant process of either fire, vultures or *aqua-fortis* (the latter the prevailing method of the Parsis in days of old) was as beneficent in its results as it was wise, since it was the best and most necessary sanitary precaution against epidemics. The Christians might do worse than borrow that law from the "Pagans," since no further than a few years back, a whole province of Russia was nearly depopulated, in consequence of the crowded condition of its burial grounds. Too numerous interments within a limited space and a comparatively short time saturate the earth with the products of decomposition to such a degree, as to make it incapable of further absorbing them, and the decomposition under such a condition being retarded its products escape directly into the atmosphere, bringing on epidemic diseases and plagues. "Let the dead bury their dead"—were wise words though to this day no theologian seems to have understood their real and profound meaning. There were no funeral rites or ceremonies at the death of either Zoroaster, Moses or Buddha, beyond the simple putting out of the way of the living corpses of them who had gone before.

Though neither the *Dabistan* or the *Desatir* can, strictly speaking, be included in the number of orthodox Parsi books—the contents of both of these if not the works themselves anteceding *by several milleniums* the ordinances in the *Avesta* as we have now good reasons to know—we yet find the first command repudiated but the second corroborated in the latter. In *Fargard* VIII (Verse "74" 233 of *Vendidad*) Ahura Mazda's command: "They shall kill the man that burns the corpse," &c., is thus commented upon— "He who burns Nasá (dead matter) must be killed. . . . Burning Nasá from the dead is a capital crime [*Fargard* I, 17 (63)] for . . . Thereupon came Angra Mainyu, who created by his witchcraft a sin for which there is no atonement, the (*immediate*) burning of corpses."[1] Ahriman being man's own ignorance and selfishness.

But as regards the rites observed after the funeral of the corpse, we find no more than this—a repetition of the injunction given in the *Book of Abad* (*Desatir*). "An Athravan . . . shall say aloud these fiend-smiting words:—Yathâ ahû vairyô—the riches of Vohu-manô (paradise; *vohu-mano* or Good Thought being the doorkeeper of heaven—see *Farg.* XIX, 31)—shall be given to him who works in this world for Mazda and wields agreeably to the will of Ahura the power he gave to him to relieve the poor (*Farg.* VIII, v. 19-49).

Thus while abrogating the Fersendajian usage of burning the dead among the devotees of Mah-Abad, Zerdusht the 13th (of

---

1 Twelve hours at least had to elapse between the death of the person and the burning or the destruction by any other means of the corpse of the dead. This old law was equally forgotten by the Brahmins as by the Zoroastrians. It was not the act of *burning* that was forbidden, but the burning before the corpse was empty, viz., before the inner principles had that time to get entirely liberated. As the *aqua-fortis* was thought possessed of an occult property to that effect, hence the preliminary burning of the flesh by this means—with the Fersendajians.

the Persian prophets) *who introduces* many improvements and reforms, yet he commands no other rites than charity. [IV, 222.]

The air is thronged with *shells*—the pale reflections of men and women who lived and whose *reliquiæ* are magnetically drawn to those whom they had loved on earth.

As to the efficacy of *Pindam* [offerngs to the dead] or *Shraddha* we deny it most emphatically. The custom of such *post-mortem* offerings having been in existence for long centuries and forming part and parcel of the Hindu religion, they produce effects, only owing to the strong belief in them of the offerers, or the *pujarees*. It is the latter who cause unconsciously the production of such phenomena. Let there only be a strong medium in the midst of pilgrims (something that happens invariably in a country so full of sensitives as India is), and the intensity and sameness of their thoughts bent constantly and simultaneously upon the object of their pilgrimage, will affect the throng of the elementaries around them. They will repeat that which they find in their friends' brains and clamour for *Pindam*. After which, following the same idea which develops in the pilgrim's thought, *i.e.,* that the offering will bring on deliverance —they, "the ghosts," will promise a sign of it, and perform the promise mechanically and unconsciously as a parrot would repeat a word, or any trained animal perform an act, led on by the superior intelligence of the master mind, that had trained it to this.

What is it that puts an end to the unrestfulness of the "Ghost?" Nothing particular, most probably: neither the magnetism of the place devoted to the *Pindam,* nor the strong will of the person who offers it; but simply the absence of any idea connected with the reappearance of the "ghost," the firm assurance, the implicit confidence of the medium that the "ghost" having been comforted by the offering of the *Pindam* can no longer return, or feel unrestful. That's all. It is the medium's brain, his own creative power of imagination that calls forth out of the normal subjectivity into *abnormal objectivity* the ghosts that appear, except in the cases of the apparitions of *real spirits* at the moments immediately following their death. No living being, no god or goddess has the power of impeding the immutable law of nature called *karma,* especially after the death of the person that evolved it.

We would be pleased to see an infuriated *asura* shaking in its wrath "the world to its foundation." Many a day, during the invasions of and attacks upon cities by the armies of an enemy, have the shrines remained without any offering as they have often been destroyed, and yet the world moveth not. It is the presiding and hungry, when not simply *greedy,* geniuses of the shrines, the Brahmins, who need the *Pindam,* we should say, more than the Godadharâs and the *omnia gatherum* of such. The masses claimed for the quieting of the souls of Christian ghosts paid in hard cash instead of being rewarded mostly in nature are of the same kind and efficacy. And if we are asked to give our honest opinion upon both the modes adopted by the priests of every religion to make the living spend their money in useless ceremonies upon their dead, we say, that both means are in our sight no better than a legal and authorized extortion, the tribute paid by credulity to cunning. Change the name and the story is told of civilized Christians as it is of half-civilized Hindus. But—*Mundus vult decipi*—and who can prevent a willing man from hanging himself! [V, 24.]

———————•———————

To realize the conditions of spiritual existence of any sort it is necessary to get above the plane of merely physical perceptions. One cannot see the things of the spirit with the eyes of the flesh, and one cannot successfully appreciate subjective phenomena by help only of those intellectual reflections which appertain to the physical senses.

"How can a conscious existence without *activity or pursuit* be one of satisfaction or enjoyment?" It would only emphasize the mistaken idea which this question embodies if one were to ask instead, "how can a conscious existence without athletic sports and hunting be one of enjoyment?" The cravings of man's animal or even bodily human nature are not permanent in their character. The demands of the mind are different from those of the body. In physical life an ever recurring desire for change impresses our imagination with the idea that there can be no continuity of contentment without variety of occupation and amusement. To realize completely the way in which a single vein of spiritual consciousness may continue for considerable periods of time to engage the attention—not only the contented, but the delighted attention—of a spiritual entity, is probably possible only for persons who already in life have developed certain inner faculties, dormant in mankind at large.

But meanwhile—as explained in recent essays on the subject —that one sort of variety is developed in Devachan in a very high degree; *viz,* the variety which naturally grows out of the simple themes set in vibration during life. Immense growths for example, of knowledge itself are possible in Devachan, for the spiritual entity which has begun the "pursuit" of such knowledge during life. Nothing can happen to a spirit in Devachan, the keynote of which has not been struck during life; the conditions of a subjective existence are such that the importation of quite external impulses and alien thoughts is impossible. But the seed of thought once sown—the current of thoughts once set going (the metaphor may freely be varied to suit any taste)—then its developments in Devachan may be infinite, for the sixth sense there, and the sixth principle, are our instructors, and in such society there can be no isolation, as physical humanity understands the term. The spiritual ego in fact, under the tuition of his own sixth principle, need be in no fear of being dull, and would be as likely to sigh for a doll's house or a box of ninepins as for the harps and palm-leaves of the mediaeval Heaven. [IV, 202.]

The reader is reminded in this connection that neither Devachan nor Avitchi is a locality, but a *state* which affects directly the being in it and all others only by *reaction.* [IV,270.]

Though we may purge our individual natures of evil, it can never be extirpated but must still linger in the whole expanse of the *Kosmos,* as the opposing power to active goodness, which maintains the equilibrium in Nature—in short, the equal balancing of the scales, the perfect harmony of discords. [I, 184.]

Magnetic emanations are constantly radiating from every human being. Their influence is present in the person's shadow, in his photo or picture as well as every thing else with which his aura comes into contact. It is interesting in this connection to refer to the "Chaya grahini" (Shadow Catcher), mentioned in *Ramayana* which was able to arrest the aerial progress of Hanuman by seizing on his shadow on the surface of the sea. It is well-known that the figure of a person or his picture is a great help to a black magician who intends to affect him by his infernal art. [VI, 221.]

The "higher attributes" of the 5th principle are evolved in it during the lifetime of the Personality, by its more or less close assimilation with the *sixth*, by the development, or rather the spiritualization by the *Buddhi* of the intellectual capacities which have their seat in the *Manas* (the fifth). When the spiritual monad striving to enter the Devachanic state is being subjected to the process of purification, what happens is this; personal consciousness, which alone constitutes the personal Ego, has to rid itself of every earthly speck of grossly material taint before it becomes capable of living "in spirit" and as a spirit. Therefore while the upper consciousness with all its noblest higher feelings—such as undying love, goodness, and all the attributes of divinity in man, even in their latent state—are drawn by affinity towards, follow and merge into the monad, thus endowing it—which is part and parcel of universal consciousness and has therefore no consciousness of its own—with a personal self-consciousness—the dross of our earthly thoughts and cares, "the material tastes, emotions and proclivities" are left to lurk behind in the shell. It is, so to say, the pure incense, the spirit of the flame, disengaging itself from the ashes and cinders of the burnt-up fires. . . .

The "Soul when laden with unsatisfied desires" will remain "earthbound" and suffer. If the desire is on a purely earthly plane, the separation may take place notwithstanding and the shell alone be left wandering: if it were some act of justice and beneficence, such as the redress of a wrong, it can be accomplished only through visions and dreams, the spirit of the impressed person being drawn within the spirit of the Devachanee, and by assimilation with it, first instructed and then led by Karma to redress the wrong. But in *no* case is it a good or meritorious action for "living friends" to encourage the simulacra, whether shells or entities, to communicate. For, instead of "smoothing the path of its spiritual progress," they impede it. In days of old, it was the *initiated* hierophant under whose guidance the mediums of the *adyta,* the sybils, the oracles and the seers acted. In our days there are no initiated priests or adepts at hand to guide the blind instincts of the mediums; themselves the slaves of yet blinder influences. The ancients knew more about those matters than we do. There must be some good reason why every old religion prohibits intercourse with the dead as a crime. Subjective, purely spiritual "Mediumship" is the only harmless kind, and is often an elevating gift that might be cultivated by every one. [VI, 110.]

THE FIVE-POINTED STAR

Of late numerous letters have been received in the THEOSOPHIST office concerning the efficacy of the mysterious Pentagram. Our Eastern readers are perhaps unaware of the great importance given by the Western Kabalists to that sign, and, therefore, it may be found expedient to say a few words about it just now, when it is coming so prominently before the notice of our readers. Like the six-pointed star which is the figure of the *macrocosm*, the five-pointed star has its own deep symbolic significance, for it represents the *microcosm*. The former—the "double triangle" composed of two triangles respectively white and black—crossed and interlaced (our Society's symbol)—known as "Solomon's Seal" in Europe,—and as the "Sign of Vishnu" in India,—is made to represent the universal spirit and matter, one *white* point which symbolizes the former ascending heavenward, and the two points of its *black* triangle inclining earthward.* The Pentagram also represents spirit and matter but only as manifested upon earth. Emblem of the *microcosm* (or the "little universe") faithfully mirroring in itself the *macrocosm* (or the great cosmos), it is the sign of the supremacy of human intellect or spirit over brutal matter.

Most of the mysteries of Kabalistic or *ceremonial* magic, the gnostical symbols and all the Kabalistic keys of prophecy are summed up in that flamboyant Pentagram, considered by the practitioners of the Chaldeo-Jewish Kabala as the most potent magical instrument. In magical evocation during which the slightest hesitation, mistake or omission, becomes fatal to the operator, the star is always on the altar bearing the incense, and other offerings, and under the tripod of invocation. According to the position of its points, it "calls forth good or bad spirits, and expels, retains or captures them"—the Kabalists inform us. "Occult qualities are due to the agency of *elemental* spirits," says the *New American Cyclopædia* in article "Magic," thus making use of the adjective

---

*The double triangle on the right corner of the THEOSOPHIST was by a mistake of the engraver reversed, *i.e.*, placed upside down. So is the Egyptian *Tau* with the snake coiled round it, in the opposite corner of the title-page cover. The latter double sign when drawn correctly represents the anagram of the Society—a T. S.—and the head of the snake ought to turn the opposite way.—ED. THEOS.

"Elemental" for certain spirits—a word which, by the bye, the spiritualists accused the Theosophists of having coined, whereas the *N. A. Cyclopædia* was published twenty years before the birth of the Theosophical Society. "This mysterious figure (the five-pointed star) must be consecrated by the four elements, breathed upon, sprinkled with water, and dried in the smoke of precious perfumes, and then the names of great spirits, as Gabriel, Raphael, Oriphiel and the letters of the sacred tetragram and other Kabalistical words, are whispered to it, and are inscribed upon it"—adds the *Cyclopædia* copying its information from the books of old Mediæval Kabalists, and the more modern work of Eliphas Levi—*Dogmes et Rituel de la Haute Magie*. A modern London Kabalist, styling himself an "Adept,"—a correspondent in a London Spiritual paper, derides Eastern Theosophy and would—if he could—make it subservient to the Jewish Kabala with its Chaldeo-Phenikœan Angelology and Demonology. That new Cagliostro would probably explain the power and efficacy of the "five-jointed star" by the interference of the good "genii," evoked by him; those *jins* which Solomon-like he has apparently bottled up by sealing the mouth of the vessel with King "Solomon's Seal" servilely copied by that mythical potentate from the Indian Vaishnava sign, together with other things brought out by him from the no-less mythical Opher if his vessels ever went there. But the explanation given by the Theosophists for the occasional success obtained in relieving pain (such as scorpion-bites) by the application of the Pentagram—a success, by the bye, which with the knowledge of the cause producing it might with some persons become permanent and sure—is a little less *supernatural,* and rejects every theory of "Spirit" agency accomplishing it whether these spirits be claimed *human or elemental.* True, the *five-pointed shape* of the star has something to do with it, as will be now explained, but it depends on, and is fully subservient to, the chief agent in the operation, the *alpha* and the *omega* of the "magical" force—HUMAN WILL. All the paraphernalia of ceremonial magic,—perfumes, vestments, inscribed hieroglyphics and mummeries are good, but for the beginner; the neophyte whose powers have to be developed, his mental attitude during the operations defined, and his WILL educated by concentrating it on such symbols. The Kabalistic axiom that the magician can become the master of the Elemental Spirits only by surpassing them in courage and audacity in their own elements, has an allegorical meaning. It was but to test the moral strength and daring of the candidate that the terrible trials of initiation into ancient mysteries were invented by the hierophants; and hence the neophyte who had proved fearless in water, fire, air and in the terrors of a Cymmerian darkness, was recognised as having become the master of the Undines, the Salamanders, Sylphs and Gnomes. He had "forced them into obedience," and "could evoke the spirits" for having studied and acquainted himself with the ultimate essence of the occult or hidden nature and the respective properties of the Elements, he could produce at will the most wonderful manifestations or "occult" phenomena by the combination of such properties, combinations hitherto unknown to the profane, as progressive and exoteric science which proceeds slowly and cautiously, can marshal its discoveries, but one by one and in their successive order, for hitherto it has scorned to learn from those who had grasped all the mysteries of nature for long ages before. Many are the occult secrets ferreted out by her and wrung from the old magic, and yet it will not give it credit even for that which has been proved to have been known by the ancient esoteric scientists or "Adepts." But our subject must not be digressed from, and we now turn to the mysterious influence of the Pentagram.

"What is in a sign?" will our readers ask. "No more than in a name" we shall reply—nothing except that as said above it helps to concentrate the attention, hence to nail the WILL of the operator to a certain spot. It is the magnetic or mesmeric fluid flowing out of the finger's ends of the hand tracing the figure which cures or at least stops the acute pain in benumbing the nerves and not the figure *per se*. And yet there are some proficients who are able to demonstrate that the *five-pointed* star, whose points represent the five cordial limbs or those channels of man—the head, the two arms and the two legs—from whence the mesmeric currents issue the strongest, the simple tracing of that figure (a tracing produced with far more efficacy with the finger ends than with ink, chalk or pencil) helped by a strong desire to alleviate pain, will very often force out unconsciously the healing fluid from all these extremities, with far more force than it otherwise would. *Faith* in the figure is transformed into intense will, and the latter into energy; and energy from whatsoever feeling or cause it may proceed, is sure to rebound somewhere and strike the place with more or less force; and naturally enough that place will be the locality upon which the attention of the operator is at that moment concentrated; and hence —the cure attributed by the self-ignorant mesmeriser to the PENTAGRAM. Truly remarks Shelling that "although magic has ceased to be an object of serious attention, it has had a history which links it on the one hand with the highest themes of symbolism, theosophy and early science, as well as on the other with the ridiculous or tragical delusions of the many forms of demonomania. . . . In Greek theurgy the ruins of a superior intelligence and even of a perfect system are to be found, which would reach far beyond the horizon which the most ancient written records present to us . . . and *portions* of the same system may be discovered in the Jewish Kabala." . . . That "perfect system" is now in the hands of a few proficients in the East. The legitimacy of "Magic" may be disputed by the bigots, its reality as an art, and especially as a science, can scarcely be doubted. Nor is it at all doubted by the whole Roman Catholic Clergy, though their fear of its becoming a terrific witness against the legitimacy of their own ascendency forces them to support the argument that its marvels are due to malignant spirits or "fallen angels." In Europe it has still "a few learned and respectable professors and adepts" admits the same *Cyclopædia*. And, throughout the "Pagan" world we may add its reality is almost universally admitted and its proficients are numerous, though they do try to avoid the attention of the sceptical world. [II, 240.]

———◆———

To the Editor of The Theosophist:

MADAME,—In the last issue of your valuable Journal, a member of the New York Theosophical Society seeks to be enlightened as to the cause of a bright spot of light which he has often seen. I am also equally curious to have an explanation. I attribute it to the highest *concentration* of the soul. As soon as I place myself in *that* prescribed attitude, suddenly a bright spot appears before me which fills my heart with delight,—indeed, that being regarded as a special sign by the Indian devotee that he is in the right path, leading to ultimate success in the Yoga practice—that he is blessed by the special grace of the Almighty.

One evening, sitting on the ground cross-legged, in that state of innate concentration when the soul soars into the high regions, I was blessed with a shower of flowers—a most brilliant sight, and which I long to see again. I moved to catch at flowers so rare, but they eluded my grasp and suddenly disappeared, leaving me much disappointed. Finally two flowers fell on me, one touching my head and the other my right shoulder but this time also the attempt to seize them was unsuccessful. What can it be, if not a response that God has been pleased with his worshipper, meditation being, I believe, the unique way of spiritual worship.

—P.

September 18, 1881

It depends. Those of our orthodox native contributors, who worship some particular God,—or, if they so prefer, the one IswAR under some particular name—are too apt to attribute every psychological effect brought on by mental concentration during the hours of religious meditation to their special deity, whereas, in 99 cases out of 100, such effects are due simply to purely *psycho-physiological* effects. We know a number of mystically-inclined people who see such "lights" as that as soon as they concentrate their thoughts. Spiritualists attribute them to the agency of their departed friends; Buddhists—who have no personal God—to a *pre-nirvanic* state; pantheists and Vedantins to *Maya*—illusion of senses; and Christians—to a foresight of the glories of Paradise. The modern Occultists say that, when not directly due to cerebral action whose normal functions are certainly impeded by such an artificial mode of deep concentration—these lights are glimpses of the Astral Light, or, to use a more *scientific* expression—of the "Universal Ether" firmly believed in by more than one man of science, as proved by Mr. Balfour Stewart's *Un-seen Universe*. Like the pure blue sky closely shrouded by thick vapours on a misty day —is the Astral Light concealed from our physical senses, during the hours of our normal, daily life. But when concentrating all our spiritual faculties, we succeed, for the time being, to paralyze their enemy—physical senses, and the inner man becomes, so to say, distinct from the man of matter, then, the action of the ever-living spirit, like a breeze that clears the sky from its obstructing clouds— sweeps away the mist which lies between our normal vision and the Astral Light, and, we obtain glimpses into, and of, that light.

The days of "smoking furnaces" and "burning lamps" which form part of the Biblical visions are well gone by and—to return no more. But, whosoever, refusing natural explanations, prefers *supernatural* ones, is, of course, at liberty to imagine that an "Almighty God" amuses us with visions of flowers, and sends burning lights before making "covenants" with his worshippers. [III, 45.]

———————•———————

[A lengthy report in a French Spiritualist journal on the physical phenomena of "stone showers," contributed by M. Riko, a Dutch correspondent of good education and wide repute, was reprinted by H.P.B. in the *Theosophist* and made the basis for extensive comments.—Eds.]

Meanwhile, M. Riko will perhaps permit us a word. The last sentence of his letter proves clearly that even he, a spiritist, is unable to trace such a uniformly senseless, idiotic phenomenon— one that periodically occurs in every part of the world and without the slightest cause for it, as without the least *moral* effect upon those present,—to the agency of disembodied *human spirits*. We well know that, while most of the spiritists will attribute it to the *Esprits malins* (malicious disembodied spirits) the Roman Catholic world and most of the pious Protestants—at least who may have convinced themselves of the facts—will lay it at the door of the *devil*. Now for argument's sake, and allowing the idea of such creatures as the "malicious human souls" of the spiritist and the "demons" of the Christian theology to exist elsewhere than in imagination, how can both these classes of believers account for the contradictions involved? Here are beings which or who—whether devils, or malicious ex-human imps—are evidently wicked. Their object—if they have any at all—must be to derive cruel pleasure from tormenting mortals? They cannot be less bent upon mischief or more careful of possible results than ordinary mischievous school-boys. Yet we see the stones, or whatever the missiles may be, *carefully avoiding contact* with those present. They fall all around without "even grazing" the little Javanese girl—evidently *the medium* in the case observed by General Michiels. They fall thick among the ranks of the soldiers at "Fort Victoria"; and pass incessantly for several days before the very noses of the police agents at Paris and the Hague, without ever touching, let alone hurting, any one! What does this mean? *Malicious* human spirits, to say nothing of devils, would certainly have no such delicate care for those they were bent upon tormenting. What are they then, these invisible persecutors? Ordinary human "spirits?" In such a case human intelligence would be but a name; a word devoid of meaning as soon as it gets separated from its physical organs. It would become a blind force, a remnant of intellectual energy that was, and we would have to credit every liberated soul with insanity!

Having disposed of the theory of "spirits," "imps" and "devils" on the score of the idiocy and total absence of malevolence in the proceedings, once that the genuineness of the phenomenon is proved, to what else can it be attributed in its *causation* or origin, but to a *blind* though living force; one subjected to an intransgressible law of attraction and repulsion—in its course and *effects* —a law which exact science has yet to discover; for it is one of innumerable correlations due to magnetic conditions which are supplied only when both animal and terrestrial magnetism are present; meanwhile the former has to fight its way step by step for recognition, for science *will not* recognize it in its *psychological* effects,—do what its advocates may. The Spiritualists regard the phenomena of the stone-showers as irregular. We, Theosophists, answer that although their occurrence at a given place may appear to be very irregular, yet from a comparison of those in all parts of the world it might be found, if carefully recorded, that hitherto they have been uniform or nearly so. Perhaps they may be aptly compared with the terrestrial magnetic perturbations called by Science "fitful," and distinctly separated by her, at one time, from that other class she named "periodical"; the "fitful" now being found to recur at as regular periods as the former. The cause of these variations of the magnetic needle is as entirely unknown to physical science as are the phenomena of stone showers to those who study psychological Science; yet both are closely connected. If we are asked what we mean by the comparison—and indignant may be the question on the part of both, Science and Spiritualism—we will humbly answer that such is the teaching of *Occult* Science. Both classes of our opponents have yet much to learn, and the Spiritualists—to first *unlearn* much in addition. Did our friends the believers in "spirits" ever go to the trouble of first studying "mediumship" and only then turning their attention to the phenomena occurring through the sensitives? We, at least, never heard that such is the case, not even during the most scientific investigation of mediumistic powers that ever took place—

Professor Hare's and Mr. Crookes' experiments. And yet, had they done so, they might have found how closely related to and dependent on the variation of terrestrial magnetism are those of the mediumistic or animal magnetic state. Whenever a true medium fails to get phenomena it is immediately attributed by the Spiritualists, and oftener by the "Spirits" themselves to "unfavorable conditions." The latter are lumped together in a single phrase; but never did we hear the real scientific and chief cause for it given: the unfavorable variations of the terrestrial magnetism. The lack of harmony in the "circle" of investigators; various and conflicting magnetisms of the "sitters" are all of secondary importance. The power of a real, strongly *charged* medium[1] will always prevail against the animal magnetism which may be adverse to it; but it cannot produce effects unless it received a fresh supply of molecular force, an impress from the invisible body of those we call blind "Elementals" or Forces of Nature, and which the Spiritualists in every case regard as the "spirits of the dead." Showers of stones have been known to take place where there was not a living soul—consequently no medium. The medium charged by the atmospheric legion of "correlations" (we prefer calling them by the new scientific term) will attract stones within the periphery of his force, but will at the same time repel them, the polaric condition of his body preventing the missiles from touching it. And its own molecular condition will temporarily induct with its properties all the other human and even non-sensitive bodies around it. Sometimes there may be an exception to the rule produced by some chance condition.

This explanatory postscript may be closed with the remark to M. Riko that we do not regard the Elementals of the Kabalists as properly "beings." They are the active Forces and correlations of Fire, Water, Earth, and Air, and their shape is like the hues of the chameleon which has no permanent colour of its own. Through the interplanetary and interstellar spaces, the vision of almost every *clairvoyant* can reach. But it is only the trained eye of the profi-

---

1 We hold that a "physical medium," so called, is but an organism more sensitive than most others to the terrestrial electro-magnetic induction. That the powers of a medium for the production of phenomena fluctuate from one hour to another is a fact proven by Mr. Crookes' experiments and, believing though we do in the existence of innumerable other so-called Spiritual Forces besides and quite independent of human spirits, we yet firmly maintain that *physical* mediums have very little, if anything to do with the latter. Their powers are purely physical and conditional; *i.e.*, these powers depend almost entirely on the degree of receptivity, and chance polarization of the body of the medium by the electro-magnetic and atmospheric currents. Purely psychological manifestations are quite a different thing.

cient in Eastern Occultism, that can fix the flitting shadows and give them a shape and a name. [II, 232-33.]

————•————

[The following comment responds to a reader's request for the "esoteric point of view" concerning William Underwood, an American who could "generate fire through the medium of his breath."—Eds.]

The exhalation of fire from the mouth is one of the stock illusions of the itinerant jugglers of various countries. In their case the dried powder of *Lycopadium* is employed, we believe, and the same substance is used in theatrical performances when it is desired to simulate either fire or lightning flashes. It may be that the American human volcano in question employs some such agent to impose upon his spectators, and we are always bound to exhaust the theories of the possible before venturing upon those of the seemingly impossible. Yet, personal character being a prime factor always, we must take it for granted that Mr. Underwood is above such trickery, since his phenomenon has such respectable endorsement. If then, we turn to occult science to seek for an explanation, we will find that there are cases of record of individuals who emit from their persons a luminous vapour or aura, under high states of nervous exaltation. Sometimes it appears as a wild radiance, sometimes as a lambent flame, and in others as an electric or rather odic corruscation. Rarely it is observed by day, but most frequently by night, and still oftener while the subject is deeply engaged in his devotions. A noted example is that of the fasting Peter of Alcantara, a Catholic devotee. The halo, or nimbus which painters depict about the heads and bodies of saints, yogis, gods and goddesses, is familiar to every one, and is a memento of this natural phenomenon. But the light in these instances is of an odic character, and though flaming and flickering like fire, has none of its combustive property. Writers upon sorcery and mediumship have frequently recorded anecdotes of the bursting forth of flames from the doors, windows, chimneys or roofs of buildings without apparent cause, and in fact at times when there was no fire in any part of the house, nor any articles stored within, such as cotton, cotton-waste, greased rags, or other substances liable to spontaneous combustion. These mysterious burnings have been some-times attended with stone-showers or throwings, equally unac-countable. The Spiritualists affirm that the agents in all these cases have been spirits; but unless they be fire-elementals or Salaman-ders of the Rosicrucians, they must be queer "Spirits." Among modern Western mediums, equally with Hindus of the same class, are many who can handle burning coals, red-hot iron, and molten metal with perfect impunity, and walk through beds of blazing fire unscathed. In America there is a female medium named Mrs. Swydam, who has this gift, and in Europe a late, and the most noted of male mediums, has not only exhibited the feat of handling hot coals without receiving harm, but even laid them upon the heads of non-mediums in the company present or upon newspapers or books, without injury to person or property. The explanation in both classes of cases is that the fire-proof individual is a me-dium for these fire elementals, and contains in himself an unusual proportion of Salamandrine properties, the result of an abnormal combination of elemental forces in his foetal development. Nor-mally, a human being contains the elementals of all the four king-doms in almost equal proportions, any slight preponderance of one or the other determining the so-called "temperament." [IV, 280.]

THE expression "physico-materialism," as well as its pendant "spirito" or "metaphysico-materialism," may be newly coined words, but some such are rigorously necessary in a publication like the *Theosophist* and with its present non-English editor. If they are not clear enough, we hope C.C.M. or some other friend will suggest better. In one sense every Buddhist as well as every Occultist, and even most of the educated Spiritualists, are, strictly speaking, Materialists. The whole question lies in the ultimate and scientific decision upon the nature or essence of FORCE. Shall we say that FORCE *is*—Spirit, or that Spirit is—a force? Is the latter physical or spiritual, *Matter* or SPIRIT? If the latter is some-thing—it must *be* material, otherwise it is but a pure abstraction, a *no*-thing. Nothing which is capable of producing an effect on any portion of the physical,—objective or subjective—Kosmos can be otherwise than material. Mind—whose enormous potentiality is being discovered more and more with every day, could produce *no* effect were it not material; and believers in a personal God, have themselves either to admit that the deity in doing its work has to use material force to produce a physical effect, or—to advocate miracle, which is an absurdity. As A. J. Manley, of Minnesota, very truly observes in a letter:—

"It has ever been an impossibility with me to realize or comprehend an effect, which requires motion or force, as being produced by 'nothing'. The leaves of the forest are stirred by the gentlest breeze, and yet withhold the breeze, and leaves cease to move. While gas continues to escape from the tube, apply the match and you will have a brilliant light; cut off the supply and the wonderful phenomenon ceases. Place a magnet near a compass, and the needle is attracted by it; remove the former and the needle will resume its normal condition. By will-power the mesmerist compels his subject to perform various feats, but who becomes normal again when the will is withdrawn.

"I have observed in all physical phenomena, that when the propelling force is withdrawn, the phenomena invariably cease. From these facts, I infer that the producing causes must be material, though we do not see them. Again, if these phenomena were produced by 'nothing,' it would be impossible to withdraw the producing force, and the manifestations would never cease. Indeed, if such manifestations ever existed, they must of necessity be perpetual."

Concurring fully with the above reasoning, it thus becomes of the utmost necessity for us, and under the penalty of being constantly accused of inconsistency, if not of flat contradictions, to make a well marked difference between those *materialists* who, believing that nothing can exist outside of matter in however sublimated a state, the latter yet believe in various subjective forces unknown to, only because as yet undiscovered by, science; rank sceptics and those *transcendentalists* who, mocking at the majesty of truth and fact fly into the face of logic by saying that "nothing is impossible to God"; that he is an extra-cosmic deity who created the universe out of nothing, was never subject to law, and can produce a *miracle* outside of all physical law and whenever it pleases him, etc. [IV, 105-6 fn.]

. . . the events [in "Can the 'Double' Murder?" printed in *Occult Tales*] actually occurred, and they possess a very deep interest for the student of psychological science. They show in a marked degree the enormous potentiality of the human will upon mesmeric subjects whose whole being may be so imbued with an imparted intellectual preconception that the "double," or *mayavi-rupa,* when projected transcorporeally, will carry out the mesmerizer's mandate with helpless subserviency. The fact that a mortal wound may be inflicted upon the inner man without puncturing the epidermis will be a novelty only to such readers as have not closely examined the records and noted the many proofs that death may result from many psychical causes besides the emotions whose lethal power is universally conceded. [IV, 99.]

It is precisely because we claim to know something of "practical" Occultism in addition to being a Theosophist that we answer without in the least "evading the question" that a mortal wound may be inflicted "not only *upon,* but also by one" inner man upon another. This is the A.B.C. of esoteric mesmerism. The wound is inflicted by neither a real dagger or a hand of flesh, bones and blood, but simply *by*—WILL. It is the intense will of the "Gospoja" that guided the astral or inner body, the *Mayavi-rupa* of Frozya.* It is the passively obedient action of the latter's "double" that scanning space and material obstacles, followed the "trail" of, and found the real murderers. It is again that WILL shaped by the incessant thought of the revenger, that inflicted the internal wounds which though unable to kill or even to hurt the inner man, yet by reaction of the interior *physical* body proved mortal to the latter. If the fluid of the mesmerizer can cure, it can also kill. And now we have "established the fact as scientifically"—as science which generally disbelieves in and rejects such mesmeric phenomena will permit it. For those who believe in, and know something of, mesmerism, this will be plain. As to those who deny it the explanation will appear to them as absurd as any other psychological claim: as much so as the claims of Yogism with its beatitudes of *Samadhi* and other states, for the matter of that. [IV, 246 fn.]

An important point for the student of occult science should not be overlooked. The law of physics, that action and reaction tend

---

* "Gospoja" and "Frozya" are characters in H.P.B.'s "Can the 'Double' Murder?", first published as one of the *Occult Tales* in 1876-77 in New York and later reprinted in the *Theosophist* (January, 1883).—Eds.

to equilibrate each other, holds in the realm of the occult. This has been fully explained in "Isis Unveiled" and other works of the kind. A current of Akas, directed by a sorcerer at a given object with an evil intent, must either be propelled by such intensity of will as to break through every obstacle and overpower the resistant will of the selected victim, or it will rebound against the sender, and afflict him or her in the same way as it was intended the other should be hurt. So well is this law understood that it has been preserved to us in many popular proverbs, such as the English ones, 'curses come home to roost,' 'The biter's bit,' etc. This reversal of a maleficent current upon the sender may be greatly facilitated by the friendly interference of another person who knows the secret of controlling the Akasic currents—if it is permissible for us to coin a new word that will soon be wanted in the Western parlance. [I, 203.]

In view of the fact that occult science explains the mysteries of bird-flying and fish-swimming on principles entirely opposed to the accepted scientific theory of the day, one might well hesitate before putting out the true explanation. However, since we already stand so low in the favour of the orthodox scientists, we will say a few words upon the subject; but they must be few indeed. "If," writes our correspondent, "we take the position that birds have the power to make themselves light or heavy *at will,* the phenomenon of their flight becomes easy to comprehend."

And why not take up such a position? Whether by *instinct* or *will,* whether an effect identical with another is produced consciously or unconsciously, by animal or man, the cause underlying that invariable and identical *result* must be one and the same, barring diversity of conditions and exceptions as to unimportant details. The action of certain fishes which, by swallowing large draughts of air, distend an internal bag and thereby, becoming specifically lighter, float above the surface of the water, does not militate against the scientific theory of swimming, when it concerns such fish, man or a bladder filled with air. But we are left as wise as ever, when it is a question of rapid sinking, to the bottom, whether by man or whale. In the former case such sinking might be ascribed to *volition.* But man's inability to sink as rapidly and to such a depth, even though a most experienced diver, —who *has* to sink himself by a stone—proves that there must be something more than blind instinct or conscious volition. What is it? Occult science tells us the word: it is "a change of polarity and of normal gravity," not yet admissible by science. With birds and animals—as instinctive a mechanical action as any other they execute; with man, when he thus defies the familiar conditions of gravity, it is something he can acquire, in his training as a Yogi. Though the former act unconsciously, and he changes his polarity *at will,* the same cause is made operative, and both produce an identical effect. There are certainly alternating changes of polarity going on in the bird while ascending or dropping, and a maintenance of the same polarity while sailing at any given altitude. [III, 271-72.]

To such "impossible" facts, belong the phenomena of Hypnotism, which have created such a new stir in Germany, Russia and France, as well as the manifestations (belonging to the same kind) produced and observed by Dr. Charcot upon his hysterical patients. With the latter phenomena we must class those induced by the so-called *metaloscopy* and *xiloscopy.* Under the former are meant in medicine the now firmly established facts proving the characteristic influence on the animal organism of various metals and of the magnet, through their simple contact with the skin of the patient: each producing a different effect. As to *xiloscopy,* it is the name given to the same effects produced by various kinds of woods, especially by the quinine bark. *Metaloscopia* has already given birth to *Metalotherapia*—the science of using metals for curative means. The said "impossibilities" begin to be recognized as facts, though a Russian medical *Encyclopædia* does call them "monstrous." The same fate awaits other branches of the occult sciences of the ancients. Hitherto rejected, they now begin to be—although still reluctantly—accepted. Prof. Ziggler of Geneva has well nigh proved the influence of metals, of quinine and of some parts of the living organisms (the ancient fascination of flowers) upon plants and trees. The plant named *Drosera,* the quasi invisible hairs of which are endowed with partial motion, and which was regarded by Darwin as belonging to the insect-eating plants, is

shown by Ziggler as affected even at a distance by animal magnetism as well as by certain metals, by means of various con-
ductors. And a quarter century ago M. Adolphe Didier, the famous
French somnambule and author, reports that an acquaintance of
his met with much success in the experimental application of the
mesmeric aura to flowers and fruits to promote their growth, color,
flavour, and perfume. Miss C. L. Hunt, who quotes this fact approvingly in her useful "Compendium of Mesmeric Information,"
mentions (p. 180, foot-note) that there "are persons who are
unable to wear or handle flowers, as they begin to wither and
droop directly, as though the vitality of the plant were being
appropriated by the wearer, instead of being sustained." To cor-
roborate which foregoing observations by Western authorities,
our Brahmin readers need only be reminded of the imperative
injunction of their ancient *Sutras* that if any one should even
salute a Brahmin when on his way to the river or tank for his
morning puja (devotions), he must at once throw away the flowers
he is carrying according to the ritualistic custom, return home and
procure fresh flowers. This simple explanation being that the
magnetic current projected towards him by the salutor taints the
floral aura and makes the blossoms no longer fit for the mystical
psychic ceremony of which they are necessary accessories. [IV,
107 fn.]

The power of the Yogi to quit his own body and enter and animate that of another person, though affirmed by Patânjali and included among the Siddhis of Krishna, is discredited by European-
ized young Indians. Naturally enough, since, as Western biologists
deny a soul to man, it is an unthinkable proposition to them that
the Yogi's soul should be able to enter another's body. That such
an unreasoning infidelity should prevail among the pupils of
European schools, is quite reason enough why an effort should be
made to revive in India those schools of Psychology in which the
Aryan youth were theoretically and practically taught the occult
laws of Man and Nature. We, who, have at least some triffling
acquaintance with modern science, do not hesitate to affirm our
belief that this temporary transmigration of souls is possible. We
may even go so far as to say that the phenomenon has been experi-

mentally proved to us—in New York, among other places. And, since we would be among the last to require so marvellous a statement to be accepted upon any one's unsupported testimony, we urge our readers to first study Aryan literature, and then get from personal experience the corroborative evidence. The result must inevitably be to satisfy every honest enquirer that Patânjali and Sankaracharaya did, and Tyndall, Carpenter and Huxley do not, know the secrets of our being. [I, 89.]

An unmistakable error. . . . confounds the *Raja* with the *Hatha* Yogins, whereas the former have nothing to do with the physical training of the *Hatha* nor with any other of the innumerable sects who have now adopted the name and emblems of *Yogins*. Wilson in his *Essays on the Religions of the Hindus* falls into . . . confusion and knows very little, if anything at all, of the true *Raja Yogins* who have no more to do with *Siva* than with *Vishnu* or any other deity. Alone, the most learned among the *Sankara's Dandis* of Northern India, especially those who are settled in Rajputana who would be able—if they would to give some correct notions about the *Raja Yogins*. . . . If, in speaking of the *Dandis,* we have used above the phrase beginning with the conjunction "if," it is because we happen to know how carefully the secrets of the real *Yogins*—nay even their existence itself—are denied within this fraternity. It is comparatively but lately that the usual excuse adopted by them, in support of which they bring their strongest authorities, who affirm that the *Yogi* state is unattainable in the present or *Kali* age—has been set afloat by them. "From the unsteadiness of the senses, the prevalence of sin in the *Kali,* and the shortness of life, how can exaltation by the *Yoga* be obtained?" enquires *Kasikhanda*. But this declaration can be refuted in two words and with their own weapons. The duration of the present *Kali Yuga* is 432,000 years of which 4,979 have already expired. It is at the very beginning of *Kali Yuga* that Krishna and Arjuna were born. It is since Vishnu's eighth incarnation that the country had all its *historical* Yogis, for as to the prehistoric ones, or claimed as such, we do not find ourselves entitled to force them upon public notice. Are we then to understand that none of these numerous saints, philosophers and ascetics from Krishna down to the late Vishnu Brahmarchári Báwa of Bombay had ever reached the "exaltation by Yoga?" To repeat this assertion is simply suicidal in their own interests. [II, 31.]

IT is not that among the *Hatha* Yogins—men who at times had reached through a physical and well-organized system of training the highest powers as "wonder-workers"—there has never been a man worthy of being considered as a true Yogin. What we say, is simply this: the *Raja Yogin* trains but his mental and intellectual powers, leaving the physical alone, and making but little of the exercise of phenomena simply of a physical character. Hence it is the rarest thing in the world to find a real Yogi boasting of being one, or willing to exhibit such powers—though *he does acquire them as well as the one practising Hatha Yoga, but through another and far more intellectual system.* Generally, they deny these powers pointblank, for reasons but too well-grounded. The latter need not even belong to any apparent order of ascetics, and are oftener known as private individuals than members of a religious fraternity, nor need they necessarily be Hindus. Kabir, who was one of them, fulminates against most of the later sects of mendicants who occasionally become warriors when not simply brigands, and sketches them with a masterly hand:

"I never beheld such a *Yogi,* Oh, brother! who forgetting his doctrine roves about in negligence. He follows professedly the faith of MAHADEVA and calls himself an eminent teacher; the scene of his abstraction is the fair or market. MAYA is the mistress of the false saint. When did DATTATRAYA demolish a dwelling? When did SUKHADEVA collect an armed host? When did NARADA mount a matchlock? When did VYASADEVA blow a trumpet? etc." [II, 31.]

It certainly is not worth the while of any sensible man to spend time in learning such puerilities as are above described [in a report of phenomena produced by a fakir]. These are the baser branches of occultism. A Yogi who gets frightened at any threat is *no* Yogi, but one of those who learn to produce effects without knowing or having learnt what are the causes. Such men, if not tricksters, are simply *passive* mediums—not adepts! [II, 144.]

If an ascetic prefers a subterranean cave to the open fresh air, takes (apparently) the vow of silence and meditation, refuses to touch money or anything metallic, and, lastly, passes his days in what appears the most ludicrous occupation of all, that of concentrating his whole thoughts on the tip of his nose,—he does this, neither for the sake of playing an aimless comedy nor yet out of mere unreasoned superstition, but as a physical discipline, based on strictly scientific principles. Most of the thousands of fakirs, gosseins, bayraguis and others of the mendicant order, who throng the villages and religious fairs of India in our present age, may be and undoubtedly are worthless and idle vagabonds, modern clowns, imitating the great students of the philosophic ages of the past. And, there is but little doubt that, though they ape the postures and servilely copy the traditional customs of their nobler brethren, they understand no more *why* they do it than the sceptic who laughs at them. But, if we look closer at the origin of their school and study Patanjali's *Yoga Vidya*—we will be better able to understand and hence appreciate their seemingly ridiculous practices. If the ancients were not as well versed in the details of physiology as are our physicians of the Carpenterian modern school,—a question still *sub judice*—they may perhaps be proved, on the other hand, to have fathomed this science in another direction by other methods far deeper than the former; in short, to have made themselves better acquainted with its occult and exceptional laws than we are. That the ancients of all countries were intimately acquainted with what is termed in our days "hypnotism" or self-mesmerisation, the production, in a word, of voluntary trance—cannot be denied. One of the many proofs is found in the fact that the same method, described here, is known as tradition and practised by the Christian monks at Mount Athos even to this very day. These, to induce "divine visions," concentrate their thoughts and fix their eyes on the navel for hours together. A number of Russian travellers testify to such an occupation in the Greek convents, and writers of other nationalities, who have visited this celebrated hermitage, will bear out our assertion. . . . [I, 315.]

As the science and study of Yoga Philosophy pertains to Buddhist, Lamaic and other religions supposed to be atheistical, *i.e.,* rejecting belief in a personal deity, and as a Vedantin would by no means use such an expression, we must understand the term "absorption into God" in the sense of union with the *Universal Soul,* or *Parama Purusha*—the Primal or One Spirit. [II, 72.]

. . . The physical body incarnates and disincarnates—that is its elements change—continually from the time of foetal existence until death. The life principle acts from the time of conception until death, the lower principles are fed continually during that time from the astral plane; that which constitutes the individual monad reincarnates at the time of birth, but whether or not the highest principles may assimilate with that germ during a lifetime, and to which extent they will either assimilate or be lost, will depend on the will and the exertions of the individual. [VI, 71.]

———•———

Human hibernation belongs to the Yoga system and may be termed one of its many results, but it cannot be called "Yoga." [I, 314.]

In reference to the arrest of the growth of the hair, some adepts in the secret science, which is generally known in India under the name of *Yoga,* claim to know something more than this. They prove their ability to completely suspend the functions of life each night during the hours intended for sleep. Life then is, so to say, held in total abeyance. The wear and tear of the inner as well as the outer organism being thus artificially arrested, and there being no possibility of waste, these men accumulate as much vital energy for use in their waking state as they would have lost in sleep during which state, if natural, the process of energy and expanse of force is still mechanically going on in the human body. In the induced state described, as in that of a deep swoon, the brain no more dreams than if it were dead. One century, if passed, would appear no longer than one second, for all perception of time is lost for him who is subjected to it. Nor do the hairs or nails grow under such circumstances, though they do for a certain time in a body actually dead, which proves, if anything can, that the atoms and tissues of the physical body are held under conditions quite different from those of the state we call death. For, to use a physiological paradox, life in a dead animal organism is even more intensely active than it ever is in a living one, which as we see, does not hold good in the case under notice. Though the average skeptic may regard this statement as sheer nonsense, those who have experienced this in themselves know it is an undoubted fact. Two certain fakirs from Nepaul once agreed to try the experiment. One of them, previous to attempting the hibernation, underwent all the ceremonies of preparation . . . and took all the necessary precautions; the other simply threw himself by a process known to himself and others into that temporary state of complete paralysis, which imposes no limits of time, may last months as well as hours, and which is known in certain Tibet lamaseries as . . . The result was that while the hair, beard, and nails of the former had grown at the end of six weeks, though feebly yet perceptibly, the cells of the latter had remained as closed and inactive as if he had been transformed for the lapse of time into a marble statue. Not having personally seen either of the two men, or the experiment, we can vouch only in a general way for the possibility of the phenomenon, not for the details of this peculiar case, though we would as soon doubt our existence as the truthfulness of those from whom we have the story. We only hope that among the skeptical and materialistic who may scoff, we may not find either people who, nevertheless accept with a firm and pious conviction the story of the resurrection of the half-decayed Lazarus and other like miracles, or yet those who, while ready to crush a theosophist for his beliefs, would never dare scoff at that of a Christian. [II, 146.]

This system, evolved by long ages of practice until it was brought to bear the above-described results, was not practised in India alone in the days of antiquity. The greatest philosophers of all countries sought to acquire these powers; and certainly, behind the external ridiculous postures of the Yogis of today, lies concealed the profound wisdom of the archaic ages; one that included among other things a perfect knowledge of what are now termed physiology and psychology. Ammonius Saccas, Porphyry, Proclus and others practised it in Egypt; and Greece and Rome did not shrink even at all in their time of philosophical glory, to follow suit. Pythagoras speaks of the celestial music of the spheres that one hears in hours of ecstacy; Zeno finds a wise man who having conquered all passions, feels happiness and emotion, but in the midst of torture. Plato advocates the man of meditation and likens his powers to those of the divinity; and we see the Christian ascetics themselves through a mere life of contemplation and self-torture acquire powers of levitation or aethrobacy, which, though attributed to the miraculous intervention of a personal God, are nevertheless real and the result of physiological changes in the human body. "The Yogi," says Patanjali, "will hear celestial sounds, the songs and conversations of celestial choirs. He will have the perception of their touch in their passage through the air,"—which translated into a more sober language means that the ascetic is enabled to see with the spiritual eye in the Astral Light, hear with the spiritual ear subjective sounds inaudible to others, and live and feel, so to say, in the *Unseen Universe*.

"The Yogi is able to enter a dead or a living body by the path of the senses, and in this body to act as though it were his own." The "path of the senses"—our physical senses supposed to originate in the astral body, the ethereal counterpart of man, or the *jivatma,* which dies with body—the senses are here meant in their spiritual sense—volition of the higher principle in man. The true Raj Yogi is a Stoic; and Kapila, who deals but with the latter—utterly rejecting the claim of the *Hatha* Yogis to converse during Samadhi with the *Infinite* Iswar—describes their state in the following words:—"To a Yogi, in whose mind all things are identified as spirit, what is infatuation? what is grief? He sees all things as one; he is destitute of affections; he neither rejoices in good nor is offended with evil. . . . A wise man sees so many false things in those which are called true, so much misery in what is called happiness, that he turns away with disgust. . . . He who in the body has obtained liberation (from the tyranny of the senses) is of no caste, of no sect, of no order, attends to no duties, adheres to no shastras, to no formulas, to no works of merit; he is beyond the reach of speech; he remains at a distance from all secular concerns; he has renounced the love and the knowledge of sensible objects; he flatters none, he honours none, he is not worshipped, he worships none; whether he practises and follows the customs of his fellowmen or not, this is his character."

And a selfish and a disgustingly misanthropical one this character would be, were it that for which the TRUE ADEPT would be striving. But, it must not be understood *literally* . . . [II, 75.]

———•———

Will you kindly let me know whether females can attain to adeptship, and whether female adepts exist at all?

"An INQUIRER"

Note.—It is difficult to see any good reason why females should not become Adepts. None of us, Chelas, are aware of any physical or other defect which might entirely incapacitate them from undertaking the dreary ordeal. It may be more difficult, more dangerous for them than it is for men, still not impossible. The Hindu sacred books and traditions mention such cases, and since the laws of Nature are immutable, what was possible some thousand years ago must be possible now. If our correspondent had referred to the Editorial Notes, page 148, Vol. III, "Re-Incarnation in Tibet,"* he would have found the existence of a female Adept hinted at— the pious Chinese Princess who, after living for ten years a married life, renounced it with her husband's consent and became a *Gelungma,* or Ani, *i.e.,* a nun. She is believed to be still re-incarnating herself *"in a succession of female Lamas."* The late Tde-Shoo Lama's sister is said to be one of such re-incarnations. From this lady-Adept, the Superior of the Nunnery on the Palte-Lake—a Tibetan pedlar of Darjeeling acknowledged to some Bengal Theosophists, who visited that place last year, to have received a talisman. . . . In Nepaul, we all know, there is a high female Adept. And in Southern India, flourished at a recent date, another great female Initiate named Ouvaiyar. Her mysterious work in Tamil on Occultism is still extant. It is styled *Kural,* and is said to be very enigmatically written, and consequently inexplicable. In Benares too lives a certain lady, unsuspected and unknown, but to the very few to whom reference has been made in the *Theosophist,* (page 47, Vol. II). Further information about these few already mentioned or any other female Adepts we may know of, we do not feel at liberty to give. . . . D.K.M. [V, 29.]

Some enquire how the world is to go on if all were to become occultists, one of the vital conditions of that order being celibacy. Others say that the ancient Rishis married, quoting some of the names mentioned in the Hindu religious books; and argue therefrom, that celibacy is not an essential condition for progress in *practical* occultism. Generally, they put a literal interpretation upon what is beautifully conveyed by means of an allegory and insist upon the dead-letter sense being correct, whenever such a course is profitable in their narrow interests. They find it difficult to control the lower animal desires; and, in order to justify their conduct of persistence in hankering after sensual pleasures, they resort to these books as their authority, interpreting them in a manner most convenient to themselves. Of course, when any passages, even in their exoteric sense, conflict with the dictates of their "lower self," then others are quoted, which *esoterically* convey the same sense, although *exoterically* supporting their peculiar views.

---

*See *H.P.B. Articles,* Vol. III, 356.

The question of the marriage of the *Rishis* is one of such disputed points. The readers of the *Theosophist* may recall here, with advantage, a passage occurring in the article under the heading of "Magicon," where one of the occultists is said to have rejected the hand of a beautiful young lady, on the ground of his having taken the vow of celibacy, although he himself confesses further on to be courting a virgin whose name was "Sophia." Now, it is explained there that "Sophia" is wisdom or the *Buddhi*—the spiritual soul (our sixth principle). This principle is everywhere represented as a "female," because it is passive in as much as it is merely the vehicle of the seventh principle. This latter—which is called *Atma* when spoken of in connection with an individual and *Purush* when applied in its relation to the Universe—is the active male, for it is the CENTRE OF ENERGY acting through and upon its female vehicle, the sixth principle.

The occultist, when he has identified himself thoroughly with his *Atma,* acts upon the *Buddhi,* for, according to the laws of Cosmic Evolution, the *Purusha*—the universal seventh principle—is perpetually acting upon and manifesting itself through *Prakriti*—the universal sixth principle. Thus the MAHATMA, who has become one with his seventh principle—which is identical with *Purusha,* since there is no isolation in the spiritual monad—is practically a creator, for he has identified himself with the evoluting and the manifesting energy of nature. It was in this sense that the *Rishis* are said to have married. And the union of *Siva* and *Sakti* represents the same allegory. *Siva* is the *Logos,* the *Vach,* manifested through the *Sakti;* and the union of the two produces the phenomenal creation, for until the Son is born, the Father and the Mother are non-existent. Now Sakti being a female principle, it is *fully* manifested through a woman, although, properly speaking, the *inner* man is neither male, nor female. It is only the preponderance of either of the two principles (positive and negative) which determines the sex. Now, this preponderance is determined by the Law of Affinity; and hence in a woman is manifested abnormally the occult power represented by *Sakti*. She is moreover gifted with a wonderfully vivid imagination—stronger than man's. And as the phenomenal is the realisation or rather the manifestation of the IDEAL, which can be properly and strongly conceived only by a *powerful* IMAGINATION—a WOMAN-ADEPT can produce high occultists—a race of "Buddhas and Christs," born "without sin." The more and the sooner the animal sexual affinities are given up, the stronger and the sooner will be the manifestation of the higher occult powers which alone can produce the "immaculate conception." And this art is practically taught to the occultists at a very high stage of initiation. The "Adept," whether the *Sthula Sarira* be male or female, is then able to bring a new being into existence by the manipulation of cosmic forces. *Anusúya,* a female adept of the ancient times, is thus said to have conceived immaculately *Dúrvasa, Dattatraya* and *Chandra*—the three distinct types of Adeptship. Thus it will be seen that the marriage of the occultist (who is, as already explained, neither male nor female) is a "holy union," devoid of sin, in the same manner as Krishna's union with thousands of *Gopies.* Sensual-minded men have taken this fact up too literally; and, out of a wrong interpretation of the text, has arisen a sect which indulges in the most degrading practices. But, in fact, *Krishna* represents the seventh principle, while the *Gopies* indicate the innumerable powers of that principle manifested through its "vehicle." Its union "without sin," or rather the action or manifestation of each of these powers through the "female principle" gives rise to the phenomenal appearances. In such a union the occultist is happy and "without sin" for the "conception" of his other-half—the female principle—is "immaculate." The very fact, that this stage pertains to one of the very highest initiations, shows that the time—when ordinary humanity, during the course of cosmic evolution, will, in this manner, be able to produce a race of "Buddhas," &c, born "without sin"—is yet very, very far off— perhaps attainable in the sixth or the seventh "round." But when once this possibility and the actuality of this fact is recognised, the course of living and education may be so moulded as to hasten the approach of that eventful day when on this earth will descend "the Kingdom of Heaven." [V, 264.]

Neither the Tibetan nor the modern Hindu Mahatmas for the matter of that, ever meddle with politics, though they may bring their influence to bear upon more than one momentous question in the history of a nation—their mother country especially. If any Adepts have influenced Washington or brought about the great

American Revolution, it was not the "Tibetan Mahatmas" at any rate; for these have never shown much sympathy with the Pelings of whatever Western race, except as forming a part of Humanity in general. Yet it is as certain though this conviction is merely a *personal* one, that several Brothers of the Rosie Cross—or "Rosicrucians," so called—did take a prominent part in the American struggle for independence, as much as in the French Revolution during the whole of the past century. We have documents to that effect, and the proofs of it are in our possession. But these Rosicrucians were Europeans and American settlers who acted quite independently of the Indian or Tibetan Initiates. And the "Exasiatic" who premises by saying that his statements are made entirely upon his own personal responsibility—settles this question from the first. He refers to Adepts *in general* and not to Tibetan or Hindu Mahatmas necessarily, as our correspondent seems to think.

No Occult theosophist has ever thought of connecting Benjamin Franklin, or "Brother Benjamin" as he is called in America, with theosophy; with this exception, however, that the great philosopher and electrician seems to be one more proof of the mysterious influence of numbers and figures connected with the dates of the birth, death and other events in the life of certain remarkable individuals. Franklin was born on the 17th of the month (January, 1706) died on the 17th (April, 1790) and was the youngest of the 17 children of his parents. Beyond this, there is certainly nothing to connect him with modern theosophy or even with the theosophists of the 18th century—as the great body of alchemists and Rosicrucians called themselves.

Again neither the editor nor any member of the Society acquainted even superficially with the rules of the Adepts— [the former individual named, disclaiming emphatically the rather sarcastic charge of the writer to her being *"alone* to enjoy or claim the extraordinary felicity of personal communication with the Adepts"]—would believe for one moment that any of the cruel, blood-thirsty heroes —the regicides and others of English and French history—could have ever been inspired by any Adept—let alone a Hindu or Buddhist Mahatma. The inferences drawn from the article "The Adepts in America in 1776," are a little too far-fetched by our imaginative correspondent. President Bradshaw—if such a cold, hard and impassive man can be suspected of having ever been influenced by any power outside of, and foreign to, his own soulless entity—must have been inspired by the "lower Jehovah" of the old Testament—the Mahatma and Paramatma, or the "personal" god of Calvin and those Puritans who burnt to the greater glory of their deity—"ever ready for a bribe of blood to aid the foulest cause"— alleged witches and heretics by hundred of thousands. Surely it is not the living Mahatmas but "the Biblical one living God," he who, thousand of years ago, had inspired Jepthah to murder his daughter, and the weak David to hang the seven sons and grandsons of Saul "in the hill before the Lord"; and who again in our own age had moved Guiteau to shoot President Garfield—that must have also inspired Danton and Robespierre, Marat and the Russian Nihilists to open eras of Terror and turn Churches into slaughterhouses.

Nevertheless, it is our firm conviction based on historical evidence and direct inferences from many of the *Memoirs* of those days that the French Revolution is due to *one* Adept. It is that mysterious personage, now conveniently classed with other "historical *charlatans*" (*i.e.,* great men whose occult knowledge and powers shoot over the heads of the imbecile majority), namely, the Count de St. Germain—who brought about the just outbreak among the paupers, and put an end to the selfish tyranny of the French kings—the "elect, and the Lord's anointed." And we know also that among the *Carbonari*—the precursors and pioneers of Garibaldi there was more than one *Freemason* deeply versed in occult sciences and Rosicrucianism. To infer from the article that a claim is laid down for Paine "to *supernatural* visitors" is to misconstrue the entire meaning of its author; and it shows very little knowledge of theosophy itself. There may be Theosophists who are also Spiritualists, in England and America who firmly believe in *disembodied* visitors; but neither they nor we, Eastern Theosophists, have ever believed in the existence of *supernatural* visitors. We leave this to the *orthodox* followers of their respective religions. It is quite possible that certain arguments adduced in this journal in proof of the existence of our Mahatmas, "have failed to bring conviction home" to our correspondent; nor does it much matter if they have not. But whether we refer to the Mahatmas he *believes* in, or to those whom we personally *know*— once that a man has raised himself to the eminence of one, unless he be a sorcerer, or a Dugpa, he can never be an inspirer of sinful acts. To the Hebrew saying, "I, the Lord create evil," the Mahatma answers,—"I, the Initiate try to counteract and destroy it." [V, 80.]

———•———

The belief in a personal god may do some good under certain circumstances, but it may also do a great deal of harm according to the attributes which we give to that personal god. A personal god without personal attributes is unthinkable and illogical; because it is his personal attributes, which constitute him a "personal" god. If we believe that such a god is passionate, revengeful and changeable, if we believe that he favors some and condemns others, that he can be persuaded to forgive our sins and thereby act contrary to the law of justice, such a belief not only impedes our own progress, but is highly pernicious.

The words "right" and "wrong" may be used in the absolute or in the relative sense. Generally speaking it is the intention with which the act is done, that constitutes its right or wrong. If it is in accordance with the law of justice, it cannot be wrong; but we cannot obtain a perfect sense of justice without a corresponding degree of knowledge. [VI, 18.]

Rather than believe in *such* a "God," many good men have ceased to believe in one at all. It is against the *interpretations* of the words of Jesus of Nazareth and not the words themselves (which mean quite a different thing) that so many ex-Christians have rebelled. [IV, 272 fn.]

We cannot conceive of an *"All-pervading* whole," being separate from its part. The idea . . . is of course the theistic, but not very philosophical doctrine which teaches the relation of man to God as that between father and child.

. . . How can Parabrahma be "the ever-active state of the whole" when the only attribute—an absolutely negative one—of Parabrahma is passivity, unconsciousness, etc. And how can Parabrahma, the *one* principle, the universal Essence of the Totality be only a "state of the WHOLE" when it is itself the WHOLE, and when even the Vedantic Dwaitees assert that Iswara is but a mere manifestation of, and secondary to, Parabrahma which is the "All-Pervading" TOTAL?

. . . If the whole is *"all-pervading"* and "infinite," all its parts must be indivisibly linked together. The idea of separation involves the possibility of a vacuum—a portion of space or time where the *whole* is supposed to be absent from some given point. Hence the absurdity of speaking of the parts of one Infinite being also infinite. To illustrate geometrically, suppose there is an infinite line, which has neither a beginning nor end. Its parts cannot also be infinite, for when you say "parts," they must have a beginning and end; or, in other words, they must be finite, either at one or the other end, which is as evident a fallacy as to speak of an *immortal* soul which was at some time *created*—thus implying a beginning to that which, if the word has any sense, is eternal.

Would it not be better and far more philosophical to resort, in such a case, to the oft-repeated simile of the ocean? If we suppose for a moment, infinity to be a vast and *all-pervading* ocean, we can conceive of the individual existence of each of the drops composing that sea. All are alike *in essence,* but their *manifestations* may and do differ according to their surrounding conditions. In the same manner, all human *individualities,* although alike in nature, yet differ in *manifestations* according to the vehicles and the conditions through which they have to act. The *Yogi,* therefore, so far elevates his other principles, or let us call them vehicles, if preferred, as to facilitate the manifestation of his individuality in its original nature. [IV, 228.]

FROM "LUCIFER"

THOUGHTS ON THEOSOPHY

"THE letter killeth, but the spirit giveth life," this is the key-note of all true reform. Theosophy is the vehicle of the spirit that gives life, consequently nothing *dogmatic* can be truly *theosophical*.

It is incorrect, therefore, to describe a *mere* unearthing of dead letter dogmas as "Theosophic work."

When a word, phrase, or symbol, having been once used for the purpose of suggesting an idea *new* to the mind or minds being operated on, is insisted upon irrespective of the said idea, it becomes a dead letter dogma and loses its vitalising power, and serves rather as an obstruction to, than as vehicle of the spirit; but, alas, this insistence upon the letter is too often carried on under the honoured name of "Theosophy."

A man cannot acquire an idea *new to him* unless it *grows* in his mind.

The mere familiarity with the *sound* of a word, or a phrase, or the mere familiarity with the *appearance* of a symbol, does not, of *necessity,* involve the possession of the idea properly associated with the said word, phrase or symbol. To insist, therefore, on the contrary cannot be theosophical; but would be better described as *un*theosophical.

It would certainly be theosophical work to point out kindly and temperately how certain words, phrases and symbols appear to have been misunderstood or misapplied, how various claims and professions may be excessive or confused as a consequence of ignorance or vanity, or both. But it is quite another thing to condemn a man or a body of men *outright,* for certain errors in judgment or action; even though they were the result of vanity, greed or hypocrisy; indeed such wholesale condemnation would, on the contrary, be untheosophical.

The one eternal, immutable law of life alone can judge and condemn a man absolutely. "Vengeance is *mine,* saith the Lord."

Were I asked how I would dare attempt "to dethrone the gods, overthrow the temple, destroy the law which feeds the priests and props the realm; I should answer as the Buddha is made to answer in the *Light of Asia:* 'What thou bidst me keep is form which passes while the free truth stands; get thee to thy darkness.' "

"What good gift hath my brother but it comes from search and strife (inward) and loving sacrifice."

*
*   *

Lucifer, October, 1887

SOME WORDS ON DAILY LIFE
(Written by a Master of Wisdom)

IT is divine philosophy alone, the spiritual and psychic blending of man with nature, which, by revealing the fundamental truths that lie hidden under the objects of sense and perception, can promote a spirit of unity and harmony in spite of the great diversities of conflicting creeds. Theosophy, therefore, expects and demands from the Fellows of the Society a great mutual toleration and charity for each other's shortcomings, ungrudging mutual help in the search for truths in every department of nature—moral and physical. And this ethical standard must be unflinchingly applied to daily life.

"Theosophy should not represent merely a collection of moral verities, a bundle of metaphysical ethics, epitomized in theoretical dissertations. Theosophy *must be made practical;* and it has, therefore, to be disencumbered of useless digressions, in the sense of desultory orations and fine talk. Let every Theosophist only do his duty, that which he can and ought to do, and very soon the sum of human misery, within and around the areas of every Branch of your Society, will be found visibly diminished. Forget SELF in working for others—and the task will become an easy and a light one for you.

"Do not set your pride in the appreciation and acknowledgement of that work by others. Why should any member of the Theosophical Society, striving to become a Theosophist, put any value upon his neighbour's good or bad opinion of himself and his work, so long as he himself knows it to be useful and beneficent to other people? Human praise and enthusiasm are short-lived at best; the laugh of the scoffer and condemnation of the indifferent looker-on are sure to follow, and generally to out-weigh, the admiring praise of the friendly. Do not despise the opinion of the world, nor provoke it uselessly to unjust criticism. Remain rather as indifferent to the abuse as to the praise of those who can never know you as you really are, and who ought, therefore, to find you unmoved by either, and ever placing the approval or condemnation of your own

Inner Self higher than that of the multitudes.

"Those of you who would know yourselves in the spirit of truth, learn to live alone even amidst the great crowds which may sometimes surround you. Seek communion and intercourse only with the God within your own soul; heed only the praise or blame of that deity which can never be separated from your *true* self, as it *is verily that God itself:* called the HIGHER CONSCIOUSNESS. Put without delay your good intentions into practice, never leaving a single one to remain only an intention—expecting, meanwhile, neither reward nor even acknowledgement for the good you may have done. Reward and acknowledgement are in yourself and inseparable from you, as it is your Inner Self alone which can appreciate them at their true degree and value. For each one of you contains within the precincts of his inner tabernacle the Supreme Court—prosecutor, defense, jury and judge—whose sentence is the only one without appeal; since none can know you better than you do yourself, when once you have learned to judge that Self by the never wavering light of the inner divinity—your higher Consciousness. Let, therefore, the masses, which can never know your true selves, condemn your outer selves according to their own false lights.

"The majority of the public Areopagus is generally composed of self-appointed judges, who have never made a permanent deity of any idol save their own personalities—their lower selves; for those who try in their walk in life, to follow their *inner light* will never be found judging, far less condemning, those weaker than themselves. What does it matter, then, whether the former condemn or praise, whether they humble you or exalt you on a pinnacle? They will never comprehend you one way or the other. They may make an idol of you, so long as they imagine you a faithful mirror of themselves on the pedestal or altar which they have reared for you, and while you amuse or benefit them. You cannot expect to be anything for them but a temporary *fetish,* succeeding another fetish just overthrown, and followed in your turn by another idol. Let, therefore, those who have created that idol destroy it whenever they like, casting it down with as little cause as they had for setting it up. Your Western Society can no more live without its Khalif of an hour than it can worship one for any longer period; and whenever it breaks an idol and then besmears it with mud, it is not the model, but the disfigured image created by its own foul fancy and which it has endowed with its own vices, that Society dethrones and breaks.

"Theosophy can only find objective expression in an all-embracing code of life, thoroughly impregnated with the spirit of mutual tolerance, charity, and brotherly love. Its Society, as a body, has a task before it which, unless performed with the utmost discretion, will cause the world of the indifferent and the selfish to rise up in arms against it. Theosophy has to fight intolerance, prejudice, ignorance, and selfishness, hidden under the mantle of hypocrisy. It has to throw all the light it can from the torch of Truth, with which its servants are entrusted. It must do this without fear or hesitation, dreading neither reproof nor condemnation. Theosophy, through its mouthpiece, the Society, has to tell the TRUTH to the very face of LIE; to beard the tiger in its den, without thought or fear of evil consequences, and to set at defiance calumny and threats. *As an Association,* it has not only the right, but the duty to uncloak vice and do its best to redress wrongs, whether through the voice of its chosen lecturers or the printed word of its journals and publications—making its accusations, however, as impersonal as possible. But its Fellows, or Members have *individually* no such right. Its followers have, first of all, to set the example of a firmly outlined and as firmly applied morality, before they obtain the right to point out, even in a spirit of kindness, the absence of a like ethic unity and singleness of purpose in other associations or individuals. No Theosophist should blame a brother, whether within or outside of the association; neither may he throw a slur upon another's actions or denounce him, lest he himself lose the right to be considered a Theosophist. For, as such, he has to turn away his gaze from the imperfections of his neighbour, and centre rather his attention upon his own shortcomings, in order to correct them and become wiser. Let him not show the disparity between claim and action in another, but, whether in the case of a brother, a neighbor, or simply a fellow man, let him rather ever help one weaker than himself on the arduous walk of life.

"The problems of true Theosophy and its great mission are, first, the working out of clear unequivocal conceptions of ethic ideas and duties, such as shall best and most fully satisfy the right and altruistic feelings in men; and, second, the modeling of these conceptions for their adaptation into such forms of daily life, as shall offer a field where they may be applied with most equitableness.

"Such is the common work placed before all who are willing to act on these principles. It is a laborious task, and will require strenuous and persevering exertion; but it must lead you insensibly to progress, and leave you no room for any selfish aspirations outside the limits traced. . . . Do not indulge personally in unbrotherly comparison between the task accomplished by yourself and the work left undone by your neighbours or brothers. In the fields of Theosophy *none is held to weed out a larger plot of ground than his strength and capacity will permit him.* Do not be too severe on the merits or demerits of one who seeks admission among your ranks, as the truth about the actual state of the inner man can only be known to Karma, and can be dealt with justly by that all-seeing Law alone. Even the simple presence amidst you of a well-intentioned and sympathizing individual may help you magnetically. . . . You are the free volunteer workers on the fields of Truth, and as such must leave no obstruction on the paths leading to that field."

*   *   *   *   *

"The degree of success or failure are the landmarks the Masters have to follow, as they will constitute the barriers placed with your own hands between yourselves and those whom you have asked to be your teachers. The nearer your approach to the goal contemplated—the shorter the distance between the student and the Master."

Lucifer, January, 1888

THE THREE DESIRES

THE first three of the numbered rules of "Light on the Path" must appear somewhat of an unequal character to bracket together. The sense in which they follow each other is purely spiritual. Ambition is the highest point of personal activity reached by the mind, and there is something noble in it, even to an Occultist. Having conquered the desire to stand above his fellows, the restless aspirant, in seeking what his personal desires are, finds the thirst for life stands next in his way. For all that are ordinarily classed as desires has long since been subjugated, passed by, or forgotten, before this pitched battle of the soul is begun. The desire for life is entirely a desire of the spirit, not mental at all; and in facing it a man begins to face his own soul. But very few have even attempted to face it; still fewer can guess at all at its meaning.

The connection between ambition and the desire of life is of this kind. Men are seldom really ambitious in whom the animal passions are strong. What is taken for ambition in men of powerful physique is more often merely the exercise of great energy in order to obtain full gratification of all physical desires. Ambition pure and simple is the struggle of the mind upwards, the exercise of a native intellectual force which lifts a man altogether above his peers. To rise—to be pre-eminent in some special manner, in some department of art, science, or thought, is the keenest longing of delicate and highly-tuned minds. It is quite a different thing from the thirst for knowledge which makes of a man a student always—a learner to the end, however great he may become. Ambition is born of no love for anything for its own sake, but purely for the sake of oneself. "It is I that will know, I that will rise, and by my own power."

> Cromwell, I charge thee, fling away ambition;
> By that sin fell the angels.

The place-seeking for which the word was originally used, differs in degree, not in kind, from that more abstract meaning now generally attached to it. A poet is considered ambitious when he writes for fame. It is true; so he is. He may not be seeking a place at court, but he is certainly seeking the highest place he knows of. Is it conceivable that any great author could really be anonymous, and remain so? The human mind revolts against the theory of the Baconian authorship of Shakespeare's works, not only because it deprives the world of a splendid figure, but also because it makes of Bacon a monster, unlike all other human beings. To the ordinary intelligence it is inconceivable that a man should hide his light in this purposeless manner. Yet it is conceivable to an occultist that a great poet might be inspired by one greater than himself, who would stand back entirely from the world and all contact with it. This inspirer would not only have conquered ambition but also the abstract desire for life, before he could work vicariously to so great an extent. For he would part with his work for ever when once it had gone to the world; it would never be his. A person who can imagine making no claim on the world, neither desiring to take pleasure from it nor to give pleasure to it, can dimly apprehend the condition which the occultist has reached when he no longer desires to live. Do not suppose this to mean that he neither takes nor gives pleasure; he does both, as also he lives. A great man, full of work and thought, eats his food with pleasure; he does not dwell on the prospect of it, and linger over the memory, like the gluttonous child, or the gourmand pure and simple. This is a very material image, yet sometimes these simple illustrations serve to help the mind more than any others. It is easy to see, from this analogy, that an advanced occultist who has work in the world may be perfectly free from the desires which would make him a part of it, and yet may take its pleasures and give them back with interest. He is enabled to give more pleasure than he takes, because he is incapable of fear or disappointment. He has no dread of death, nor of that which is called annihilation. He rests on the waters of life, submerged and sleeping, or above them and conscious, indifferently. He cannot feel disappointment, because although pleasure is to him intensely vivid and keen, it is the same to him whether he enjoys it himself or whether another enjoys it. It is pleasure, pure and simple, untarnished by personal craving or desire. So with regard to what occultists call "progress"—the advance from stage to stage of knowledge. In a school of any sort in the external world emulation is the great spur to progress.

The occultist, on the contrary, is incapable of taking a single step until he has acquired the faculty of realizing progress as an abstract fact. Someone must draw nearer to the Divine in every moment of life; there must always be progress. But the disciple who desires that he shall be the one to advance in the next moment, may lay aside all hope of it. Neither should he be conscious of preferring progress for another or of any kind of vicarious sacrifice. Such ideas are in a certain sense unselfish, but they are essentially characteristic of the world in which separateness exists, and form is regarded as having a value of its own. The shape of a man is as much an *eidolon* as though no spark of divinity inhabited it; at any moment that spark may desert the particular shape, and we are left with a substantial shadow of the man we knew. It is in vain, after the first step in occultism has been taken, that the mind clings to the old beliefs and certainties. Time and space are known to be non-existent, and are only regarded as existing in practical life for the sake of convenience. So with the separation of the divine-human spirit into the multitudes of men on the earth. Roses have their own colours, and lilies theirs; none can tell why this is when the same sun, the same light, gives the colour to each. Nature is indivisible. She clothes the earth, and when that clothing is torn away, she bides her time and re-clothes it again when there is no more interference with her. Encircling the earth like an atmosphere, she keeps it always glowing and green, moistened and sunlit. The spirit of man encompasses the earth like a fiery spirit, living on Nature, devouring her, sometimes being devoured by her, but always in the mass remaining more ethereal and sublime than she is. In the individual, man is conscious of the vast superiority of Nature; but when once he becomes conscious that he is part of an indivisible and indestructible whole, he knows also that the whole of which he is part stands above nature. The starry sky is a terrible sight to a man who is just selfless enough to be aware of his own littleness and unimportance as an individual; it almost crushes him. But let him once touch on the power which comes from knowing himself as part of the human spirit, and nothing can crush him by its greatness. For if the wheels of the chariot of the enemy pass over his body, he forgets that it is his body, and rises again to fight among the crowd of his own army. But this state can never be reached, nor even approached, until the last of the three desires is conquered, as well as the first. They must be apprehended and encountered together.

Comfort, in the language used by occultists, is a very comprehensive word. It is perfectly useless for a neophyte to practice discomfort or asceticism as do religious fanatics. He may come to prefer deprivation in the end, and then it has become his comfort. Homelessness is a condition to which the religious Brahmin pledges himself; and in the external religion he is considered to fulfill this pledge if he leaves wife and child, and becomes a begging wanderer, with no shelter of his own to return to. But all external forms of religion are forms of comfort, and men take vows of abstinence in the same spirit that they take pledges of boon companionship. The difference between these two sides of life is only apparent. But the homelessness which is demanded of the neophyte is a much more vital thing than this. It demands the surrender from him of choice or desire. Dwelling with wife and child, under the shelter of a familiar roof-tree, and fulfilling the duties of citizenship, the neophyte may be far more homeless, in the esoteric sense, than when he is a wanderer or an outcast. The first lesson in practical occultism usually given to a pledged disciple is that of fulfilling the duties immediately to hand with the same subtle mixture of enthusiasm and indifference as the neophyte would imagine himself able to feel when he had grown to the size of a ruler of worlds and a designer of destinies. This rule is to be found in the Gospels and in the *Bhagavad Gita*. The immediate work, whatever it may be, has the abstract claim of duty, and its relative importance or non-importance is not to be considered at all. This law can never be obeyed until all desire of comfort is forever destroyed. The ceaseless assertions and re-assertions of the personal self must be left behind forever. They belong as completely to the character of this world as does the desire to have a certain balance at the bank, or to retain the affections of a loved person. They are equally subject to the change which is characteristic of this world; indeed, they are even more so, for what the neophyte does by becoming a neophyte is simply to enter a forcing-house. Change, disillusionment, disheartenment, despair will crowd upon him by invitation; for his wish is to learn his lessons quickly. And as he turns these evils out they will probably be replaced by others worse than themselves—a passionate longing for separate life, for sensation, for the consciousness of growth in his own self, will rush in upon him and sweep over the frail barriers which he has raised. And no such barriers as asceticism, as renunciation, nothing indeed which is negative, will stand for a single moment against this powerful tide of feeling. The only barrier is built up of new desires. For it is perfectly useless for the neophyte to imagine he can get beyond the region of desires. He cannot; he is still a man; Nature must bring forth flowers while she is still Nature, and the human spirit would loose its hold on this form of existence altogether did it not continue to desire. The individual man cannot wrench himself instantly out of that life of which he is an essential part. He can only change his position in it. The man whose intellectual life dominates his animal life, changes his position; but he is still in the dominion of desire. The disciple who believes it possible to become selfless in a single effort, will find himself flung into a bottomless pit as the consequence of his rash endeavour. Seize upon a new order of desires, purer, wider, nobler; and so plant your foot upon the ladder firmly. It is only on the last and topmost rung of the ladder, at the very entrance upon Divine or Mahatmic life, that it is possible to hold fast to that which has neither substance or existence.

The first part of "Light on the Path" is like a chord in music; the notes have to be struck together though they must be touched separately. Study and seize hold of the new desires before you have thrust out the old ones; otherwise in the storm you will be lost. Man while he is man has substance and needs some step to stand on, some idea to cling to. But let it be the least possible. Learn as the acrobat learns, slowly and with care, to become more independent. Before you attempt to cast out the devil of ambition— the desire of something, however fine and elevated, outside of yourself,—seize on the desire to find the light of the world within yourself. Before you attempt to cast out the desire of conscious life, learn to look to the unattainable or in other language to that which you know you can only reach in unconsciousness. In knowing that your aim is of this lofty character, that it will never bring conscious success, never bring comfort to you, that it will never carry you *in your own temporary personal self* to any haven of rest or place of agreeable activity, you cut away all the force and power of the desires of the lower astral nature. For what avail is it, when these facts have been once realised, to desire separateness, sensation or growth?

The armour of the warrior who rises to fight for you in the battle depicted in the second part of "Light on the Path," is like the shirt of the happy man in the old story. The king was to be cured of all his ills by sleeping in this shirt; but when the one happy man in his kingdom was found, he was a beggar, without care, without anxiety—and shirtless. So with the divine warrior. None can take his armour and use it, for he has none. The king could never find happiness like that of the careless beggar. The man of the world, however fine and cultivated he may be, is hampered by a thousand thoughts and feelings which have to be cast aside before he can even stand on the threshold of occultism. And, be it observed, he is chiefly handicapped by the armour he wears, which isolates him. He has personal pride, personal respect. These things must die out as the personality recedes. The process described in the first part of "Light on the Path," is one which takes off that shell, or armour, and casts it aside forever. Then the warrior arises, armourless, defenseless, offenseless, identified with the afflicters and the afflicted, the angered and the one that angers; fighting not on any side, but for the Divine, the highest in all.

Lucifer, February, 1888

WHAT GOOD HAS THEOSOPHY DONE IN INDIA?

> The race of mankind would perish, did they cease to aid each other. From the time that the mother binds the child's head, till the moment that some kind assistant wipes the death-damp from the brow of the dying, we cannot exist without mutual help. All, therefore, that need aid, have a right to ask it from their fellow-mortals. No one who holds the power of granting, can refuse it without guilt.
>
> —SIR WALTER SCOTT

SEVERAL correspondents and enquirers have lately asked us "What good have you done in India?" To answer it would be easy. One has but to ask the doubters to read the January Number, 1888, of the Madras *Theosophist*—our official organ—and, turning to the report in it on the Anniversary Meeting of the Theosophical Society, whose delegates meet yearly at Adyar, see for himself. Many and various are the good works done by the 127 active branches of the Theosophical Society scattered throughout the length and breadth of India. But as most of those works are of a moral and reformatory character, the ethical results upon the members are difficult to describe. Free Sanskrit schools have been opened wherever it was possible; gratuitous classes are held; free dispensaries—homœopathic and allopathic—established for the poor, and many of our Theosophists feed and clothe the needy.

All this, however, might have been done by people without belonging to our Brotherhood, we may be told. True; and much the same has been done before the T.S. appeared in India, and from time immemorial. Yet such work has been hitherto done, and such help given by the wealthier members of one caste or religious community exclusively to the poorer members of the same caste and religious denomination. No Brahmin would have held brotherly intercourse even with a Brahmin of another division of his own high caste, let alone with a Jain or Buddhist. A Parsee would only protect and defend his own brother follower of Zoroaster. A Jain would feed and take care of a lame and sick animal, but would turn away from a Hindu of the Vaishnava or any other sect. He would spend thousands on the "Hospital for Animals" where bullocks, old crippled tigers and dogs are nursed, but would not approach a fellowman in need unless he was a Jain like himself. But now, since the advent of the Theosophical Society, things in India are, slowly it is true, yet gradually, becoming otherwise.

We have, then, to show rather the good moral effect produced by the Society in general, and each branch of it in its own district on the population, than to boast of works of charity, for which India has ever been noted. We shall not enter even into a disquisition upon the benefits to be reaped by the establishment of a Sanskrit, or rather an Oriental and European library at Adyar, which, thanks to the indefatigable efforts of the President-Founder and his colleagues, begins now to assume quite hopeful proportions. But we will draw at once the attention of the enquirers to the ethical aspect of the question; for all the visible or objective works, whether of charity or any other kind, must pale before the results achieved through the influence of the chief universal, ethical aim and idea of our Society.

Yes; the seeds of a true *Universal Brotherhood* of man, not of brother-religionists or sectarians only, have been finally sown on the sacred soil of India! The letter that follows these lines proves it most undeniably. These seeds have been thrown since 1881 into that soil, which, for thousands of years, has stubbornly and systematically ejected everything foreign to its system of caste, and refused to assimilate any heterogeneous element alien to Brahmanism, the chief master of the soil of Aryavarta, or to accept any ideas not based upon the Laws of Manu. The Orientalist and the Anglo-Indian, who know something of that tyranny of caste which has hitherto formed an impassable barrier, an almost fathomless gulf between Brahmanism and every other religion, know also of the great hatred of the orthodox "twice born," the *dwija* Brahmin, to the Buddhist *nastika* (the atheist, he who refuses to recognise the Brahminical gods and idols); and they, above all others, will realise, even if they do not fully appreciate, the importance of what has now been achieved by the Theosophical Society. It took several years of incessant efforts to bring about even the beginning of a *rapprochement* between the Brahmin and Buddhist theosophists. A few years ago the President-Founder of the Society, Colonel H. S. Olcott, had almost succeeded in making a breach in the Chinese wall of Brahmanism. It was an unprecedented event; and it created a great stir among the natives, a sincere enthusiasm among the "Heathen," and much malicious opposition, gossip, and slanderous denial from those who, above all men, ought to work for the idea of Universal Brotherhood preached by their Master—the *good* Christian Missionaries. Colonel Olcott had succeeded in arranging a kind of preliminary reconciliation between the Brahminical Theosophical Society of Tinevelly and their brother Theosophists and neighbors of Ceylon. Several Buddhists had been brought from Lanka, led by the President, carrying with them, as an emblem of peace and reconciliation, a sprout of the sacred *rajah* (king) cocoanut-tree. This actually was to be planted in one of the courts of the Tinevelly pagoda, as a living and growing witness to the event. It was an extraordinary and imposing sight that day, namely October 25th, 1881, when, before an immense crowd numbering several thousands of Hindus and other natives, the Delegates of the Buddhist Theosophical Societies of Ceylon, met with their brother Theosophists of the Tinevelly Branch and their Brahmin priests of the pagoda. For over 2,000 years an irreconcilable religious feud had raged between the two creeds and their respective followers. And now they were brought once more together on Hindu soil, and even within the thrice sacred, and to all strangers almost impenetrable, precincts of a Hindu temple, which would have been, only a few days previous to the occurrence, regarded as irretrievably desecrated had even the very shadow of a Buddhist *nastika* fallen upon its outward walls. Signs of the times, indeed! The cocoanut sprout was planted with great ceremony, and to the sounds of the music of the pagoda orchestra. After that, year after year, Hindus and Buddhists met together at Adyar, at the Annual Conventions for the Anniversary Meetings of the Theosophical Parent Society; but no Brahmin Theosophist had hitherto returned the visit to Ceylon to his Buddhist Brethren. The ice of the centuries had been split, but not sufficiently broken to permit anyone to dive deep enough under it to call this an entire and full reconciliation. But the impressive and long-expected and wished-for event has at last taken place. All honour and glory to the son of Brahmins—the proudest, perhaps, of all India, the Northern Brahmins of Kashmir —who was the first to place the sacred duties of Universal Brotherhood above the prejudices, as potent as they are narrow, of caste and custom. . . .

But after reading extracts from his own address, which appeared in *Sarasavisandaresa,* the Cinghalese organ of the Buddhists of Ceylon,* let not our critics rise once more against the policy of the Theosophical Society, and take the opportunity of calling it intolerant and uncharitable *only as regards one creed, namely Christianity.* . . . No Theosophist has ever spoken against the teachings of Christ, no more than he did against those of Krishna, Buddha, or Sankaracharya; and willingly would he treat every Christian as a Brother, if the Christian himself would not persistently turn his back on the Theosophist. But a man would lose every right to the appellation of a member of the Universal Brotherhood, were he to keep silent in the fact of the crying bigotry and falseness of all the theological, or rather sacerdotal, systems—the world over. We, Europeans, expatiate loudly and cry against Brahminical tyranny, against caste, against infant and widow marriage, and call every religious dogmatic rule (save our own) idiotic, pernicious, and devilish, and do it orally as in print. Why should not we confess and even denounce the abuses and defects of Christian theology and sacerdotalism as well? How dare we say to our "brother"—Let me cast out the mote of thine eye, and refuse to consider "the *beam that is in our own eye?"* Christians have to choose—Either they "shall not judge that they be not judged," or if they do—and one has but to read the missionary and clerical organs to see how cruel, unchristian, and uncharitable *their* judgments are—they *must be prepared to be judged in their turn.* . . .

"There is but ONE Eternal Truth, one universal, infinite and changeless Spirit of Love, Truth and Wisdom, impersonal, therefore bearing a different name with every nation, one Light for all, in which the whole Humanity lives and moves, and has its being. Like the spectrum in optics, giving multicoloured and various rays, which are yet caused by one and the same sun, so theologies and sacerdotal systems are many. But the Universal religion *can only be one,* if we accept the real, primitive meaning of the root of that word. We, Theosophists, so accept it; and therefore say, "We are all brothers—by the laws of Nature of birth, and death, as also by

—————
*Reprinted as a portion of this article.—Eds.

the laws of our utter helplessness from birth to death in this world of sorrow and deceptive illusions. Let us, then, love, help, and mutually defend each other against this spirit of deception; and while holding to that which each of us accepts as his ideal of truth and reality—*i.e.*, to the religion which suits each of us best— let us unite ourselves to form a practical 'nucleus of a Universal Brotherhood of Humanity WITHOUT DISTINCTION OF RACE, CREED, OR COLOUR'."

Lucifer, April, 1888

A MASTER'S LETTER

[H.P.B. printed in *Lucifer* some extracts from a Letter written a few weeks previously by the Master, K.H., to H.S. Alcott. The correctness of the extracts was certified by Colonel Olcott. The ostensible occasion for the Letter was an "interference" by H.P.B. with the affairs of a Theosophical Society in Paris, where a bitter quarrel was going on. Col. Olcott resented both the "interference" of H.P.B. and the action taken by her. His attitude supplied the *mise en scene* for the Letter. Students of Theosophy may be able to read much within the words of the Letter if they are informed on theosophical history during the years that have intervened since the Letter was written.

Colonel Olcott's version of the Paris difficulties and his comments on H.P.B. in connection therewith, may be found in his article, "Old Diary Leaves," in the *Theosophist* for February, 1900.—Eds.]

". . . Misunderstandings have grown up between Fellows both in London and Paris which imperil the interests of the movement. You will be told that the chief originator of most, if not of all of those disturbances is H.P.B. This is not so, though her presence in England has, of course, a share in them. But the largest share rests with others, whose serene unconsciousness of their own defects is very marked and much to be blamed. . . . Observe your own case, for example. . . . But your revolt, good friend, against her 'infallibility'—as you once thought it—has gone too far, and you have been unjust to her, for which I am sorry. . . .

"Try to remove such misconceptions as you will find, by kind persuasion and an appeal to the feelings of loyalty to the cause of truth, if not to us. Make all these men feel that we have no favourites, nor affections for persons, but only for their good acts and Humanity as a whole. But we employ agents—the best available. Of these, for the last thirty years, the chief has been the personality known as 'H.P.B.' . . . imperfect and very troublesome, no doubt, she proves to some; nevertheless, *there is no likelihood of our finding a better one for years to come,* and your theosophists should be made to understand it. . . .

"Since 1885 I have not written, nor caused to be written, save through her agency, direct or remote—*a letter or a line to anybody in Europe or America,* nor have I communicated orally with, or through any third party. Theosophists should learn it. You will understand later the significance of this declaration, so keep it in mind. . . . Her fidelity to our work being constant, and her sufferings having come upon her through it, neither I nor any of my brother associates will desert or supplant her. As I once before remarked, ingratitude is not among our vices . . . to help you in your present perplexity: H.P.B. has next to no concern with administrative details, and should be kept clear of them. . . . But *this you must tell to all: with occult matters she has everything to do.* . . . We have *not* 'abandoned her'; she is *not* 'given over to chelas.' *She is our direct agent.* . . . In the adjustment of this European business you will have two things to consider—the external and administrative, and the internal psychical. Keep the former under *your* control, and that of your most prudent associates, jointly; *leave the latter to her.* You are left to devise the practical details. . . . Only be careful, I say, to discriminate when some emergent interference of hers in practical affairs is referred to your appeal between that which is merely exoteric in origin and effects and that which, beginning on the practical, tends to beget consequences on the spiritual plane. As to the former you are the best judge; as to the latter, she. . . ."

(This letter) . . . is merely given you as a warning and a guide; . . . you may use it discreetly, if needs be. . . . Prepare, however, to have the authenticity of the present denied in certain quarters.

(Signed) K. H.

(Extracts correctly copied.—H. S. OLCOTT)

Lucifer, October, 1888

CONSCIOUSNESS

CONSCIOUSNESS is the seat of the real life of the human individual. The mere carrying on of his bodily functions is not his life. Those functions are the channels and avenues through which his real being has communion with the phenomenal world, and with other units of consciousness similar to his own. Through them his life is greatly affected; by their means his thoughts are fed, his feelings modified, his actions suggested. But let us consider the modes in which consciousness may work, and the specific forms in which it may manifest itself. Observation of human modes and objects of life indicates three classes of consciousness. In other words, there are three modes of existence which the consciousness of an individual may fall into, or work itself into, and the adoption of the particular mode, knowingly and deliberately, or the contrary, determines the character and intrinsic value of the consciousness.

The elementary or simplest mode of consciousness we designate as *lineal*. In this, the feelings, thoughts, and energies of the individual lie not only on one plane but merely in one direction on that plane.

The consciousness which belongs to this class is limited to the faculty of moving *backwards or forwards in a straight line*. It is bound like a railway train to its special track. This form of consciousness is very common. It is the lot of those who have only one aim in life, and that a personal one. Whatever the chief aim of the life may be, whether that of the shopkeeper, merely to earn money, or of the professional man in his special sphere, or of society men and women, in their incessant flittings to and fro in the whirl of pleasure and excitement, it matters nothing; the consciousness, which is the essence of the individual, exercises itself and possesses power only in the limited sphere described. It is simply necessary to look around to observe many examples of this class. A very large number of men and women of the present day belong to it.

In the second class the consciousness enjoys a wider freedom.

The dimensions of the realm over which it rules lie in two directions; for, in addition to backward and forward movement, the consciousness may traverse regions that lie to the right and to the left.

This form of consciousness we shall term the *superficial;* it has length and breadth, but no depth. It is the possession of those who, while devoted to one special employment which absorbs their chief energies, also occupy themselves, as adjuncts of life, in other spheres having for them a particular interest. This consciousness predominates largely amongst men and women who, following a daily avocation to supply the main needs of life, have sufficient mental or emotional activity to lead them into secondary engagements that exercise thought or fulfil an aim. The persons possessing this form of consciousness are active and seem to follow a purpose, though the purpose may not be noble or of intrinsic value. Naturally, this consciousness enjoys much more of life than the form belonging to the class designated as lineal. Men of business, not wholly immersed in the getting of money, clergymen and ministers of wise sympathies, teachers not limited to one peculiar tendency of thought, and persons whose lives generally are useful and active, are those who belong to the second class of superficial consciousness.

The consciousness, the nature of which remains to be described, is of vastly greater extent than either of the two classes already discussed.

Its dimensions lie in three directions. Not only does it exist in all directions superficially, but it further penetrates below the surface in possessing the quality of *depth.* It is true that the superficial area may vary in extent. This may appear, to the observer, but limited, or it may seem to spread far and wide, but the circumstance of depth in its nature and extent will be recognized only by the few, and not even by them to its full extent. The territory below the surface can neither be seen nor gauged, except by the faculties of a consciousness of similar nature. In the depth of an object there is capacity for substance, and consciousness is of a nature so real that wherever it exists in depth it is as true substance. The objects with which the lineal and superficial forms of consciousness deal are but temporal character and will pass away, but those that are the possession of the solid form are secure beyond possibility of removal.

Within that deep region, and corresponding to its intricacy and in the extent to which it penetrates, there are tracks of infinite variety and number.

In exploring these, the consciousness may find unending employment. This class of consciousness gives to the world those men from whom it learns, whose depth of nature is the abyss from which spring fountains and rills that irrigate life, and turn its wheels, and cause it to be fruitful.

Such men are the richest of earthly beings; their wealth is inexhaustible and imperishable. That depth, in which their consciousness revels, belongs to another world than that of ordinary human existence; it is the universe of eternal and infinite life, of which they are already subjects.

The first-named form of consciousness we should term sensuous, or that which operates merely through the senses and the nervous system; the second form we should call the intellectual or inner-sensuous; the third form is the spiritual or super-sensuous.

Sensuous consciousness delights merely in the external forms of objects and receives impressions only from those forms as they are found.

Intellectual consciousness finds its exciting cause not so much in the forms of external objects as in their movements and the effects of those movements upon the objects themselves.

The spiritual consciousness moves amidst the *hidden causes* of the sensuous and intellectual.

—I.

Lucifer, October, 1888

THE FUNCTION OF ATTENTION IN
PERSONAL DEVELOPMENT

TRUE study of any branch of knowledge consists in giving the matter of that branch such repetitions of *attentive* consideration that it at length becomes an integral part of the domain of the consciousness, and can at any time, under any correlated stimulus, be made use of by automatic mental action.

True Study of an Art consists, primarily in the *attentive* repetitions of the action of the physiological organs, involved in the productions of that Art, until that action becomes automatic, and is as well and so naturally performed as any original reflex physiological function.

In these definitions the word qualifying the necessary processes is the adjective *attentive,* denoting the presence of *attention* in the operation. Without this word the definitions would not merely be imperfect, they would be essentially incorrect and misleading.

Only in the quality of being *attentive* can the reiterated consideration and the reiterated action, respectively, result in the *possession,* on the one hand, of a new realm of knowledge, or, on the other hand, of a new area of power.

What is the *nature and manner of expression* of this supreme quality Attention?

An appreciative intellectual grasp of the answer to this question and a realisation of the function of its subject in the processes of human personal evolution, should be recognised as fundamental elements in the knowledge and understanding of the true educationist, be he teacher or not.

The word Attention is used largely, but loosely, in educational employments, yet we have no other word with which, habitually, to express that *attitude of the consciousness* which, in any study or acquisition of power, is absolutely and continuously demanded, in order to ensure intrinsic results. The term *concentration* is more literally correct in this relation, but concentration has, with most persons, too limited and too special an application to render it available for ordinary use instead of Attention.

Yet the Attention we are discussing, the attention of all knowledge-acquiring processes, may perhaps be better understood and realized if it is regarded as *Concentrated Attention.*

Attention is that condition or attitude of consciousness in which its rays are *steadily and unintermittently centred* upon the thing being done or the subject of study. This may be presented to the consciousness by one or more of the special senses, or it may already be a content of the mind; the special element in the attitude being *the intentness with which the consciousness operates.* This intentness of gaze must proceed to such a degree that all other sensible or mental objects, except *the one,* become excluded from its range.

In the effort to do this—to *maintain* concentrated attention, the Will of the individual is brought into play, and its function in the process may be compared to that played by a burning-glass held between the sun and the surface of an object. If it is intended that the sun's rays shall produce, through the burning-glass, a definite and observable effect, the glass must be held in such a relation to the object that the rays of light converge upon *one spot.* This spot, or focus, then receives the whole force of the rays that pass through the glass; it alone, of all that surrounding surface, is brought out into relief and operated upon. In like manner the Will, in sustaining attention, focuses the rays of the consciousness, with all their inherent dynamic forces, upon one circumscribed area, physiological, mental, or moral, as the case may be, wherein lies the work to be done.

Thus we see that Attention is intentness of Mental Vision, concentrated and maintained by action of the Will. It is not a separate function or property of the mind, like perception, imagination, reason, &c., as some psychologists might lead us to suppose, but *a mode of action,*—the true mode of the Will's action. In other words it is the *definite, efficient expression of the Volition or Will-force* of the individual.

The functions perception, conception, imagination, &c., are *instruments* of the Ego for operating upon the phenomenal world and upon mental appropriations of that world; when one or more of these thus operates with all its force, undiverted from its employment by any surrounding object, then Attention is exhibited.

Will is the manifestation or action of the *real human Ego;* Attention designates the mode in which that manifestation is functionally exhibited, and by which alone permanent results are produced.

In relation to the psychological realm in which Attention is a feature, we may formulate the following scheme. This scheme may serve to make the general bearings of the subject clearer and to more definitely indicate the part played by Attention in all psychological phenomena.

The *source* of mental movement
        arises in   Emotion=the desire to know.

The *direction* of the movement
        lies with   Reason=how and what to know.

The *machinery* of the movement
    is provided by   The mental=the means by which
                  activities   the knowledge is
      (Perception, etc.)   gained.

The *maintaining force* of the
    movement resides in the   Will=the mode by
                (the Energy   which continuity of
            of the Ego.)   operation is ensured.

The efficient relation of the two last groups of factors to each other, and their joint relation to the object under study, are expressed by our term Attention. The Will holds the mental activities employed *rigidly and persistently* to their work.

The Ego, through Volition, can only establish relations with objects external to itself *through the mental activities,* Perception, Conception, Judgment, Imagination, &c., and to effect this, the latter must be maintained in operation in a direct line between the Ego, represented by Volition, and the object to be studied; just as the gun of the sportsman must be held with exact precision longitudinally between his eye and the object he desires to hit. If the gun be allowed to deviate in the least degree from the exact line of vision, the sportsman misses his object, so, also, if Perception, or Conception, or Judgment, or Imagination, whichever of these activities or faculties is in use, is permitted to lose its *direct* bearing upon the work in hand absolute failure of purpose ensues. In this illustration the steady maintenance of the gun in precise position is a parallel to the psychological action of Attention.

When we grasp the full bearing of the truths here pointed out, we cannot fail to perceive the significant relation which the mental attitude of Attention holds to *all* educational processes and employments, nor can we assign it too prominent a position in laying down true and efficient methods of culture. Let Volition, the Mental Activities, the Light of Reason, the Physiological System of nerves and muscles, and vast mines of possible knowledge, all be provided; what intrinsic and permanent result can be accomplished amongst them if the manner in which they are used does not include Attention?

Modern Education fails, as evident to all thoughtful observers of human life, very largely because of its neglect to maintain this essential factor of personal evolution in its due place. The desultoriness, aimlessness and mental commonplaceness of the general adult life around us, spring from this omission.

Modern Education, in its multitude of subjects, in its haste in passing from one subject to another, and in its lack of precise aim, exhibits *desultoriness* in employment of time and faculty.

Desultoriness is the antithesis of Systematic Attention.

Modern Education rules over an area from which nothing new arises as the fruit of *its* fostering care, it brings no new thing into being from out its world of chaos.

This results from its desultoriness of method and action.

The Human Will is, however, a natural *creator* when it operates through *Concentrated Attention,* but education fails in its true mission as a stimulus and guide to individual creative force, because of this unreasonable neglect of a fundamental principle.

Every area of acquired skill is a new creation; it has a real, patent existence and is an object of possession and use in the world of human life, which did not exist previous to its evolution by the personal Will operating through the mental activities upon a physiological chaos.

To prevent possible confusion of thought in tracing out the subject, it may be remarked here that there is a mental attitude to which the term, Attention is commonly applied. This may be termed Passive Attention.

Passive Attention rules the consciousness when one listens to an eloquent speech or interesting lecture.

In such instances the Will is in abeyance, the consciousness being probably held entranced by forces which the Occultist might term *Mantramic.*

Passive attention also rules when the mind follows an absorbing train of thought. But this form is not that demanded for personal growth; educationally it is of slight value and without necessary relation to our subject.

Attention plays its necessary part in each one of the realms or planes of life to which the human individual belongs:—

1.   On the physical plane;—in the physiological realm of the special senses and the nervous and muscular systems. Conscious action under its rule in this realm results in *skill,* the basis not only of all art and artistic performance, but of every nicely adapted movement of the human limbs and frame for practical purpose or for the display of agility and gracefulness.

2. On the mental plane;—in the psychological realm of concepts, comparisons, judgments, deductions, speculations and ideals. On this plane intellectual energy under the control of Attention, creates logical systematic and consecutive forms of thought, true panoramic fields of vision out of detached intellectual details, and new emotional forms of power and beauty.

3.   On the moral plane;—in the spiritual realm of supreme truths, vital principles, gropings after the Infinite, the laws of human relationships, and the application of all these to the entire conduct of the personal life. In this supreme area the moral sentiments and spiritual aspirations after perfection of life, concentrate their attention upon *definite details* of personal thought and behaviour, the production of grace of spirit, reliability of disposition, agreement of conduct with principle, altruism in all its effective forms, and the development of a personal influence ever tending towards the evolution of a vitalizing social harmony.

In the evolution of personal life, when the object of its action is an area or detail of any one of these realms, Attention may be termed *specific,* and when the control of the adopted *purpose of existence as a whole* is maintained through its means, establishing an efficient and well-ordered unity amongst the many divisions and details of that purpose, then we may designate Attention as *supreme*.

"Genius" has been defined as "an infinite capacity for *taking pains*." The expression "taking pains" is merely a synonym for "close attention to *minute details*." "Close attention to details" takes each brick of which the "mansion for all lovely forms,"—the structure of personal knowledge, capacity and ability, is to be built, and carefully places it in *its due position, cementing it there at once*. The structure so put together is substantial, capacious, beautiful, and efficient.

This structure, the result of infinite pains long continued, is that which the world wonders at and worships and calls Genius. Nearly all men, if first guided and supported along the toilsome track and afterwards urged along it by pressure of their own Wills, might develop some form of power and skill which would elevate them considerably towards that height from which Genius looks down, and thus render the ordinary world much less commonplace, monotonous and unskillful than it is at present. To sum up:—

Concentrated Attention is the expression of the Will, and Will is the central, animating force proceeding from the Ego. Will, operating under the condition of Attention upon the chaos of its attendant world, and co-ordinating the energies, forces and movements of that world, converts it into a realm of form, power, and purpose, centering around the Ego.

This constitutes Personal Evolution resulting at length in a perfected Individuality, the *creation of its own Will*.

—I.

Lucifer, November, 1888

THE GENESIS OF EVIL IN HUMAN LIFE

EVIL is a mysterious subject, and of universal interest; it is continually presenting itself for discussion, and men exercise their minds very greatly upon it. It affects man deeply in his thoughts and speculations, because it is so large a factor in his life, and the cause of so much sorrow and suffering.

It is also an element which, though permeating his present existence as a canker, and paralysing and marring his happiness and the realisation of his ideals, man recognises *must* be eliminated from his life to the greatest possible extent, and especially in certain of its forms, in preparation for existence in a spiritual sphere. This recognition is one of the chief factors in the domain of personal religion, and the special aspect in which it is viewed determines the true or false conception of the means of salvation from evil.

The false conception of the means of salvation from evil rests upon the assumption that a *vicarious atonement* is essential; hence the religion of many is based, primarily, upon faith in the crucifixion of another being—an objective Christ—and only secondarily, and very indifferently, upon actual personal effort and suffering.

The true conception of salvation is based upon the literal acceptance of the exhortation of St. Paul: "Work out your own salvation in fear and trembling."*

Instead of resting complacently upon the sufferings of another, nailed upon a material cross by the hands of violent, unspiritually-minded men, its gaze is turned inwards, the arena of crucifixion is seen to be *there,* and the pain-giving nails and piercing spear are to pass through the sensitive forms of cherished personal desires, appetites, and subtler indulgences, not of the flesh only, but also of the mind and heart, extending and fixing them as to a cross until they expire.

---

* Philippians ii., 12.

But whence comes this canker, this cause of discord, confusion and paralysis, which we term evil? How has it arisen in the sphere of human existence?

In viewing the unlimited potentialities in man, in their number and extent, and in observing the boundless resources by which he is surrounded in his various domains of external activity, of thought, of emotion, and of personal cultivation, we can readily perceive that, were the discord of evil absent, his life would be bright, happy and full of intelligent purpose.

So it is continually asked what it is that has produced a world of activity and of feeling so inharmonious in its movments, so disjointed in its mutual inner relations, and so accompanied by sadness and fruitlessness? And the *wise* go further and ask, as the most pertinent and momentous of life-questions, how can the discords be resolved, the canker of disunion eliminated, and the vitalizing elements of true wisdom and purpose introduced?

At the outset of any enquiry respecting evil it is essential to recognise that *it is not itself a thing,* but is the *form* which a certain thing, *i.e.,* man's behaviour, individually and collectively, has taken. *Apart from that behaviour it does not exist;* let the form of that behaviour be changed, so that it becomes an expression of the Supreme Law of Life, reflecting the beauty and harmonious operation of that Law, and Evil will no longer exist. Whence has this form arisen, and what has attached it to the area of human existence?

And further, why is the inner life of each individual man the arena of a continual struggle? How is it that there is within him an incessant conflict as to *which form,* the good or the evil, shall characterise the weaving fabric of his permanent individuality? Why is there not smoothness of movement, concord and peace in the world of thought, feeling and action, of which man is the centre and the creator?

On considering the nature and ways of man's life, we find that he shares with the lower animals those principles of existence and motives of action which minister to self-preservation—provision of the necessaries of existence, protection from danger, and continuation of the species. In the brutes these principles and motives act without disorder. The animals obey their instincts, or inherent impulses, for the purposes of preservation, protection and continuation, but they obey their instincts *within a well-defined limit,* laid down by the exigencies and impulses of the moment.

No consciousness of the future plays any part in the action of animals, leading them to lay up store for the future or modifying in any marked manner other uses of their instincts; while their intercourse with each other is simple and obedient to certain natural impulses.

Man possesses these same impulses and instincts; but, in addition, he has been endowed with another group of qualities of greater range and force: memory, realistic perception of objects and of acts, prevision, and an infinite power of adaptation.

These make him master of countless resources, and give him conscious command over the past for the purposes of the present and the future.

But the animal nature in him retains its strength and is still an essential part of his being, connecting him with the objective world and prompting him to acts necessary to his existence.

So strong is this original nature that it tends to assert supremacy over the faculties of greater range and power, pressing them into its service and subordinating them to the ministration of its demands and needs. And the whole principle of the animal nature is *self;* this is the beginning, middle and end of animal existence. In the arena of animal life, whatever conflicts with Self, or opposes obstacles to its desires, is treated as antagonistic: if the opponent be weak or the obstacle slight, it is crushed; if the opposite, it is fled from or avoided.

In all such conditions, however, there is but the one feeling of antagonism, which, if opposition be continued, passes at once into the ultimate stage of either fear or anger. The realm of the animal world, where Self is the natural ruler, is thus one of very simple arrangement and of few governing principles. In it right and wrong do not exist, but in their place, as sole arbiters of action, we find *Necessity* where self-preservation and propagation of the species are concerned, and where individual relations are involved we find *Expediency.*

In the obtaining of food, or in the assertion of possession or of supremacy, no law but that of the stronger or more cunning is recognised. Only the impulse to obtain that which is desired is obeyed, except when an instinct of weakness or of inferiority causes fear and either paralyses or instigates to flight.

When, therefore, the animal nature found itself in alliance with the higher attributes of intelligence, memory, foresight and resource, with which man is endowed, the strength of its emotions and the acuteness of its sensuous experiences, would become accentuated; and these, intensified by reflection from the more widely extended consciousness, would lead it to assert supremacy over the forces of higher range, in order that its several individual instincts might be the more effectually ministered to and gratified.

Memory and intelligence would enhance the pleasure found in gratifying desire, by seeking and providing those elements and conditions in which the pleasure was consciously found to exist, and by repetition of indulgence merely for the sake of individual enjoyment and advantage. Thus, the faculty of prevision and more acutely conscious participation in definite acts, could of themselves, in union with the original animal nature, only accentuate and enlarge the principle and power of Self and aid in developing that course of life which tended to exalt and strengthen it.

Had the evolution of man ever presented a stage of this nature, he would have been nothing more than an animal of exaggerated selfish desires gratified without restraint.

It is true that Modern Education, in its systems, methods and appliances, treats man as if he were a being actually in such a stage of development, practically ignoring, in its bearing upon him, his possession of any further endowments beyond these; but unhappily, Modern Education, being chiefly controlled by amateur educationists and self-appointed directors, is quite unrelated to its subject—and treats it unworthily and ignorantly.

But with the endowments of which we have spoken and which alone would have made him *an animal of more definite consciousness merely,* a higher principle was also bestowed which carried with it a Law of Existence the very antithesis of the animal principle or Principle of Self. This higher principle, like Light in the physical world, appears as a simple essence in its complete form, but may, like Light, be dispersed into many beautiful and energizing rays by refraction through suitable media. In its simple form, as a unit of force, this principle is *Spiritual Wisdom.** It

---

* "The wisdom that is from above is first pure, then peaceable, gentle and easy to be entreated, full of mercy and of good works."—James iii., 17.

illumines life fully and truly, and beneath its brilliant rays the true character of the individual and of the world in which he moves—its objects, paths, movements and destiny, arrange themselves before the inner vision in their real nature and relationship.

This Spiritual Principle, embracing as one of its rays the transforming force of Universal Love, the charity of St. Paul, is, as already noted, the direct opposite of the Principle of Self.

Yet the two principles are found to exist side by side in the constitution of man; the one essentially of the flesh and the world and adapted only for a sensuous physical existence, the other infinite both in capacity and in duration, and allying him with the ever-unfolding world of beauty, wisdom and power.

But they cannot thus exist within the same territory and remain passive in attitude towards each other; nor can they compromise their antagonistic claims and assert rule over departments of being entirely detached from each other. The rule they both strive to assert is over that *which is the very man himself;* each of them claims the Ego, the enduring essence within the visible and transient personality; that which, according to its own absolute choice and decision, will suffer or enjoy, decay or grow, drift at the mercy of every idle wind or steadily ascend the Mount of God.

The one or the other of these forces struggling within the breast of man must become supreme in ultimate rule. By one he is drawn towards this mode of life, by the other to a mode of life diametrically opposite.†

The higher principle with which he is endowed strives to reveal to his understanding that another destiny is intended for him than that of living the mere animal life of Self; and at times glimpses come to him of a world totally different in nature from that with which his external senses connect him. By degrees he learns that the *Life of Self* is destructive of all that is true and enduring, that it is false and delusive, and that it prevents the resolution of the discords of life into a full and complete harmony.

He recognizes, also, that to yield to this disintegrating force, to that which produces chaos and decay instead of vitality, must be contrary to the law of his being, and will ever hinder the fulfillment of his destiny, *the union of his will and his intelligence with the Fount of Wisdom, Beauty and Power.*

---

† "The flesh lusteth against the spirit, and the spirit against the flesh."—Gal. v. 18.

The antagonism and energy of the contending forces become accentuated from the discovery of these truths, and confusion and unrest are generated within the arena of the struggle. The conscious object of this conflict cannot escape from the discomfort, perplexity and sadness it engenders, and he realizes, sooner or later, that his decision must needs be made, and his Will definitely and permanently allied with the One Principle, or surrendered with unstable weakness to the other.

And here we may note that not only do the merely intellectual endowments furnish the nature below them with fuller means of gratification, but they add special areas of personal life in which self-glorification may run riot. One of these is the area of self-seeking emulation, which in these days is crowded with vulgar activity, and which has been *criminally** extended, by the gratuitous appropriation of prizes and examinations, into the period of life nature demands for the normal training of every unit of the human race.

In another of these areas arise conditions which instigate to the display of imagined personal superiority and the enjoyment of meretricious and disintegrating social distinctions, manifested not only in the craving for titles and other individualising terms, but even in the active search for them, and in the pleasure derived from their use, exhibited in all the middle and upper grades of social, political and professional life. However plausible, however universal, this action of the lower mental endowments of man may be, it is a surrender to the Principle of Self, and one of the forms in which it is worshipped.

On this plane also arises the common display of personal arrogance and self consequence, which, through tyrannical and ar-

---

* We have used the word *criminally* advisedly. The term is a just one, because of the disintegrating and deteriorating effect of the system alluded to upon mankind, individually and in its social groups. The system has not been imposed and maintained in ignorance. It was commenced and is maintained in defiance of the emphatic teachings of the New Testament, and embodiment of precepts asserted by those "who profess and call themselves Christians," to be based upon the highest authority and to have been taught by One for whom they profess the highest reverence. (See Matthew xx., 20-28; xxiii., 12; Luke xii., 34; xiv., 7-12; xvi., 15; John xiv., 15; Philippians ii., 3; James iii., 14-16, &c.)

The spirit as well as the letter of those precepts is entirely against personal emulation and the struggle for notoriety, while the teachings which accompany them are, in many instances, illustrations of the moral and spiritual disasters which result from their infringement, and of the condemnation which eventually awaits him who transgresses. In spite of this clear and definite teaching, personal emulation is made a chief factor in a *normal, universal experience* of mankind, and at a period when virtues and vices, habits and impulses, receive their form and strength, and give the bias of the motives which will eventually rule the whole earth-life, and probably also the life beyond. We ask: Are the plants of a well-cultivated garden ruled by this plan, and stimulated to grow *each better than its neighbour,* or is each trained and fostered *to its own best possible development?*

bitrary acts, creates new forms of conflict in the arena of human thought and feeling, sets in motion ever-widening circles of mischief, calls into play the forces of "spiritual wickedness in high places," and leaves the actor himself at still greater variance with the supreme Law of Life.† This is the emphasised, more spiritual form of self-worship—the most deadly enemy of the soul of man, and the greatest obstacle to its attainment of true blessedness.

An honest and thorough investigation of the truths and facts now set forth, both as regards the individual centres of life and of force with which man is endowed, and the relation of his Ego towards them and its use of them, leaves us in no doubt as to the origin of Evil, its true nature, and the logical character of its consequences. There is *that* within man, or overshadowing him, which presses towards rendering him master of himself and of life, by making him a true servant of the Deity; for only when he is the servant of the Most High will man cease to be the servant of the blind, self-centering forces which operate within him. "Ye *cannot* serve God and Mammon."

And man is conscious of this overshadowing by the Supreme Principle of the Universe—Divine Knowledge and Divine Motive —"the Light which lighteth every man that cometh into the world." He *would* receive it,* he even dallies with it, but alas! the lower forces are *more present* with him; he yields to them and assents to life on their plane; he yields to the motives which they create, though, while yielding, he knows that *he is destroying* the rule of God and is helping to flood the world with disease, darkness and death.

Thus, voluntarily choosing, or allowing himself to be led into,

---

† The act of a late bishop of the English Church may serve as an illustration of what is here meant. He disinherited his only daughter, "to mark," as he said in his will, *"his* sense of her conduct."* This daughter, in the exercise of her personal inherent rights and responsibilities, which no parental assumption can abrogate or remove, had married the man whom she loved, and her father had, from that time, refused all intercourse with her. She appealed to him in vain. Acts of this imperious and arrogant nature are, in varying degree, only too common.

They set in motion currents of evil and misery of which no one can foresee the end or the consequences. It is the forces underlying such acts which originate dogmatism, persecution, priestly assumption, and all forms of inquisition into personal life and personal convictions. Have these not wrought sorrow, pain, social chaos, and national anarchy? Are they not still in operation around us? What said Jesus about personal arrogance and Phariseeism?

* "The good that I would I do not: but the evil which I would not, that I do." "I delight in the law of God after the inward man: but I see another law in my members, warring against the law of my mind, and bringing me into captivity to the law of sin which is in my members."—Romans vii., 19, 23-4. The force of the lower nature *becomes the law of sin,* of which St. Paul speaks, by surrender of the individual life of thought, feeling and motive to its control.

that which opposes his union with the Supreme Principle of Life—
the Absolute in Wisdom, Knowledge and Power,—he determines
for himself and his race the resulting future; sowing persistently
false seeds of life out of his own tainted heart,† is it strange that
he should reap their natural fruit in sadness and dismay?§

> "Sow an act, and you reap a habit,
> Sow a habit, and you reap a character,
> Sow a character and you reap a destiny."

—I.

Lucifer, January, 1889

---

† "For out of the heart proceed evil thoughts," &c.—Matt. xv., 19.

§ "Be not deceived; God is not mocked: for whatsoever a man soweth, that shall he also reap. For he that soweth to his flesh shall of the flesh reap corruption; but he that soweth to the Spirit shall of the Spirit reap life everlasting."—Ephesians vi., 7-8.

THOUGHTS ON KARMA AND REINCARNATION

In man there are arteries, thin as a hair split a 1000 times,
filled with fluids blue, red, green, yellow, etc. The tenuous invo-
lucrum (the base or ethereal frame of the astral body) is lodged
in them, and the ideal residues of the experiences of the former
embodiments (or incarnations) adhere to the said tenuous invo-
lucrum, and *accompany it in its passage from body to body*.

—Upanishads

JUDGE of a man by his questions rather than by his answers,"
teaches the wily Voltaire. The advice stops half-way in our
case. To become complete and cover the whole ground we
have to add, "ascertain the motive which prompts the questioner."
A man may offer a query from a sincere impulse to learn and to
know. Another person will ask eternal questions, with no better
motive than a desire of cavilling and proving his adversary in
the wrong.

Not a few among the "inquirers into Theosophy," as they
introduce themselves, belong to this latter category. We have
found in it Materialists and Spiritualists, Agnostics and Christians.
Some of them, though rarely, are "open to conviction"—as they
say; others, thinking with Cicero that no liberal, truth-seeking man
should ever impute a charge of unsteadiness to anyone for having
changed his opinions—become *really* converted and join our ranks.
But there are those also—and these form the majority—who, while
representing themselves as *inquirers,* are in truth *carpers.* Whether
owing to narrowness of mind or foolhardiness they intrench themselves behind their own preconceived and not unseldom shallow
beliefs and opinions, and will not budge from them. Such a
"seeker" is hopeless, as his desire to investigate the truth is a
pretext, not even a fearless mask, but simply a *false nose.* He has
neither the open determination of an avowed materialist, nor the
serene coolness of a "Sir Oracle." But—

You may as well
Forbid the sea for to obey the moon,
As, or by oath remove, or counsel shake,
The fabric of his folly . . .

Therefore, a "seeker after truth" of this kind had better be severely left alone. He is intractable, because he is either a skin-deep sciolist, a self-opinionated theorist or a fool. As a general rule, he talks reincarnation before he has even learnt the difference between *metempsychosis,* which is the transmigration of a human Soul into an animal form, and Reincarnation, or the rebirth of the same Ego in successive human bodies. Ignorant of the *true* meaning of the Greek word, he does not even suspect how absurd, in philosophy, is this purely exoteric doctrine of transmigrations into animals. Useless to tell him that Nature, propelled by Karma, never recedes, but strives ever forward in her work on the physical plane; that she may lodge a human soul in the body of a man, morally ten times lower than any animal, but she will not reverse the order of her kingdoms; and while leading the irrational monad of a beast of a higher order into the human form at the first hour of a Manvantara, she will not guide that Ego, once it has become a man, even of the lowest kind, back into the animal species—not during that cycle (or Kalpa) at any rate.*

The list of queer "investigators" is by no means exhausted with these amiable *seekers.* There are two other classes—Christians and Spiritualists, the latter being in some respects, more formidable than any. The former having been born and bred believers in the Bible and supernatural "miracles" on *authority,* or "thirty-seventh hand evidence," to use a popular proverb, are often forced to yield in the face of the first-hand testimony of their own reason and senses; and then they are amenable to reason and conviction. They had formed *a priori* opinions and got crystallized in them as a fly in a piece of amber. But that amber has cracked, and, as one of the signs of the times, they have bethought themselves of a somewhat tardy still sincere search, to either justify their early opinions, or else part company with them for good. Having found out that *their* religion—like that of the great majority of their fellow men—had been founded on *human* not *divine* respect, they come to us as they would to surgical operators, be-

---

*Occult Science teaches that the same order of evolution for man and animals—from the first to the seventh planet of a chain, and from the first to the end of the seventh round—takes place on every *chain* of worlds in our Solar system from the inferior to the superior. Thus the highest as the lowest Ego, from the monads selected to people a new chain in a Manvantara, when passing from an inferior to a superior "chain" has, of course, to pass through every animal (and even vegetable) form. But once started on its cycle of births no human Ego will become that of an animal during any period of the seven rounds.—Vide *Secret Doctrine.*

lieving that theosophists can remove all the old cobwebs from their bewildered brains. Sometimes it does so happen; once made to see the fallacy of first accepting and identifying themselves with any form of belief, and then only seeking, years later, for reasons to justify it, they very naturally try to avoid falling again into the same mistake. They had once to content themselves with such interpretations of their time-honoured dogmas as the fallacy and often the absurdity of the latter would afford; but now, they seek to learn and understand before they believe.

This is the right and purely theosophical state of mind, and is quite consistent with the precept of Lord Buddha, who taught never to believe merely on authority but to test the latter by means of our personal reason and highest intuition. It is only such seekers after the eternal truth who can profit by the lessons of old Eastern Wisdom.

It is our duty, therefore, to help them to defend their new ideals by furnishing them with the most adequate and far-reaching weapons. For they will have to encounter, not only Materialists and Spiritualists, but also to break a lance with their ex-coreligionists. These will bring to bear upon them the whole of their arsenal, composed of the pop-guns of biblical casuistry and interpretations based on the dead-letter texts and the disingenuous translation of *pseudo* revelation. They have to be prepared. They will be told, for instance, that there is not a word in the Bible which would warrant belief in reincarnation, or life, more than once, on this earth. Biologists and physiologists will laugh at such a theory, and assure them that it is opposed by the fact that no man has a glimpse of recollection of any *past* life. Shallow metaphysicians, and supporters of the easy-going Church ethics of this age, will gravely maintain the injustice there would be in a posterior punishment, in the present life, for deeds committed in a previous existence of which we know nothing. All such objections are disposed of and shown fallacious to anyone who studies seriously the esoteric sciences.

But what shall we say of our ferocious opponents, the Kardecists, or the reincarnationists of the French school, and the *anti*-reincarnationists, *i.e.,* most of the Spiritualists of the old school. The fact, that the first believe in rebirth, but in their own crude, unphilosophical way, makes our task the more heavy. They have made up their minds that a man dies, and his "spirit," after a few

visits of consolation to the mortals he left behind him, may reincar-
nate at his own sweet will, in whom and whenever he likes. The
Devachanic period of no less than a 1,000, generally 1,500 years,
is a vexation of mind and a snare in their sight. They will have
nothing of this. No more will the Spiritualists. These object on
the highly philosophical ground that "it is *simply impossible.*"
Why? Because it is so unpalatable to most of them, especially to
those who know themselves to be the personal Avatar, or the
reincarnation of some historically great hero or heroine who flourished within the last few centuries (rebirth from, or into, the scums
of Whitechapel, being for them out of question). And "it is so
cruel," you see, to tell fond parents that the fancy that a *still-born*
child, a daughter of theirs, who, they imagine, having been reared
in a nursery of Summerland, has now grown up and comes to visit
them daily in the family seance-room, is an absurd belief, whether
reincarnation be true or not. We must not *hurt their feelings* by
insisting that every child who dies before the age of reason—when
only it becomes a responsible creature—reincarnates immediately
after its death—since, having had no personal merit or demerit in
any of its actions, it can have no claim upon Devachanic reward
and bliss. Also, that as it is irresponsible till the age of, say, seven,
the full weight of the Karmic effects generated during its short life
falls directly upon those who reared and guided it. They will hear
of no such philosophical truths, based on eternal justice and Karmic action. "You hurt our best, our most devotional feelings.
Avaunt!" they cry, "we will not accept your teachings."

E pur se muove! Such arguments remind one of the curious
objections to, and denial of, the sphericity of the earth used by
some clever Church Fathers of old. "How can the earth, forsooth,
be round?" argued the saintly wiseacres—the "venerable Bedes"
and the Manichean Augustines. "Were it so the men *below* would
have to walk with their heads downward, like flies on a ceiling.
Worse than all, they could not see the Lord descending in his
glory on the day of the second advent!" As these very logical arguments appeared irrefutable, in the early centuries of our era, to
Christians, so the profoundly philosophical objections of our
friends the *Summerland* theorists, appear as plausible in this century of Neo-Theosophy.

And what are your proofs that such series of lives ever take
place, or that there is reincarnation at all?—we are asked. We re-

ply: (1) the testimony of every seer, sage and prophet, throughout an endless succession of human cycles; (2) a mass of *inferential* evidence appealing even to the profane. True, this kind of evidence—although not seldom men are hung on no better than such *inferential* testimony—is not absolutely reliable. For, as Locke says: "To infer is nothing but by virtue of one proposition, laid down as true, to draw in another as true." Yet all depends on the nature and strength of that first proposition. The Predestinarians may lay down as true their doctrine of predestination;—that pleasant belief that every human being is pre-assigned by the will of our "Merciful Father in Heaven," to either everlasting Hell-fire, or the "Golden Harp," on the pinion-playing principle. The proposition from which this curious belief is inferred and laid down as true, is based, in the present case, on no better foundation than one of the nightmares of Calvin, who had many. But the fact, that his followers count millions of men, does not entitle either the theory of total depravity, or that of predestination, to be called a universal belief. They are still limited to a small portion of mankind, and were never heard of before the day of the French Reformer.

These are pessimistic doctrines born of despair, beliefs artificially engrafted on human nature, and which, therefore, cannot hold good. But who taught mankind about soul transmigration? Belief in successive rebirths of the human *Ego* throughout the cycles of life in various bodies is a universal belief, a certainty innate in mankind. Even now, when theological dogmas of human origin have stifled and well-nigh destroyed this natural inborn idea from the Christian mind, even now hundreds of the most eminent Western philosophers, authors, artists, poets and deep thinkers still firmly believe in reincarnation. In the words of George Sand, we are:

> Cast into this life, as it were, into an alembic, where after a previous existence which we have forgotten, we are condemned to be remade, renewed, tempered by suffering, by strife, by passion, by doubt, by disease, by death. All these evils we endure for our good, for our purification, and, so to speak, to make us perfect. From age to age, from race to race, we accomplish a tardy progress, tardy but certain, an advance of which, in spite of all the skeptics say, the proofs are manifest. If all the imperfections of our being and all the woes of our estate drive at discouraging and terrifying us, on the other hand, all the more noble faculties, which have been bestowed on us that we might seek after perfection, do make for our salvation, and deliver us

from fear, misery and even death. Yea, a divine instinct that always grows in light and strength helps us to comprehend that nothing in the whole world wholly dies and that we only vanish from the things that lie about us in our earthly life, to reappear among conditions more favorable to our eternal growth in good.

———

Writes Professor Francis Bowen, as quoted in *Reincarnation, A Study of Forgotten Truths,** uttering a great truth:

> The doctrine of metempsychosis may almost claim to be a natural or innate belief in the human mind, if we may judge from its wide diffusion among the nations of the Earth and its prevalence throughout the historical ages.

The millions of India, Egypt, China, that have passed away, and the millions of those who believe in reincarnation today, are almost countless. The Jews had the same doctrine; moreover, whether one prays to a *personal,* or worships in silence an impersonal deity, or a Principle and a Law, it is far more reverential to believe in this doctrine than not. One belief makes us think of "God" or "Law" as a synonym of Justice, giving to poor little man more than one chance for righteous living and for the atoning of sins, whether of omission or commission. Our disbelief, credits the Unseen Power instead of equity with fiendish cruelty. It makes of *it* a kind of sidereal Jack the Ripper or Nero doubled with a human monster. If a *heathen* doctrine honors the Deity and a Christian dishonors it, which should be accepted? And why should one who prefers the former be held as—an *infidel?*

But the world moves on now as it has always moved, and along with it move the ideas in the heads of the fogies. The question is not whether a fact in nature fits, or not, some special hobby, but whether it is really a *fact* based on, at least, inferential evidence. We are told by those special *hobbyists* that it is not. We reply, study the questions you would reject, and try to understand our philosophy, before you dismiss our teachings *a priori.* Spiritualists complain, and with very good reasons, of men of science who, like Huxley, denounce wholesale their phenomena whilst knowing next to nothing of them. Why do they do likewise, with regard to propositions based on the psychological experiences of thousands of generations of seers and adepts? Do they know anything of the laws of Karma—the great Law of Retribution, that mysteri-

———

*We advise every disbeliever in reincarnation, in search of proofs, to read this excellent volume by Mr. E. D. Walker. It is the most complete collection of proofs and evidences from all the ages that was ever published.

ous, yet, in its effects, quite evident and palpable action in Nature which, sooner or later, brings back every good or bad deed of ours to rebound on us, as the elastic ball, thrown against a wall, rebounds back on the one who throws it? They do not. They believe in a personal God, whom they endow with intelligence, and who rewards and punishes in their ideas, every action of ours in life. They accept this *hybrid* deity (finite, because they endow it most unphilosophically with conditioned attributes, while insisting on calling it Infinite and Absolute), regardless of, and blind to, the thousand and one fallacies and contradictions in which the theological teachings concerning that deity involve us. But when offered a consistent, philosophical and quite logical substitute for such an imperfect God, a complete solution of most of the insoluble problems and mysteries in human life, they turn away in idiotic horror. They remain indifferent or opposed to it, only because its name is KARMA instead of Jehovah; and that it is a tenet which emanates from Aryan philosophy—the deepest and profoundest of all the world philosophies—instead of from the Semitic cunning and intellectual jugglery, which has transformed an astronomical symbol into the "one living God of Gods." "We do not want an *impersonal* Deity," they tell us; "a negative symbol such as 'Non-Being' is incomprehensible to Being." Just so. "The light shineth in darkness; but the darkness comprehendeth it not." Therefore they will talk very glibly of their *immortal* spirits; and on the same principle that they call a personal God *infinite* and make of him a gigantic *male,* so they will address a human phantom as "Spirit"—Colonel Cicero Treacle, or "Spirit" Mrs. Amanda Jellybag, with a vague idea that both are at least sempiternal.

It is useless, therefore, to try and convince such minds. If they are unable or unwilling to study even the broad general idea contained in the term *Karma,* how can they comprehend the fine distinctions involved in the doctrine of reincarnation, although, as shown by our venerable brother, P. Iyaloo Naidu of Hyderabad, Karma and Reincarnation are, "in reality, the A B C of the Wisdom-Religion." It is very clearly expressed in the January *Theosophist,* "Karma is the sum total of our acts, both in the present life and in the preceding births." After stating that Karma is of three kinds, he continues:

Sanchita Karma includes human merits and demerits accumulated in the preceding births. That portion of the *Sanchita Karma* destined to influence human life . . . in the present incarnation is called *Prarabdham*. The third kind of Karma is the result of the merits or demerits of our present acts. *Agami* extends over all your words, thoughts and deeds. What you think, what you speak, what you do, as well as whatever results your thoughts, words and acts produce on yourself, and on those affected by them, fall under the category of the present Karma, which will be sure to sway the balance of your life for good or for evil in your future development (or reincarnation).

Karma thus is simply *action,* a concatenation of *causes and effects.* That which adjusts each effect to its direct cause; that which guides invisibly and as unerringly these effects to choose, as the field of their operation, the *right person in the right place,* is what we call *Karmic law.* What is it? Shall we call it the hand of Providence? We cannot do so, especially in Christian lands, because the term has been connected with, and interpreted theologically as, the *foresight* and *personal design* of a personal god; and because in the active laws of Karma—*absolute Equity* based on the Universal Harmony—there is neither foresight nor desire; and because again, it is our own actions, thoughts, and deeds which *guide that law,* instead of being guided by it. "Whatever a man soweth, that shall he reap." It is only a very unphilosophical and illogical theology which can speak in one breath of *free will,* and grace or damnation being *pre-ordained* to every human *from* (?) eternity, as though eternity could have a beginning *to start from!* But this question would lead us too far into metaphysical disquisitions. Suffice it to say that Karma leads us to rebirth, and that rebirth generates new Karma while working off the old, *Sanchita* Karma. Both are indissolubly bound up, one in the other. Let us get rid of *Karma,* if we would get rid of the miseries of rebirths or—REINCARNATION.

Lucifer, April, 1889

THE VISION OF SCIPIO

A Version of Cicero's "Somnium Scipionis"

THE short fragment of Cicero generally known as the Vision of Scipio to those who are seeking for the scattered pearls, which once adorned the sacred bosom of the pure virgin of the mysteries, before she was defiled and her robe and jewels trampled in the mire of the sty, is perhaps the most interesting record in the voluminous writings of the great Roman orator.

Whence Tully derived his information, whether from the writings of the outer schools of Pythagorean and Platonic philosophy, or from private sources, is in the present case immaterial.

Antiquity has appealed to a higher tribunal in these later days for justification, and, as a witness in this all important case, we welcome the noble Scipio, and bid him come into the fair and open court of LUCIFER, there to plead his cause in words so eloquent, wise and clear, that the jury, LUCIFER's good readers, will require no further comment.[1]

For those who like dates and facts, and the anatomical processes of modern chronicle-ism, with its dry-boned rattle, it may be stated that the occasion of the vision was as follows.

At the outbreak of the third Punic War 149 B.C., P. Corn. Scipio Æmilianus Africanus Minor, the philosopher and polished man of letters, accompanied the Roman army to Africa, and there met with the aged Massinissa, prince of Numidia, the friend of his great-grandfather by adoption, the renowned Africanus (Major). After spending the day in discussing the political institutions of their respective countries and in recollections by the aged prince of the elder Africanus, for whom he still retained the most lively affection, Scipio, wearied by the lengthy conversation and exhausted by his journey, retired to his couch and soon fell into a profound sleep. And while he slept the vision of his grandsire appeared to him, in that form which was more familiar to Scipio from his statue than from his own person, and after foretelling the fu-

---

1 The most remarkable passages are printed in italics.

ture exploits of his adopted grandson and the incidents of his death in full detail, continued (Scipio narrating the story):

"But that you may be the readier to protect your country, know this of a surety. All who have preserved, helped or increased their country, have in heaven a certain and assigned place, there in blessedness to enjoy a sempiternal age. For to the Supreme Deity, which rules the whole of this universe, nothing on earth is more acceptable than the assemblies and gatherings of men united by law, which are called states. It is from this region that the rulers and preservers of States proceed and hither do they return."

Hereupon, although excessively frightened, I asked whether my father Paulus too and others, whom we thought annihilated, still lived.[1]

"To be sure they do," answered Africanus, "for they have flown from the chains of their bodies, as out of a prison. That which you call life is death. But behold your father Paulus approaching you."

And when I saw my father, I burst into a great flood of tears. But he, folding me to his breast, with kisses, forbade me to weep. And as soon as I had dried my tears and began to be able to speak, I said: "Prythee, most reverend and excellent father, since this is a state of life, as I hear from Africanus, why do I tarry on earth and not hasten to join you in this state?"[2]

"It may not be," he replied, "for unless that Deity, whose temple is the whole of this, which you behold, shall free you from those ties which keep you in the body; the way hither cannot be open to you. For this is the law which governs the birth of men; that they should maintain that globe, which you see is the middle one in this temple, and which is called the earth. And a soul has been given them from those sempiternal fires, which you call constellations and stars. These being of a globular and round nature and ensouled with divine minds, perform their cycles and orbits with wonderful rapidity. Wherefore, both you, Publius, and all good men should keep their soul in the guardianship of the body, and should not quit the life of mortals without the command of that Being, by whom the soul was given to you, lest you should seem to have been untrue to that duty to mankind, which has been assigned you by the Deity.

---

1 *Extinctos,* a strong word in contradistinction to *viveret* expressing the continuance of life.

2 *Hac.*

Practice, therefore, justice and the spirit of duty,[3] like as both your grandsire here and I, your father, have done. Now duty, excellent though it is when shown to parents and relations, is best of all, when practiced towards one's country.[4] Such a mode of life is the path to Heaven and to this assembly of men, who have lived, but now freed from their body inhabit the place, which you see."

Now that place was a circle shining with dazzling splendour amid the stars,[5] which you, after the Greeks, call the Milky Way, and from it all other objects seemed to me, as I gazed, exceedingly bright and marvellous. There were stars which we have never seen from earth; and the magnitudes of all of them were such as we have never suspected. The smallest of them was the star, which being furthest from Heaven and nearest to earth, shone with a borrowed light.[6] Moreover, the stellar globes far exceeded the earth in magnitude, which now to me appeared so small, that I was grieved to see our empire contracted, as it were, into a very point.[7]

Now as I continued to gaze thereon with increasing interest, Africanus continued:

"How long will your attention be fixed earthwards? Do you not perceive into what precincts[8] you are come?

"All things are bound together with nine spheres or globes. The last of these is celestial, and embraces all the others, being that supreme Deity which restrains and contains the rest. In this sphere are fixed the sempiternal cyclic revolutions of the stars,[9] and to it are subjected the seven spheres, which revolve backwards with a contrary motion to the celestial sphere.[10] Of these the star they

---

3 *Pietas.*

4 The Roman mind saw no higher duty than this. It was necessarily the *summum bonum* of a race even in its best days of warriors and statesmen.

5 *Inter flammas, flaming bodies.*

6 Heaven (coelum) here means the *Lactaeus Orbis,* the Milky Way.

7 The above lines, as well as the still more extraordinary passage in the sequel, written some fifty years B.C., are such a stumbling block to the critics, that the wildest hypotheses have been put forward with all the parade of learning. Among others the following is interesting. "If we compare this passage with the fortieth chapter of the Prophecies of Isaiah, and with other parts of the same prophecy we shall find it difficult to believe that that inspired book had not in part, or wholly, come to the knowledge of the Romans as early as the age of Cicero." The passage of Isaiah referred to is as follows (v. 22): "It is He that sitteth upon the circle of the earth, and the inhabitants thereof are as grasshoppers." The other passages referred to have not as yet been discovered by the translator. *Verbum sapienti satis.*

8 *Templum,* signifies a portion of the heavens cut off from the rest, and was the technical term for the "Houses of the Heavens" in augury.

9 *Illi, qui volvuntur, stellarum cursus sempiterni,* a somewhat involved passage; the translation, "the original principles of those endless revolutions which the planets perform," is not warranted by the Latin.

10 See *Plato, Timaeus, XII.* " . . . . . besides which he made one of the circles external, the other internal. The motion of the exterior circle he proclaimed to be that of sameness, and that of the interior the motion of difference."

call on earth Saturnian, possesses one sphere. Next comes that splendour, which is said to be of Jupiter, propitious and salutary to the human race. Then a sphere of a red colour and terrible to the earth, which you say is of Mars. Next in order and almost under the mid region the Sun holds place, the leader and chief and director of the remaining lights, the mind of the world and its controlling principle, of such magnitude that it illumines and fills all things with its light. The two orbits of Venus and Mercury follow the Sun, as attendants. In the lowest sphere the Moon revolves, lit by the rays of the Sun. Below this there is nothing, which is not subject to death and decay, except the souls bestowed on the race of men by the gift of the gods. Above the moon, however, all things are eternal. For the Earth, which is the middle and ninth sphere, both does not move and is lowest, and all ponderable bodies are carried towards it by their natural gravity."[11]

And when I recovered myself from my amazed contemplation of these things, "What," I asked, "is this mighty and sweet harmony which fills my ears?"

And he replied: "This melody composed of unequal intervals, yet proportionately harmonized, is produced by the impulse and motion of the spheres themselves, which by blending high and low tones produces uniformly divers symphonies. Such mighty motions cannot be made in silence, and nature brings it to pass that the extremes should at one end give forth a low note, at the other a high tone. Consequently that highest star-bearing orbit of heaven which I have mentioned, whose revolution is more rapid, moves with a sharp and vigorous sound: whereas this sphere of the Moon, which is the lowest, gives forth a very grave tone. While the Earth, the ninth, remaining immovable always abides in the lowest seat, *encompassing* the middle place of the universe.[12]

---

11 If from these nine spheres we subtract the ultimate celestial and the Earth, which is perishable, we shall, as in the Eastern system, get a septenary, for the so-called first and seventh principles are really no principles. It must be left to the intuition of the student, to decide whether this echo of ancient science, this fugitive ray from the lamp of the Mysteries, is to be applied literally to the seven physical bodies called planets in ancient astronomy, or is meant as a hint for those who have ears to hear. "For the Mercury of the Philosophers is not the common mercury." In occult science the seven physical "planets" of astrology are merely symbols of the seven principles of all material bodies. —See *The Secret Doctrine*, Vol. I, 152.

12 *Complexa medium mundi locum;* this is generally translated, "occupying the central spot in the universe," a somewhat strange and unnatural rendering of *complexa*, which is never found bearing this meaning in any other context. By giving it, however, its natural signification of "embracing," a key to the tone meaning of the term, sphere, is offered. Readers who are interested in mystic harmonies, the music of the spheres, and their occult correspondences, should carefully study the opening chapters of the *Timaeus* of Plato; this, however, will prove a somewhat desperate undertaking, if the translations of the schoolmen have to be solely relied on.

"These eight orbits,[13] two of which have the same power, namely Mercury and Venus, create a scale of seven distinct intervals; *a number which is the connecting principle*[14] *of nearly all things*. And learned men imitating this mystery with strings and vocal harmonies, have won for themselves a return to this place: like as some others, who, *endowed with extraordinary natural powers, have studied divine sciences even in earth-life.*[15]

"Now mortals have become deaf to these sounds, by having their ears continually filled with them; so much so that hearing is the dullest of your senses, just as the people who dwell near the cataracts of the Nile are defective in their sense of hearing. And so this sound, which is generated by the exceedingly rapid revolution of the whole Cosmos,[16] is so stupendous, that mortal ears cannot contain it: just as you cannot look at the face of the sun without both sight and sense being overcome by its rays."

Now, though I was struck with astonishment at these things, I still kept my eyes turned to earth. Whereupon Africanus said:— "I perceive, Scipio, that you still gaze upon the seat and home of mortals. But, if it appears to you so small as it really is, it were better to keep your eyes ever fixed on these celestial sights, and disregard those of earth. For what renown from the mouths of men, or glory worth striving for, can you achieve? You see that the population of the earth is confined to scattered and narrow localities, and that vast uninhabited tracts surround the inhabited specks: that the dwellers on earth also are so cut off from one another, that mutual intercourse is impossible: but that *some stand sideways, some backwards, some directly opposite you,*[17] from whom you can certainly hope for no glory. You perceive, moreover, that the earth is also encompassed and surrounded, so to speak, with belts: *two of which separated by the greatest distance and situated at each end under the very poles of the heaven,*[18] you see are rigid with ice; but the middle zone, which is also the largest,

---

13 The celestial sphere is not included, seeing that the various tones are produced by the varying velocity of the different spheres revolving in an opposite direction to the heavenly sphere.

14 Nodus.

15 *Qui praestantibus ingeniis in vitae humana divina studio coluerunt.*

16 *Totius mundi,* an additional proof that the physical planets are not meant in the preceding description.

17 *Sed partim obliquas, partim aversos, partim etiam adversos stare vobis.* A somewhat difficult passage to do justice to; the next paragraph, however, proves beyond all doubt that the positions are referred to a spherical and not a plane surface.

18 If Cicero believed the earth was a flat surface, how could he possibly speak of *two* poles?

is burnt up with the heat of the sun. Two of these are habitable: the southern zone, the inhabitants of which *have their feet turned towards you,* [19] has no connection with your race. Of the northern (temperate) zone, however, which you inhabit, see what a small share you possess. The whole surface inhabited by you, of small extent north and south, but of greater length east and west, is an insignificant strip,[20] surrounded by the sea, which you call on earth the Atlantic, the Great Sea, or Ocean. And yet you see how small it is in spite of its great name. How, then, is it possible for either your own name, or that of any of our countrymen, to pass out of these familiar and well-known countries and either traverse the Caucasus here, which you see, or cross yonder Ganges? Who in the rest of the world, east or west, or in the extreme northern or southern regions, will hear your name? And if you subtract these, you will easily see, within what narrow limits your glory seeks to spread itself.

"How long, again, will those who speak about you, continue to do so? For even if future generations should successively desire to hand down the praises of any one of us, which they may have, in their turn, received from their fathers, yet, because of *the cataclysms of water and fire,*[21] *which must happen at fixed periods,* we can attain not even lasting renown, much less eternal glory. For what does it profit you to be spoken of by men who shall be born hereafter, when those are silent, who were born before you, not less, indeed in number, and certainly better men; when, moreover, no one even of those, who can bear our repute, is able to preserve the recollections of a single year. Now men usually measure the year by the sun, that is, by the revolution of one star; but it is only when *the rest of the constellations*[22] *have returned to their original positions,* and have brought back the same aspect of the heaven after long intervals, that the true revolution of the year can

---

19 *Quorum australis ille, in quo insistunt, adversa vobis urgent vestigia, nihil ad vestrum genus.* Surely no words could testify more clearly to the science of the ancients! Even a child might conclude the argument with a triumphant Q.E.D., and yet hear the commentator of the orthodox schools:—"This is a very curious passage, and if our author's interpreters are to be believed, he was acquainted with the true figure of the earth, a discovery which is generally thought to have been reserved for Sir Isaac Newton (?!), and to have been confirmed by some late experiments; but I own I am not without some doubts as to our author's meaning, whether he does not here speak, not of the whole face of the earth, but of that part of it which was possessed or conquered by the Romans."—GUTHRIE. Requiescat in pace!

20 *Infula,* literally a fillet or ribbon used as an ornament in the sacrifices.

21 *Propter eluriones, exustiones que terrarum.*

22 *Astra;* the term *astrum* is never applied to the planets; it generally means a constellation or a sign of the zodiac, and is used in the plural as a designation of the heavens. The usual rendering, however, is "planets"; clearly a perversion of the radical meaning.

be spoken of. In which cycle I scarcely dare say how many centuries of mortals are contained. For like as in olden days, when the soul of Romulus entered into these mansions, men saw the sun obscured and extinguished, so when the sun shall be again obscured in the same position and period, and all the signs and stars are recalled to the same origin, then must you consider the cycle complete. But you must know that not even the twentieth part of this year has completed its revolution.[23]

"Wherefore, if you have hopes of a return to this place, where great and excellent men enjoy all things; of what value, I ask, is that human glory, which can scarcely extend to the small fraction of one cycle? And so if you would look on high and fix your gaze on this state and your eternal home; you will neither devote your life to vulgar fame, nor centre the hope of your welfare in human rewards. True worth itself by its own attractions should lead you to real achievement. What others say of you, let them see to it; for talk they will. But all such fame is bounded by the narrow limits of the regions which you see. Never yet has man enjoyed lasting fame, for death destroys and the oblivion of posterity engulphs it.[24]

"And, if indeed, O, Africanus," I said, "a *side path*[25] to the highway to heaven lies open to men, who have deserved well of their country; and though heretofore from my youth up, by treading in the footsteps of yourself and my father, I have never been untrue to your honorable reputation; yet now with such a prospect before me, I will strive with even greater watchfulness."

"Strive on," said he, "with the assurance that *it is not you, who are subject to death but your body*. For that which is really yourself, is not the being which your bodily shape declares. But the real man is the *thinking principle*[26] of each, and not the form which can be pointed to with the finger. Of this, then, be sure that *thou art a God;* in as much as deity is that which has will, sensa-

---

[23] This astronomical cycle was called by the Romans *Annus Magnus* or *Annus Mundanus*. It is a period of some 25,000 common years, and the key to the mysteries of the Manvantaric cycles, rounds, races, and sub-races. The method of calculation of such cycles being one of the most important branches of occult astronomy, was jealously guarded. Even in the present Renaissance, figures are kept back.

[24] Throughout this remarkable exposition of the emptiness of fame the grand precept "kill out ambitions" re-echoes, emphasized, however, with all the logic of the practical Roman mind, so that it may stand for trial in the open court of Reason, and fight the doubter with physical facts.

[25] A hint that even true patriotism is not the *Path,* though tending in its direction.

[26] *Mens* (Manas).

tion, memory, foresight, and rules, regulates and moves the body it has in charge, just as the Supreme Deity does the universe. And like as eternal deity guides the Cosmos which is in a certain degree subject to decay,[27] so a sempiternal soul moves the destructible body. *Now that which is ever in motion is eternal.* Whereas that which communicates motion to something else, and which is set in motion by an external cause, must necessarily cease to exist, when its motion is exhausted.

"That, therefore, which has the principle of motion in itself, seeing that it can never fail itself, is the only eternal existence, and moreover is the source and causative principle of motion to all other bodies endowed with movement. The causative principle, however, can have no antecedent cause. For all things spring from this principle, which cannot in the nature of things be generated from anything else; for if it were so, it would cease to be the principal cause. And if this is without beginning, it can evidently have no end, for if the principle of causation were destroyed, it could not be reborn from anything else, nor give birth to any thing out of itself, for all things must necessarily be generated from the causative principle. The principle of motion, therefore, comes from that which is endowed with self-movement; and this can suffer neither birth nor death; otherwise every heaven would collapse, and every nature necessarily come to a standstill, seeing that it could no longer obtain that force by which it was originally impelled.

"Since, therefore, it is evident that that only is eternal which is self-motive[28] who is there to deny that this is a rational attribute of souls? For everything which is set in motion by external impulse is destitute of the soul principle,[29] whereas everything ensouled[30] is energized by an interior and self-created motion; for this is the soul's proper nature and power. And if it alone of all things has the attribute of self-movement; it surely is not subject to birth but is eternal. Exercise the soul therefore, in the highest pursuits. Now the noblest interest of a man is the welfare of his country; and if the soul is practiced and exercised in such cares,

---

27 Cosmic pralaya.

28 This is why the Absolute and the unknown deific Principle, is called "Absolute Motion" in the *Secret Doctrine*—a "motion," which has certainly nothing to do with, nor can it be explained by, that which is called motion on Earth. (Ed.)

29 *Inanimum.*

30 *Animal.*

it will the more speedily wing its flight to these mansions and its proper home. *And the time of this achievement will be greatly shortened, if even now in the prison of the body, it extends beyond, and by contemplating things which are not of the body, withdraws itself as much as possible from its earthly tabernacle.*

"For the souls of those who have given themselves up to the pleasures of the body, and have made themselves the servants of these pleasures, and under the sway of the passions, whose ruler is pleasure, have transgressed the laws of gods and men; *on quitting the body, they hover round the earth, and do not return to this heavenly haven until they have been tossed about for many ages.*"[31]

He vanished and I awoke from sleep.

—E.E.O., F.T.S.

Lucifer, July, 1889

---

[31] *i.e.,* are reincarnated.

INDIA

A TRUMPET CALL AT A CRISIS

FROM the facts that I am now the General Secretary of the American Section of the T. S. and its Vice-President, and was one of those who participated at the very first meeting of the Society in 1875, and for many years was intimately acquainted with H. P. Blavatsky and also with Col. Olcott, what I have to say on the subject of this article should have a weight it could not have if I were a new member, or unacquainted with its history, its real aims, and the aims and purposes of those who, greater than I, were and are so long in the front of its ranks. I ask for these few remarks, therefore, a serious consideration by our members in all countries, and also by such persons in India, not members, who may read this article.

Is there a crisis, and if so what is it and what does it amount to? There is a crisis not noticeable on the top of our historical wave, and which will not be perceived by those among us who are much interested in the work in their own particular Section. In some places there is no cause for any alarm, as interest is great and work goes forward. But the T. S. is not a national body; it is international; it has an object that embraces the entire race; causes at work in any one part of it may react on all with force when the time comes. We must, for that reason, look over the whole field from time to time, and not confine our estimate to what goes on merely in our own Section or Branch.

The critical spot is in India, the land where at the present time the Masters live in person, and from where went out the real impulse for our foundation and work. If India is of no consequence in our movement, then discussion is useless, for to bother about a place of no importance would be waste of time. If Western members are so enamoured of Western culture, civilization, and religion, as to look on Indian thought and philosophy as more or less fantastic, any consideration of the present would be out of place; to all such members I say, do not read this. But those who know that our forms of thought are really Indian, coloured a little by our own short lives as nations; those who realize how important in the great family of nations the Indian race is; those who see that no part of the great human mind can be left out—all those will be able to appreciate the nature of the crisis, and then will act as discreetly as possible to the end that danger may be averted.

Centuries before the West had grown out of its savagery the mighty East had grappled with all the problems that vex the men of the Western world and the nineteenth century. The solutions of these were recorded and preserved among the people of the East. This preservation has been in many ways. In stone of monuments, in books of various materials, in the arrangement of cities, in customs of the people, and last, but not least, in the very beliefs of the common people, looked on by our great men—whom many follow like sheep—as superstition and folly, and often degrading. The monuments and temples need to be read in the light of symbolism; the books are cast in a mould not quite the same as the idioms of the West, and have to be read with that in view as well as holding in the mind the fact that those who wrote them knew more of the Occult machinery of the Kosmos than we now know; they are not to be thrown on one side as folly or phantasy, but should be studied with serious care and with the help of the Hindus of today, who must naturally have some inkling of the hidden meaning. The philosophy in these books is the grandest known to man; the true religion there will be found, when the dust is cleared away, to be, as it says, the religion of Brahma, and hence the first. It will turn out to be the foundation for which the members of the T. S. are looking. But this does not mean to say that the true core and centre is just what this, that, or the other school of Vedântins say it is, for it might turn out to be different. It is hence of the highest importance that our Society should not, at any time, needlessly bring into the minds of Brâhmans the idea or belief that the T. S. is engaged covertly or openly in bringing forward any other religion, or any particular religion or philosophy. And if by accident or fortuitous circumstances Brâhmans in general acquire such an idea or belief, then it is the duty of our members to show how that is a mistake and to induce the others to alter their attitude.

But some may say that it is not of much consequence what some or many Brâhmans who do not enter the T. S. may say or think on the matter. It is of consequence, for the reason that the Brâhman in India is the natural priest, the one who is supposed to preserve the truth as to religion and religious books; and as the whole country so far as Brâhmanism is concerned moves on by and through religion, a false attitude on the part of the Brâhmans is very serious, and should be done away with if possible, by all right means and arguments. If they in their own circle, having a false idea of our movement, preach against us, we shall find a silent, subtle, untouchable influence negativing all our work. On the other hand, these teachers of the Hindû can do much work if they have a mind, as they have shown in the past. As an illustration I may cite the Ârya Samâj, which rose up from the efforts of one Brâhman, but obtained the support of many more, and learned ones also, when it was seen that the object in view was necessary.

Now, then, the crisis is that the Brâhmans in general all over India are beginning to get the idea and belief that the T. S. is merely an engine for the propagation of Buddhism. They are therefore starting an opposition by means of their own power and influence, and the consequence may be that they will keep many worthy men there from coming into the T. S. or from giving it any encouragement whatever. They are not making a new society, but are privately arguing against the T. S., and that is more subtle than public effort, because no counter argument is possible.

It is true they are not supported by the real facts, but to some extent they have arguments from appearances. A famous book in our list is called *Esoteric Buddhism,* while, in fact, it is not Buddhism at all distinctively, but is distinctively Brâhmanical. Its entitlement was due perhaps to enthusiasm about the Guru of the writer. Col. Olcott has declared himself officially and privately to be a Buddhist duly admitted by the high priest, and has written a Buddhist Catechism, a great and useful work which has the approval of the same high priest. The Colonel also is now going about a strictly Buddhist work, which has not so much to do with religious or philosophical opinion as it has with mere questions relating to a theological foundation, a temple and its appurtenances in the heart of India. If these Brâhmans were able to gauge public opinion in America they would have more arguments from the outer look of things, because here everything in respect to Indian religion is called by the generic name of "Buddhism," as the people are too hurried to distinguish between that and Hindûism, and have been accustomed to the *Light of Asia* and other works bringing forward the name of the religion of the Buddha. So much is this the case that all newspaper matter on this subject is labelled with the one name, and very often people when speaking of a Hindû will say, "Of course he is a Buddhist."

Our crisis is, then, that all our efforts may be hindered in India, and we may be deprived of the very necessary help of the Brâhmans in the attempt to bring forward to the world the great truths of the Wisdom Religion. What then is the remedy? Is any one to blame?

No one is to blame. Col. Olcott's efforts are right and proper, as he could not be rightfully asked to give up one form of his general work just for the sake of one religion or system. We all know very well that he is not engaged in trying to make the T. S. an engine for the propagation of Buddhism. For many years he laboured for Hindûism to almost the exclusion of the other system. Mr. Sinnett is not to be censured either, for his book really teaches Brâhmanism. Besides, all the work of Col. Olcott and of the book named must end in giving to the West a greater light on the subject of the Hindû religion, and in deepening the effect on the Western mind of ancient philosophy as found in the Wisdom Religion. In consequence of that, every day, more and more, the West will look for the treasures of the East, if these are not deliberately hidden away.

The remedy is for all the members who take the right view in this matter to persistently show to the Brâhman how he is mistaken, and how, in fact, the T. S. is the very best and strongest engine for the preservation of the truths of the Vedas. If the Brâhman nonmember is convinced of this, he will then encourage the community to help the T. S., and the young men under his influence to enter its ranks; he will try to discover hidden manuscripts of value and give them to us. We should also show that in the course of progress and the cycles, the time has come now when the Brâhman can no more remain isolated and the sole possessor of valuable treatises, for the West is beginning to drag these from his hands, while at the same time it is doing much to spoil the ideals of the younger generations of India, by the mechanical and material glitter of our Western civilization. Waked up fully to this he will see how necessary it is for him to seek the help of the only organization in the world broad and free enough to help him, and to give all that equal field without favour where the Truth must at last prevail.

We should all rise then at this call and do whatever we can at every opportunity to avert the danger by applying the remedy. The sincere Hindû members of the T. S., especially, should take note and act in accordance with this, and with the facts they know of their own observation, warrant, and demand.

Lucifer, April, 1893   WILLIAM Q. JUDGE

THE GREAT MASTER'S LETTER

[This article was printed in *Lucifer* without signature as "An Important Letter," prefaced by the statement that it "was circulated by H.P.B. among many of her pupils, and some quotations from it have been published from time to time." The Letter belongs to the early days of the Theosophical Society in India and was part of the correspondence received (through H.P.B.) by A. P. Sinnett and A. O. Hume from the Theosophical Adepts. His Adept-teacher introduced the letter to Mr. Sinnett as "an abridged version of the view of the Chohan on the T.S. from his own words as given last night"—in reply to objections about the conduct of the Society and especially to the "Brotherhood plank."

Although the text of the complete letter was not published until after H. P. Blavatsky and Wm. Q. Judge had left the scene, both provided a setting for the statements made, and both quoted in their magazines some passages for particular attention.—Eds.]

THE doctrine we promulgate being the only true one, must—supported by such evidence as we are preparing to give—become ultimately triumphant, like every other truth. Yet it is absolutely necessary to inculcate it gradually; enforcing its theories (unimpeachable facts for those who know) with direct inference, deduced from and corroborated by the evidence furnished by modern exact science. That is why Col. H. S. Olcott, who works to revive Buddhism, may be regarded as one who labours in the true path of Theosophy, far more than any man who chooses as his goal the gratification of his own ardent aspirations for occult knowledge. Buddhism, stripped of its superstition, is eternal truth; and he who strives for the latter is striving for Theo-Sophia, divine wisdom, which is a synonym of truth. For our doctrines to practically react on the so-called moral code, or the ideas of truthfulness, purity, self-denial, charity, etc., we have to preach and popularize a knowledge of Theosophy. It is not the individual and determined purpose of attaining Nirvana—the culmination of all knowledge and absolute wisdom, which is after all only an exalted and glorious selfishness—but the self-sacrificing pursuit of the best means to lead on the right path our neighbour, to cause to benefit by it as many of our fellow-creatures as we possibly can, which constitutes the true Theosophist.

The intellectual portion of mankind seems to be fast dividing into two classes: the one unconsciously preparing for itself long periods of temporary annihilation or states of non-consciousness, owing to the deliberate surrender of intellect, and its imprisonment in the narrow grooves of bigotry and superstition—a process which cannot fail to lead to the utter deformation of the intellectual principle; the other unrestrainedly indulging its animal propensities with the deliberate intention of submitting to annihilation pure and simple, in case of failure, and to millenniums of degradation after physical dissolution. Those intellectual classes, reacting upon the ignorant masses—which they attract, and which look up to them as noble and fit examples to be followed—degrade and morally ruin those they ought to protect and guide. Between degrading superstition and still more degrading brutal materialism, the White Dove of Truth has hardly room whereon to rest her weary unwelcome feet.

It is time that Theosophy should enter the arena. The sons of Theosophists are more likely to become in their turn Theosophists than anything else. No messenger of the truth, no prophet, has ever achieved during his life-time a complete triumph—not even Buddha. The Theosophical Society was chosen as the cornerstone, the foundation of the future religions of humanity. To achieve the proposed object, a greater, wiser, and especially a more benevolent intermingling of the high and the low, the alpha and the omega of society, was determined upon. The white race must be the first to stretch out the hand of fellowship to the dark nations, to call the poor despised "nigger" brother. This prospect may not smile for all, but he is no Theosophist who objects to this principle.

In view of the ever-increasing triumph, and at the same time the misuse, of free thought and liberty (the universal reign of Satan, Eliphas Lévi would have called it), how is the combative natural instinct of man to be restrained from inflicting hitherto unheard-of cruelty and enormous tyranny, injustice, etc., if not through the soothing influence of brotherhood, and of the practical application of Buddha's esoteric doctrines?

For everyone knows that total emancipation from the authority of the one all-pervading power, or law—called God by the priests, and Buddha, Divine Wisdom and enlightenment or Theosophy, by the philosophers of all ages—means also the emancipation from that of human law. Once unfettered and delivered from their dead-weight of dogmatism, interpretations, personal names, anthropo-morphic conceptions, and salaried priests, the fundamental doctrines of all religions will be proved identical in their esoteric meaning. Osiris, Krishna, Buddha, Christ, will be shown as different means for one and the same royal highway to final bliss—Nirvana.

Mystical Christianity teaches *Self*-redemption through one's own seventh principle, the liberated Paramatma, called by the one Christ, by others Buddha; this is equivalent to regeneration, or rebirth in spirit, and it therefore expounds just the same truth as the Nirvana of Buddhism. All of us have to get rid of our own Ego, the illusory, apparent self, to recognize our true Self, in a transcendental divine life. But if we would not be selfish, we must strive to make other people see that truth, and recognize the reality of the transcendental Self, the Buddha, the Christ, or God of every preacher. This is why even esoteric Buddhism is the surest path to lead men towards the one esoteric truth.

As we find the world now, whether Christian, Mussulman, or Pagan, justice is disregarded, and honour and mercy are both flung to the winds. In a word, how—since the main objects of the Theosophical Society are misinterpreted by those who are most willing to serve us personally—are we to deal with the rest of mankind? with that curse known as *the struggle for life,* which is the real and most prolific parent of most woes and sorrows, and all crimes? Why has that struggle become almost the universal scheme of the universe? We answer,—because no religion, with the exception of Buddhism, has taught a practical contempt for this earthly life; while each of them, always with that one solitary exception, has through its hells and damnations inculcated the greatest dread of death. Therefore do we find that struggle for life raging most fiercely in Christian countries, most prevalent in Europe and America. It weakens in the Pagan lands, and is nearly unknown among Buddhist populations. In China during famine, and where the masses are most ignorant of their own or of any religion, it was remarked that those mothers who devoured their children belonged to localities where there was none; and where the Bonzes alone had the field, the population died with the utmost indifference. Teach the people to see that life on this earth, even the happiest, is but a burden and an illusion; that it is our own Karma [the cause producing the effect] that is our own judge—our Saviour in future lives—and the great struggle for life will soon lose its intensity. There are no penitentiaries in Buddhist lands, and crime is nearly unknown among the Buddhist Tibetans. The world in general, and Christendom especially, left for 2,000 years to the *régime* of a personal God, as well as to its political and social systems based on that idea, has now proved a failure.

If the Theosophists say we have nothing to do with all this; the lower classes and the inferior races (those of India, for instance, in the conception of the British) cannot concern us, and must manage as they can, what becomes of our fine professions of benevolence, philanthropy, reform, etc.? Are those professions a mockery? And if a mockery, can ours be the true path? Shall we devote ourselves to teaching a few Europeans—fed on the fat of the land, many of them loaded with the gifts of blind fortune—the rationale of bell-ringing, of cup-growing, of the spiritual telephone, and astral body formation, and leave the teeming millions of the ignorant, of the poor and oppressed, to take care of themselves, and of their hereafter, as best they can? Never! perish rather the Theosophical Society with both its hapless Founders, than that we should permit it to become no better than an academy of magic, and a hall of occultism! That we, the devoted followers of that spirit incarnate of absolute self-sacrifice, of philanthropy, divine kindness, as of all the highest virtues attainable on this earth of sorrow, the man of men, Gautama Buddha, should ever allow the Theosophical Society to represent the embodiment of selfishness, the refuge of the few with no thought in them for the many, is a strange idea, my brothers!

Among the few glimpses obtained by Europeans of Tibet and its mystical hierarchy of perfect Lamas, there was one which was correctly understood and described. The incarnations of the Bodhisattva Padmapani or Avolokiteshvara, of Tsong-ka-pa, and that of Amitabha, relinquished at their death the attainment of Buddhahood—*i.e.,* the *summum bonum* of bliss, and of individual personal felicity—that they might be born again and again for the benefit of mankind. In other words, that they might be again and again subjected to misery, imprisonment in flesh, and all the sorrows of life, provided that they by such a self-sacrifice, repeated throughout long and weary centuries, might become the means of securing salvation and bliss in the hereafter for a handful of men chosen among but one of the many planetary races of mankind.

And it is we, the humble disciples of these perfect Lamas, who are expected to allow the Theosophical Society to drop its noblest title, that of the Brotherhood of Humanity, to become a simple school of philosophy! No, no, good brothers, you have been labouring under the mistake too long already. Let us understand each other. He who does not feel competent to grasp the noble idea sufficiently to work for it, need not undertake a task too heavy for him. But there is hardly a Theosophist in the whole Society unable to effectually help it by correcting erroneous impressions of outsiders, by himself actually propagating this idea. Oh! for noble and unselfish men to help us effectually in that divine task! All our knowledge, past and present, would not be sufficient to repay him.

Having explained our views and aspirations, I have but a few words more to add. The true religion and philosophy offer the solution of every problem. That the world is in such a bad condition, morally, is a conclusive evidence that none of its religions and philosophies, those of the civilized races less than any other, has ever possessed the truth. The right and logical explanations on the subject of the problems of the great dual principles, right and wrong, good and evil, liberty and despotism, pain and pleasure, egotism and altruism, are as impossible to them now as they were 1886 years ago. They are as far from the solution as they were; but to these problems there must be somewhere a consistent solution, and if our doctrines will show their competence to offer it, then the world will be the first to confess that *there* must be the true philosophy, the true religion, the true light, which gives truth and nothing but the truth.

Lucifer, August, 1896

NOTES FROM "LUCIFER"

[The following brief articles, notes, and replies to correspondence appeared throughout the volumes of *Lucifer* from 1887 to 1891. Too diverse in content to be grouped in any way, they are printed here in chronological order with volume and page number indicated for each note.—Eds.]

WILL AND DESIRE

WILL is the exclusive possession of man on this our plane of consciousness. It divides him from the brute in whom instinctive desire only is active.

DESIRE, in its widest application, is the one creative force in the Universe. In this sense it is indistinguishable from Will; but we men never know desire under this form while we remain only men. Therefore Will and Desire are here considered as opposed.

Thus Will is the offspring of the Divine, the God in man; Desire the motive power of the animal life.

Most men live in and by desire, mistaking it for will. But he who would achieve must separate will from desire, and make his will the ruler; for desire is unstable and ever changing, while will is steady and constant.

Both will and desire are absolute *creators,* forming the man himself and his surroundings. But will creates intelligently— desire blindly and unconsciously. The man, therefore, makes himself in the image of his desires, unless he creates himself in the likeness of the Divine, through his will, the child of the light.

His task is twofold: to awaken the will, to strengthen it by use and conquest, to make it absolute ruler within his body; and, parallel with this, to purify desire.

Knowledge and will are the tools for the accomplishment of this purification. [I, 96.]

SELF-KNOWLEDGE

The first necessity for obtaining self-knowledge is to become profoundly conscious of ignorance; to feel with every fibre of the heart that one is *ceaselessly* self-deceived.

The second requisite is the still deeper conviction that such knowledge—such intuitive and certain knowledge—can be obtained by effort.

The third and most important is an indomitable determination to obtain and face that knowledge.

Self-knowledge of this kind is unattainable by what men usually call "self-analysis." It is not reached by reasoning or any brain process; for it is the awakening to consciousness of the Divine nature of man.

To obtain this knowledge is a greater achievement than to command the elements or to know the future. [I, 89.]

———————•———————

As far as the writer knows, Occultism does not teach that the LIFE-PRINCIPLE—which is *per se* immutable, eternal, and as indestructible as the one *causeless cause,* for it is THAT in one of its aspects—can ever differentiate individually. . . . It is only each body—whether man, beast, plant, insect, bird, or mineral—which, in assimilating more or less the life principle, *differentiates it in its* own special atoms, and adapts it to this or another combination of particles, which combination determines the differentiation. The monad partaking in its universal aspect of the Parabrahmic nature, unites with its *monas* on the plane of differentiation to constitute an individual. This individual, being in its essence inseparable from Parabrahm, also partakes of the Life-Principle in its Parabrahmic or Universal Aspect. Therefore, at the death of a man or an animal, the manifestation of life or the evidences of Kinetic energy are only withdrawn to one of those subjective planes of existence which are not ordinarily objective to us. The amount of Kinetic energy to be expended during life by one particular set of physiological cells is allotted by Karma—another aspect of the Universal Principle— consequently when this is expended the conscious activity of man or animal is no longer manifested on the plane of those cells, and the chemical forces which they represent are disengaged and left free to act in the physical plane of *their* manifestation. *Jiva*—in its universal aspect—has, like *Prakriti,* its seven forms, or what we have agreed to call "principles." Its action begins on the plane of the Universal Mind (*Mahat*) and ends in the grossest of the *Tanmatric* five planes—the last one, which is ours. Thus though we may, repeating after *Sankhya* philosophy, speak of the *seven pra-kritis* (or "productive productions") or after the phraseology of the Occultists of the seven *jivas*—yet, *both Prakriti and Jiva are indivisible abstractions,* to be divided only out of condescension for the weakness of our human intellect. Therefore, also, whether we divide it into four, five or seven principles matters in reality very little. [II, 39.]

————————•————————

According to the Eastern philosophy a unity composed of "many entities, parts, or forms" is a compound unity on the plane of *Maya*—illusion or ignorance. The One universal divine Unity cannot be a differentiated whole, however much "organized into a body of harmony." Organization implies external work out of materials at hand, and can never be connected with the self-existent, eternal, and unconditioned Absolute Unity.

This ONE SELF, absolute intelligence and existence, therefore *non*-intelligence and non-existence (to the finite and conditioned perception of man), is *"impartite,* beyond the range of speech and thought and is the substract of all" teaches *Vedantasara* in its introductory Stanza.

How, then, can the *Infinite* and the *Boundless,* the unconditioned and the *absolute,* be of any *size?* The question can only apply to a dwarfed reflection of the uncreate ray on the *mayavic* plane, or our phenomenal Universe; *to one of the finite Elohim,* who was most probably in the mind of our correspondent. To the (philosoph-ically) untrained Pantheist, who identifies the objective Kosmos with the abstract Deity, and for whom Kosmos and Deity are synonymous terms, the form of the illusive objectivity must be the form of that Deity. To the (philosophically) trained Pantheist, the abstraction, or the *noumenon,* is the ever to be unknown Deity, the one eternal reality, formless, because homogeneous and *im-partite;* boundless, because Omnipresent—as otherwise it would only be a contradiction in ideas not only in terms; and the concrete phenomenal form—its *vehicle*—no better than an aberration of the ever-deceiving physical senses.

"Is nature co-eternal with God?" It depends on what is meant by "nature." If it is objective phenomenal nature, then the answer is—though ever latent in divine Ideation, but being only periodical as a manifestation, it cannot be co-eternal. But "abstract" nature and Deity, or what our correspondent calls "Self-existent cause or God," are inseparable *and even identical.* Theosophy objects to the masculine pronoun used in connection with the Self-existent Cause, or Deity. It says IT—inasmuch as that "cause" the *rootless root* of all—is neither male, female, nor anything to which an attribute—something always conditioned, finite, and limited—can be applied. The confession made by our esteemed correspondent that he "cannot think of anything of nature, Spirit (!) Soul or God (!!) without the ideas of size, form, number, and relation," is a living example of the sad spirit of anthropomorphism in this age of ours. It is this theological and dogmatic anthropomorphism which has begotten and is the legitimate parent of materialism. If once we realize that form is merely a temporary perception dependent on our physical senses and the idiosyncrasies of our physical brain and has no existence, *per se,* then this illusion that formless cause cannot be *causative of forms* will soon vanish. To think of Space in relation to any limited area, basing oneself on its three dimensions of length, breadth, and thickness, is strictly in accordance with mechanical ideas; but it is inapplicable in metaphysics and transcendental philosophy. To say then that "the truth of God is the Form of God," is to ignore even the exotericism of the Old Testament. "The Lord spake unto you *out of the midst of the fire.* Ye heard the voice of the words, *but saw no similitude."* (Deut. iv., 12.) And to think of the All-Evolver as something which has "size, form, number, and relation," *is to think of a finite and conditioned personal God,* a part only of the ALL. And in such case, why should this part be better than its fellow-parts? Why not believe in Gods—the other rays of the All-Light? To say—"Among the gods who is like Thee O Lord" does not make the God so addressed really "the god of gods" or any better than his fellow-gods; it simply shows that every nation made a god of its own, and then, in its great ignorance and superstition, served and flattered and tried to propitiate that god. Polytheism on *such* lines, is more rational and philosophical than anthropomorphous monotheism. [II, 157.]

———————•———————

There are seven classes of Pitris enumerated in the Puranas—but only three classes are composed of the progenitors (from *pitar,* father) of primeval man; one class creates the *form* of man—nay is, or rather becomes, that form (or physical man) itself; the other two are the creators of our souls and minds.

The "pitris" is a generic and collective name, and man has other progenitors more exalted and spiritual. Manu says (*iii.* 284), "The wise (the Initiated Adepts) call our fathers Vasus, our paternal grandfathers, Rudras, our paternal great grandfathers, Adityas; agreeably to the text of the Vedas." These three classes have a direct reference in Esotericism (*a*) to the creators of man in his three chief aspects (*or* principles), and (*b*) to the three primeval and serial races of men who preceded the first physical and perfect Race, which the Eastern Occultists call the Atlanteans. [II, 190fn.]

FROM A LAMRIN COMPENDIUM
BY TZON-KHA-PA

Arguments, from the consideration why Buddha's teachings should be explained on three planes; i.e., intended alike for the lowest, the mean or middle, and the highest capacities, since each man must believe according to his mental qualifications.

1. Men of vulgar capacities must believe, that there is a (personal) God, and a future life, and that they shall earn therein the fruits of their work in this, their earthly life.

2. Those who have an average intellectual capacity, besides admitting the former position, must know, that every compound thing is perishable, that there is no reality in things; that every sin is pain, and that deliverance from pain or bodily existence is bliss.

3. Those of the highest capacities must know, in addition to the above enumerated dogmas, that from the lowest form to the Supreme Soul, nothing is existent by itself. Neither can it be said that it will continue always (eternally) or cease absolutely, but that everything exists by a dependent or causal concatenation.

With respect to practice, those of vulgar capacity are content with the exercise of belief (blind faith) and the practice of the ten virtues (Ten Commandments). Those of average intellectuality, beside believing, by reason endeavor to excel in morality and wisdom. Those of the highest capacities, besides the former virtues, will exercise the six transcendental virtues (practical Occultism). [II, 242.]

A SUFI'S MYSTICAL APOLOGUE

Begging our esteemed correspondent's pardon, we believe it dangerous to leave what he says without an explanation. There is an enormous difference between the *Sophia* of the Theosophist Gichtel, an Initiate and Rosicrucian (1638-1710), and the modern Lillies, John Kings, and "Sympneumatas." The "Brides" of the Mediæval adepts are an allegory, while those of the modern mediums are astral realities of *black magic*. The "Sophia" of Gichtel was the "Eternal Bride" (Wisdom and Occult Science *personified*); the "Lillies" and others are astral spooks, semi-substantial "influences," semi-creations of the surexcited brains of unfortunate *hysteriacs* and "sensitives." No purer man ever lived in this world than Gichtel. Let any one read St. Martin's *Correspondence* (pp. 168 to 198), and he will see the difference. From Marcus, the Gnostic, down to the last mystic student of the Kabala and Occultism, that which they called their "Bride" was "Occult Truth," personified as a naked maiden, otherwise called Sophia or Wisdom. That "spouse" revealed to Gichtel all the mysteries of the outward and inward nature, and forced him to abstain from every earthly enjoyment and desire, and made him sacrifice himself for Humanity. And as long as he remained in that body which represented him on earth, he had to work for the deliverance from ignorance of those who had not yet obtained their inheritance and inward beatitude. "From that time (when he had married his 'Bride'), he gave himself up as a sacrifice, to be accursed for his brethren (men) even without knowing them," says St. Martin. Has this case any analogy with the cases of the Lillies and Rosies of the Summer Land? Sophia descends as a "bride" to the Adepts, from the higher regions of spirit; the astral Ninons de l'Enclos, from Kamaloka, to hysterical epileptics. The less one has to do with the latter class—the better. Let "sensitives" talk as poetically as they like, the naked truth is that such unnatural *sexual* unions, between the living man and the beauteous beings of the Elemental world, arise from the abnormal surexcitation of the nervous system and animal passions, through the unclean imagination of the "sensitive." In the Kabalistic world, these "celestial" brides and bridegrooms have always been called by the harsh names of *Succubi* and *Incubi;* and the difference between those creatures and the "Sympneumatas" shown in Laurence Oliphant's *Scientific Religion* is only a supposed one, and exists for no one except the author.

There are some such unions between mediums and their "controls" —we have known several such personally—and some involuntarily submitted to, under obsession. The tie is a psycho-physiological one, and can be broken by an exercise of will-power, either by the victim or a friendly mesmeriser. Colonel Olcott cured two such cases—one in America, the other in Ceylon. Amiable hysteriacs and certain religious ecstatics may give free run to their diseased fancy, and construct Sophias, Lillies, and other "Sympneumas" out of the opalescent aura of their brains; but all the same they are but unconscious sorcerers: they enjoy lustful animal feelings by *working black magic upon* themselves. If they admit that these unnatural unions, or rather hysterical hallucinations of such are *disease,* then they are on a level with insane nymphomaniacs; if they deny it, then, accepting responsibility, they place themselves on a far lower level. [III, 131.]

———————•———————

No true theosophist—the accused party least of all—believes in *miracles,* though every true theosophist ought to believe in the existence of abnormal powers in man; "abnormal" because, so far, either misunderstood or denied. All such objective physical phenomena, however, are simply psychological "glamour," *i.e.,* if not witchery, at least "a charm on the eyes and senses." This, people may call brutally "trick," but since they are *psychic,* they cannot be *physical;* hence, no conjuring or "sleight of hand." As well call "tricksters" the grave medical celebrities, who hypnotize their subjects to see things which have no reality! "Theosophical phenomena" differ from these in this; that while hypnotic hallucinations are suggested by the operator's idle fancy, occult manifestations are produced by the will of the Occultist, that one or a hundred men should see *realities,* generally hidden from the profane, *e.g.,* certain things and persons thousands of miles away, whose astral images are brought within the view of the audience. Thus a cup *may never have been broken in reality,* and yet people are made to see it shattered in atoms and then made whole. Is this a *juggler's* trick? Occult phenomena are then simply a hundred-fold intensified hypnotism, and between the hypnotic hallucinations at the *Salpêtrière* and the *magic* of the East there is chiefly a question of degree. [III, 138fn.]

So does it [Theosophy], also, warn us against ascetic retirement, save in those very rare and exceptional cases where the individual has brought over from his last preceding birth an irrepressible attraction for the life of the Spirit, and repugnance for the life of the flesh. The normal man is in normal sympathetic relation with his fellow men at each successive stage of human development. But under the law of psychical differentiation, there are in each epoch beings ahead of the average of the race at that time. From their number develop the teachers, seers and saviours of mankind. [III, 142.]

KARMA, TANHA and SKANDHAS, are the almighty trinity in one, and the cause of our re-births. The illustration of painting our own present likeness at death, and that likeness becoming the future personality is very poetical and graphic, but we claim it as an occult teaching. At the solemn moment of death no man can fail to see himself under his true colours, and no self-deception is of any use to him any longer. Thence the following thing happens. As at the instant of drowning man sees marshalled past his mind's eye the whole of his life, with all its events, effects and causes, to the minutest details, so at the moment of death, he sees himself in all his moral nakedness, unadorned by either human flattery or self-adulation, and, as he is; hence, *as he* or rather, as his astral double combined with his *Kama* principle—*shall be.* For the vices, defects and especially the passions of the preceding life become, through certain laws of affinity and transference, the germs of the future potentialities in the *animal* soul (*Kama rupa*), hence of its dependent, the astral double (*linga sharira*)—at a subsequent birth. It is the *personality* alone which changes; the real reincarnating principle, the Ego, remains always the same; and it is its KARMA that guides the idiosyncracies and prominent moral traits of the *old* "personality" that was (and that the Ego knew not how to control), to re-appear in the *new* man that will be. These traits and passions pursue and fasten on the yet plastic third and fourth principles of the child, and—unless the Ego struggles and conquers—they will develop with tenfold intensity and lead the adult man to his destruction. For it is they who are the tools and weapons of the Karmic LAW OF RETRIBUTION. Thus, the Prince says very truly that our good and bad actions "are the only tools with which we paint our likenesses at death," for the *new* man is invariably the son and progeny of the old man that was. [III, 210fn.]

It [Esoteric Section of T.S.] *is not* a lodge of *magic,* but of *training.* For however often the true nature of the occult training has been stated and explained, few Western students seem to realize how searching and inexorable are the tests which a candidate must pass before *power* is entrusted to his hands. Esoteric philosophy, the occult hygiene of mind and body, the unlearning of false beliefs and the acquisition of true habits of thought, are more than sufficient for a student during his period of probation, and those who rashly pledge themselves in the expectation of acquiring forthwith "magic powers" will meet only with disappointment and certain failure. [III, 341.]

"The six honored ones," are those of every nation which had a cult based on astronomy. The "God" was the Sun. Ahura Mazda and his six Amshaspends of the Mazdeans are the later development of the 12 Zodiacal signs divided into six double houses, the Sun being the seventh and always made the representative (or synthesis) of the six. As Proclus has it: "The Framer made the heavens six in number, and for the seventh he cast into the midst the fire of the Sun, (*Timæus*), and this idea is preeminent in the Christian (especially the Roman Catholic) idea, *i.e.,* the Sun-Christ, who is also Michael, and his six and *seven* Eyes, or Spirit of the Planets. The "six—seven" are a movable and interchangeable number and are ever made to correlate in religious symbolism. As correctly shown by Mr. G. Massey there are seven circles to Meru and six parallel ridges across it; there are seven manifestations of light and only six days of creation, etc. The mystery of the "double heaven" is one of the oldest and most Kabalistic and the six chambers, divisions, etc., in most of the temples of antiquity with the officiating priest, representing the Sun, the seventh, left abundant witnesses behind them. [III, 485fn.]

THE questions asked and the difficulties propounded in the foregoing letter arise mainly from an imperfect acquaintance with the philosophical teachings of Theosophy. They are a most striking proof of the wisdom of those who have repeatedly urged Theosophists to devote their energies to mastering, at least, the outlines of the metaphysical system upon which our Ethics are based.

Now it is a fundamental doctrine of Theosophy that the "separateness" which we feel between ourselves and the world of living beings around us is an illusion, not a reality. In every deed and truth, all men are one, not in a feeling of sentimental gush and hysterical enthusiasm, but in sober earnest. As all Eastern philosophy teaches, there is but ONE SELF in all the infinite Universe, and what we men call "self" is but the illusionary reflection of the ONE SELF in the heaving waters of earth. True Occultism is the destruction of the false idea of Self, and therefore true spiritual perfection and knowledge are nothing else but the complete identification of our finite "selves" with the Great All. It follows, therefore, that no spiritual progress at all is possible except by and through the bulk of Humanity. It is only when the whole of Humanity has attained happiness that the individual can hope to become permanently happy,—for the individual is an inseparable part of the Whole.

Hence there is no contradiction whatever between the altruistic maxims of Theosophy and its injunction to kill out all desire for material things, to strive after spiritual perfection. For spiritual perfection and spiritual knowledge can only be reached on the spiritual plane; in other words, only in that state in which all sense of separateness, all selfishness, all feeling of personal interest and desire, has been merged in the wider consciousness of the unity of Mankind.

This shows also that no blind submission to the commands of another can be demanded, or would be of any use. Each individual must learn for himself, through trial and suffering, to discriminate what is beneficial to Humanity; and in proportion as he develops spiritually, *i.e.,* conquers all selfishness, his mind will open to receive the guidance of the Divine Monad within him, his Higher Self, for which there is neither Past nor Future, but only an eternal Now.

Again, were there no "poor," far from the "benefits of civilisation being lost," a state of the highest culture and civilization would be attained, of which we cannot now form the faintest conception. Similarly, from a conviction of the impermanence of material happiness would result a striving after that joy which is eternal, and in which all men can share. Throughout the whole letter of our esteemed correspondent there runs the tacit assumption that happiness in material, physical life is all-important; which is untrue. So far from being the most important, happiness in this life of matter is of as little importance in relation to the bliss of true spiritual life as are the few years of each human cycle on earth in proportion to the millions and millions of years which each human being spends in the subjective spheres, during the course of every great cycle of the activity of our globe.

With regard to faculties and talents, the answer is simple. They should be developed and cultivated for the service of Humanity, of which we are all parts, and to which we owe our full and ungrudging service. [IV, 88.]

———•———

Between Mr. Keely calling the Sun "a dead body," and the Occult Doctrine maintaining that what we call the Sun is a reflection of untold electric brightness, the "veil which covers and conceals the *living* Sun behind," there is but a difference in the mode of expression; the fundamental idea is the same. The shadow on the wall produced by a living man or object is the inanimate, or dead effect of an animate and living cause which intercepts the rays of light. The Sun we see is "an inert mass" of adumbrations, the unreal phantom of the real Sun, which, but for this *veil,* would consume our earth, and probably all the planets with its fierce radiancy. If it has been calculated of that solar "phantom" we see, that the heat emitted by it in a single second would be enough "to melt a shell of ice covering the entire surface of the earth to a depth of 1 mile 1,457 yards," what would be the intensity of sunlight if the invisible Sun were suddenly unveiled? And this is what will happen, the Occult Doctrine teaches, when the hour of Pralaya strikes—after which the Sun himself will be disrupted. [IV, 139fn.]

———•———

It would seem probable that in the fourfold division of the human being here referred to as that which was adopted by the earliest Christians, the "spiritual body" may be identified with the

Karana Sarira, or "causal body" of Eastern philosophy. It is the inseparable and co-existent vehicle of the Monad during the periods of manifestation, and is best described, as indicated by its name, as that in which inhere all the *Karmic causes* which have been generated by that "monad."

The exact relation of this causal or spiritual body to the Monad in Devachan has never been clearly explained in any Theosophical treatise. It would seem probable, however, that during the Devachanic state this vehicle undergoes a process of *involution,* by which it assimilates all the spiritual essence of the experiences passed through during the previous life.

The spiritual body being co-existent with the Monad cannot die, but it would appear probable that the return to incarnation is caused by the termination of the process of involution just mentioned. [IV, 260.]

It is a tradition among Occultists in general, and taught as an historical fact in Occult philosophy, that what is now Ireland was once upon a time the abode of the Atlanteans, emigrants from the submerged island mentioned by Plato. Of all the British Isles, Ireland is the most ancient by several thousands of years. Inferences and "working hypotheses" are left to the Ethnologists, Anthropologists and Geologists. The master and keepers of the old science claim to have preserved genuine records, and we Theosophists—*i.e.,* most of us, believe it implicitly. Official Science may deny, but what does it matter? Has not Science begun by denying almost everything it accepts now? [IV, 347.]

Real Theosophy—*i.e.,* the Theosophy that comes to us *from the East*—is assuredly Pantheism and by no means Theism. Theosophy is a word of the widest possible meaning which differs greatly in Eastern and Western literature. Moreover, the Theosophical Society being of Eastern origin, therefore goes beyond the narrow limits of the mediæval Theosophy of the West. Members of the T. S. can, therefore, subscribe to this Western idea of Theosophy. But as the vast majority of these members accept the

Eastern ideas, this majority has given us the right of applying the term *Theosophist* only to those members who do not believe in a "personal" God. Therefore, again, it would be better, in order to avoid confusion, that a member believing in such a God should qualify the term "Theosophist" by the adjective "Western." [V, 83fn.]

The hitherto very esoteric doctrine of the *Nirmanakayas* was lately brought forward as a proof and explained in the treatise called *The Voice of the Silence*. These Nirmanakayas are the *Bodhisattvas* or late Adepts, who having reached Nirvana and liberation from rebirth renounce it voluntarily in order to remain invisibly amidst the world to help poor ignorant Humanity within the lines permitted by Karma. These are the *real* SPIRITS of the disembodied men, and we recognise no others. The rest are either *Devachanees* to whose plane the spirit of the living medium must ascend, and who therefore, can never descend to our plane, or *spooks* of the first water. But then no Nirmanakaya will influence any man for the benefit of the latter for his own weal, or to save him from anything save death, and that only if the man's life is useful. By the fruit we recognise the tree. Units are as the leaves of that tree for them; and they look forward to benefit and save *the trunk,* not to concern themselves with its every leaf, whether good, bad, or indifferent. Even living Adepts have no such right. [V, 254fn.]

NOTES ON "PROBLEMS OF LIFE"

[In December, 1890, H.P.B. began in *Lucifer* a series of articles entitled "Problems of Life." They were selections from the posthumously published *Diary* of Dr. N.I. Pirogoff, translated by H.P.B. The following is a collation of some of the notes she added to those articles.—Eds.]

Claude Bernard, one of the greatest physiologists of this age, said that organised matter was *per se* inert—*even living matter* in that sense, he explains, "has to be considered, as lacking spontaneity," although it can become and manifest its special properties of life, under the influence of excitation, for, he adds, "living matter is irritable." If so, then the materialistic negation of life and mind *outside* and *independent of* matter becomes a fallacy condemned out of its own mouth. For to excite it, there must be an agent outside of matter to do so. And if there is such an agent to irritate or excite matter, then the materialist and physiologist can no longer say that "life *is a property* of matter or of living organised substance." Dr. Paul Gibier—the latest scientific convert to transcendental psychology—objects to this and says, that "if organized, living matter were indeed *inert,* demanding an exterior stimulant to manifest its properties, it would become incomprehensible how the hepatic cell could continue, as well demonstrated, to secrete sugar long after the liver had been separated from the body." Occultism says that there is no such thing as inert, dead or even inorganic matter. As sponge is the product of water, created, living and dying in the water, whether ocean or lake, after which it changes form but can never die in its particles or elements, so is matter. It is created and informed by life in the Ocean of Life, which LIFE is but another name for Universal Mind or *Anima Mundi,* one of the *"four faces* of Brahmâ" on this manifested plane of ours, the visible universe.

Our philosophy teaches us that atoms are *not* matter; but that the smallest molecule—composed of milliards of indivisible and imponderable atoms—*is* substance. Nevertheless, the atom is not a mathematical point or a fiction; but verily an immutable Entity, *a reality within an appearance*—the molecule being in occult philosophy but a figment of that which is called *maya* or illusion. The atom informs the molecule, as life, spirit, soul, mind, inform Man. Therefore is the atom all these, and Force itself, as Dr. Pirogoff suspected. During the life-cycle, the atom represents, *according to the geometrical combinations* of its groupings in the molecule, life, force (or energy), mind and will; for each molecule in space, as each cell in the human body, is only a microcosm within (to it) a relative macrocosm. That which Science refers to as Force, conservation of energy, correlation, continuity, etc., etc., is simply the various effects produced by the presence of atoms, which are, in fact, in their collectivity, simply the (spiritual) sparks on the manifested plane, thrown out by the *Anima Mundi,* the Universal Soul or Mind (*Maha-Buddhi, Mahat*) from the plane of the Unmanifested. In short, the atom may be described as *a compact or crystalized point of divine Energy and Ideation.*

Physical Science, it seems, gives the name of "atoms" to that which we regard as particles or molecules. With us "atoms" are the inner principles and the intelligent, spiritual guides of the cells and particles they inform. This may be unscientific, but it is a fact in nature.

———•———

Occult philosophy reconciles the absurdity of postulating in the manifested Universe an active Mind without an organ, with that worse absurdity, an objective Universe evolved as everything else in it, by blind chance, by giving to this Universe an organ of thought, a "brain." The latter, although not objective to *our* senses, is none the less existing; it is to be found in the Entity called KOSMOS (Adam Kadmon, in the Kabbalah). As in the Microcosm, MAN, so in the Macrocosm, or the Universe. Every "organ" in it is a sentient entity, and every particle of matter or substance, from the physical molecule up to the spiritual atom, is a cell, a nerve centre, which communicates.

This is precisely what occult philosophy claims; our *Ego* is a ray of the Universal Mind, individualized for the space of a cosmic life-cycle, during which space of time it gets experience in almost numberless reincarnations or rebirths, after which it returns to its Parent-Source.

The Occultist would call the "Higher Ego" the immortal Entity, whose shadow and reflection is the human Manas, the mind, limited by its physical senses. The two may be well compared to the Master-artist and the pupil-musician. The nature of the Harmony produced on the "organ," the Divine melody of the harsh discord, depends on whether the pupil is inspired by the immortal Master, and follows its dictates, or, breaking from its high control, is satisfied with the terrestrial sounds produced by itself conjointly with its evil companion—the man of flesh—on the chords and keys of the brain-organ.

In the course of natural evolution our "brain-mind" will be replaced by a finer organism, and helped by the sixth and the seventh senses. Even now, there are pioneer minds who have developed these senses.

If Dr. Pirogoff, an eminent scientist, thought so, [the possibility of a fifth dimension] the occult philosophy can hardly be taken to task and declared *unscientific,* in accepting the existence of a seven dimensional space in co-ordination with the seven states of consciousness.

Mesmeric and hypnotic experiments have proven beyond doubt that sensation may become independent of the particular sense that is supposed to generate and convey it in a normal state. Whether science will ever be able to prove or not that thought, consciousness, etc., in short, the *sensus internum* has its seat in the brain, it is already demonstrated and beyond any doubt that under certain conditions our consciousness and even the whole batch of our senses, can act through other organs, *e.g.,* the stomach, the soles of the feet, etc. The "sensing principle" in us is *an entity* capable of acting outside as inside its material body; and it is certainly independent of any organ in particular, in its actions, although during its incarnation it manifests itself through its physical organs.

———•———

Our "memory" is but a general agent, and its "tablets," with their indelible impressions, but a figure of speech; the "brain-tablets" serve only as a *upadhi* or a *vahan* (basis, or vehicle) for reflecting at a given moment the memory of one or another thing. The records of past events, of every minutest action, and of passing thoughts, in fact, are really impressed on the imperishable waves of the ASTRAL LIGHT, *around us* and everywhere, not in the brain alone; and these mental pictures, images, and sounds, pass from these waves *via* the *consciousness of the personal Ego* or Mind (the lower Manas) whose grosser essence is astral, into the *"cerebral reflectors,"* so to say, of our brain, whence they are delivered by the psychic to the *sensuous* consciousness. This at every moment of the day, and even during sleep. See "Psychic and Noetic Action," in *Lucifer,* Nov. 1890, pp. 181 and 182. [*H·P·B. Articles,* Vol. II, 7-27.]

FROM "THE PATH"

SEERSHIP

THE following remarks are not intended to be a critique upon the literary merits or demerits of the poem which is taken as the subject of criticism. In 1882, *The Theosophist*[1] published a review of "The Seer, a Prophetic Poem," by Mr. H. G. Hellon, and as clairvoyance is much talked of in the West, it seemed advisable to use the verses of this poet for the purpose of inquiring, to some extent, into the western views of Seership, and of laying before my fellow seekers the views of one brought up in a totally different school.

I have not yet been able to understand with the slightest degree of distinctness what state is known as "Seership" in the language of western mysticism. After trying to analyze the states of many a "seer," I am as far as ever from any probability of becoming wiser on the subject, as understood here, because it appears to me that no classification whatever exists of the different states as exhibited on this side of the globe, but all the different states are heterogeneously mixed. We see the state of merely catching glimpses in the astral light denominated *seership,* at the same time that the very highest illustrations of that state are called *trances.*

As far as I have yet been able to discover, "Seership," as thus understood here, does not come up to the level of *Sushupti,* which is the dreamless state in which the mystic's highest consciousness— composed of his highest intellectual and ethical faculties—hunts for and seizes any knowledge he may be in need of. In this state the mystic's lower nature is at rest (paralyzed); only his highest nature roams into the ideal world in quest of food. By *lower nature,* I mean his physical, astral or psychic, lower emotional and intellectual principles, including the lower fifth.[2] Yet even the knowledge obtained during the Sushupti state must be regarded, from this plane, as theoretical and liable to be mixed, upon resuming the application of the body, with falsehood and with the preconception of the mystic's ordinary waking state, as compared with the true knowledge acquired during the several initiations.

Note.—Changes which were requested by Murdhna Joti and published by Mr. Judge in the following issue of the *Path* have been incorporated in the text of this article, as well as corrections of a few typographical errors.—Eds.

1 See *Theosophist,* Vol. III, p. 177.

2 See *Esoteric Buddhism* for the sevenfold classification adopted by many Theosophists.

There is no guarantee held out for any mystic that any experience. researches, or knowledge that may come within his reach in any state whatever, is accurate, except in the mysteries of initiation.

But all these different states are necessary to growth. *Yagrata* —our waking state, in which all our physical and vital organs, senses, and faculties find their necessary exercise and development, is needed to prevent the physical organization from collapsing. *Swapna*—dream state, in which are included all the various states of consciousness between Yagrata and Sushupti, such as somnambulism, trance, dreams, visions, &c.—is necessary for the physical faculties to enjoy rest, and for the lower emotional and astral faculties to live, become active, and develop; and *Sushupti* state comes about in order that the consciousnesses of both Yagrata and Swapna states may enjoy rest, and for the fifth principle, which is the one active in Sushupti, to develop itself by appropriate exercise.

The knowledge acquired during Sushupti state might or might not be brought back to one's physical consciousness; all depends upon his desires, and according as his lower consciousnesses are or are not prepared to receive and retain that knowledge.

The avenues of the ideal world are carefully guarded by elementals from the trespass of the profane.

Lytton makes Mejnour say:[1] "We place our tests in ordeals that purify the passions and elevate the desires. And nature in this controls and assists us, for it places awful guardians and unsurmountable barriers between the ambitions of vice and the heaven of loftier science."

The desire for physical enjoyment, if rightly directed, becomes elevated, as a desire for something higher, gradually becoming converted into a desire to do good to others, and thus ascending, ceases to be a desire, and is transformed into an element of the sixth principle.

The control by nature to which Mejnour refers is found in the natural maximum and minimum limits; there cannot be too much ascension, nor can the descent be too quick or too low. The assistance of nature is to be found in what happens immediately after the Turya or Sushupti state is over since the adept takes one step and nature helps for another.

In the Sushupti state, one might or might not find the object

---

1 *Zanoni,* Book IV, Chapter 2.

of his earnest search, and as soon as it is found, the moment the desire to bring it back to normal consciousness arises, that moment Sushupti state is at an end for the time being. But one might often find himself in an awkward position when he has left that state. The doors for the descent of the truth into the lower nature are closed. Then his position is beautifully described in an Indian proverb: "The bran in the mouth and the fire are both lost." This is an allusion to a poor girl who is eating bran, and at the same time wants to kindle the fire just going out before her. She blows it with the bran in her mouth; the bran falls on the dying ashes, extinguishing them completely, she is thus a double loser. In the Sushupti state, the anxiety which is felt to bring back the experience to consciousness acts as the bran with the fire. Anxiety to have or to do, instead of being a help as some imagine, is a direct injury, and if permitted to grow in our waking moments, will act with all the greater force on the plane of Sushupti. The result of these failures is clearly set forth by Patanjali.[1]

Even where the doors to the lower consciousness are open, the knowledge brought back from Sushupti state might, owing to the distractions and difficulties of the direct and indirect routes of ascent and descent, be lost on the way either partially or wholly, or become mixed up with misconceptions and falsehood.

But in this search for knowledge in Sushupti, there must not remain a spark of indifference or idle inquisitiveness in the higher consciousness. Not even a jot of lurking hesitation about entering into the state, nor doubt about its desirability, nor about the usefulness or accuracy of the knowledge gleaned on former occasions, or to be presently gleaned. If there is any such doubt or hesitancy, his progress is retarded. Nor can there be any cheating or hypocrisy, nor any laughing in the sleeve. In our normal wakeful state it always happens that when we believe we are earnestly aspiring, some one or more of the elements of one or more of our lower consciousnesses belie us, make us feel deluded and laugh at us, for such is the self-inconsistent nature of desire.

In this state which we are considering, there are subjective and objective states, or classes of knowledge and experience, even as there are the same in Yagrata. So, therefore, great care should be taken to make your aims and aspirations *as high as possible* while in your normal condition. Woe to him who would dare to trifle

---

1 Patanjali's *Yoga Aphorisms*, 30 & 31, Part I.

with the means placed at his disposal in the shape of Sushupti. One of the most effectual ways in which western mystics could trifle with this is to seek for the missing links of evolution, so as to bring that knowledge to the normal consciousness, and then with it to extend the domain of "scientific" knowledge. Of course, from the moment such a desire is entertained, the one who has it is shut out from Sushupti.*

The mystic might be interested in analyzing the real nature of the objective world, or in soaring up to the feet of *Manus,*[1] to the spheres where Manava intellect is busy shaping the mould for a future religion, or had been shaping that of a past religion. But here the maximum and minimum limits by which nature controls are again to be taken account of. One essential feature of Sushupti is, as far as can now be understood, that the mystic must get at all truths through but one source, or path, viz: through the divine world pertaining to his own lodge (or teacher), and through this path he might soar as high as he can, though how much knowledge he can get is an open question.

Let us now inquire what state is the seership of the author of our poem "The Seer," and try to discover the "hare's horns" in it. Later on we may try to peep into the states of Swedenborg, P. B. Randolph, and a few of the "trained, untrained, natural-born, self-taught, crystal, and magic mirror seers."

I look at this poem solely to point out mistakes so as to obtain materials for our study. There are beauties and truths in it which all can enjoy.

---

* The following from the *Kaushitaki Upanishad,* (see Max Muller's translation, and also that published in the Bibliotheka Indica, with Sankaracharya's commentary—Cowell's tran.) may be of interest to students. "Agatasatru to him: 'Bâlàki, where did this person here sleep? Where was he? Whence did he come back?' Bâlâka, did not know. And Agatasatru said to him: 'Where this person here slept, where he was, whence he thus came back, is this: The arteries of the heart called Hita extend from the heart of the person towards the surrounding body. Small as a hair divided a thousand times, they stand, full of a thin fluid of various colors, white, black, yellow, red. In these the person is when sleeping, he sees no dream (Sushupti). Then he becomes one with that prana (breath) alone.' " (Elsewhere the number of these arteries is said to be 101.) "And as a razor might be fitted in a razor case, or as fire in the fire place, even thus this conscious self enters into the self of the body, to the very hair and nails; he is the master of all, and eats with and enjoys with them. So long as Indra did not understand the self, the Asuras (lower principles in man) conquered him. When he understood it, he conquered the Asuras, and obtained the pre-eminence among all gods. And thus also he who knows this obtains pre-eminence, sovereignty, supremacy." And in the *Khandogya Upanishad,* VI Prap, 8, Kh, I: "When the man sleeps here, my dear son, he becomes united with the True—in Sushupti sleep—he is gone to his own self. Therefore they say, he sleeps (Swapita), because he is gone (apita) to his own (sva)." And in *Prasna Up.* II, 1, "There are 101 arteries from the heart; one of them penetrates the crown of the head; moving upwards by it man reaches the immortal; the others serve for departing in different directions." (ED. PATH.)

1 This opens up an intensely interesting and highly important subject which cannot be here treated of, but which will be in future papers. Meanwhile, Theosophists can exercise their intuition in respect to it. (ED. PATH.)

In ancient days it was all very well for mystics to write figur-
atively so as to keep sacred things from the profane. Then symbolism was rife in the air with mysticism, and all the allegories
were understood at once by those for whom they were intended.
But times have changed. In this materialistic age it is known that
the wildest misconceptions exist in the minds of many who are
mystically and spiritually inclined. The generality of mystics and
their followers are not free from the superstitions and prejudices
which have in church and science their counterpart. Therefore in
my humble opinion there can be no justification for writing allegorically on mysticism, and, by publication, placing such writings
within reach of all. To do so is positively mischievous. If allegorical writings and misleading novels are intended to popularize
mysticism by removing existing prejudices, then the writers ought
to express their motives. It is an open question whether the benefit resulting from such popularization is not more than counter-
balanced by the injury worked to helpless votaries of mysticism,
who are misled. And there is less justification for our present allegorical writers than there was for those of Lytton's time. Moreover, in the present quarter of our century, veils are thrown by
symbolical or misleading utterances over much that can be safely
given out in plain words. With these general remarks let us turn
to "The Seer."

In the Invocation, addressed evidently to the Seer's guru,[1]
we find these words:

> "When in delicious dreams I leave this life,
> And in sweet trance unveil its mysteries;
> Give me thy light, thy love, thy truth divine!"

Trance here means only one of the various states known as
cataleptic or somnambulic, but certainly neither Turya nor Sushupti. In such a trance state very few of the mysteries of "this life," or
even of the state of trance itself, could be unveiled. The so-called
Seer can "enjoy" as harmlessly and as uselessly as a boy who idly
swims in the lagoon, where he gains no knowledge and may end
his sport in death. Even so is the one who swims, cuts capers, in
the astral light, and becomes lost in something strange which sur-
passes all his comprehension. The difference between such a Seer
and the ordinary sensualist is, that the first indulges both his astral
and physical senses to excess, while the latter his physical senses

---

1 *Guru,* a spiritual teacher.

only. These occultists fancy that they have removed their interest from *self,* when in reality they have only enlarged the limits of experience and desire, and transferred their interest to the things which concern their larger span of life.[1]

Invoking a Guru's blessings on your own higher nature for the purpose of sustaining you in this trance state, is as blasphemous and reprehensible an act of assisting descent, and conversion of higher into lower energies, as to invoke your Guru to help you in excessive wine drinking; for the astral world is also material. To be able to solve the mysteries of any consciousness whatever, even of the lowest physical, while in trance, is as vain a boast of the hunters for such a state as that of physiologists or mesmerists. While you are in trance state, if you are not ethical enough in your nature, you will be tempted and forced, by your powerful lower elements, to pry into the secrets of your neighbors, and then, on returning to your normal state, to slander them. The surest way to draw down your higher nature into the miry abyss of your physical and astral world, and thus to animalize yourself is to go into a trance or to aspire for clairvoyance.

> "And thou, (Guru) left me looking upward through the veil,
> To gaze into thy goal and follow thee!"

These lines are highly presumptuous. It is impossible, even for a very high Hierophant, in *any of his states whatever,* to gaze into his Guru's goal,[2] his subjective consciousness can but *barely* come up to the level of the normal or objective consciousness of his Guru. It is only during the initiation that the initiated sees not only his own immediate goal, but also Nirvana, which of course includes his Guru's goal also; but after the ceremony is over he recollects only his own immediate goal for his next "class," but nothing beyond that.[3] This is what is meant by the God Jehovah saying to Moses: "And I will take away mine hand and Thou shalt see my back, but my face shall not be seen." And in The Rig Veda it is said:[4] "Dark is the path of Thee, who are bright: the

---

1 Vide *Light on the Path,* Rule 1, note, part I.

2 There is one exceptional case where the Guru's goal is seen, and then the Guru has to die, for there can be no two *equals.*

3 There is no contradiction between this and the preceding paragraph where it is said, "To see the Guru's goal is impossible." During the initiation ceremony, there is no separateness between those engaged in it. They all become one whole, and therefore even the High Hierophant, while engaged in an initiation, is no more his separate self, but is only a part of the whole, of which the candidate is also a part, and then, for the time being, having as much power and knowledge as the very highest present. (ED. PATH.)

4 *Rig Veda,* IV, VII, 9.

light is before Thee."

Mr. Hellon opens his poem with a quotation from *Zanoni*: "Man's first initiation is in trance; in dreams commence all human knowledge, in dreams he hovers over measureless space, the first faint bridge between spirit and spirit—this world and the world beyond."

As this is a passage often quoted approvingly, and recognized as containing no misconceptions, I may be permitted to pass a few remarks, first, upon its intrinsic merits, and secondly, on Lytton himself and his Zanoni. I shall not speak of the rage which prevails among mystical writers for quoting without understanding what they quote.

In *Swapna* state man gets human, unreliable knowledge, while divine knowledge begins to come in Sushupti state. Lytton has here thrown a gilded globule of erroneous ideas to mislead the unworthy and inquisitive mysticism hunters, who unconsciously price the globule. It is not too much to say that such statements in these days, instead of aiding us to discover the true path, but give rise to numberless patent remedies for the evils of life, remedies which can never accomplish a cure. Man-made edifices called true Raja Yoga,[1] evolved in trance, arise confronting each other, conflicting with each other, and out of harmony in themselves. Then not only endless disputation arises, but also bigotry, while the devoted and innocent seekers after truth are misled, and scientific, intelligent, competent men are scared away from any attempt to examine the claims of the true science. As soon as some one-sided objective truth is discovered by a Mesmer, a defender of ancient Yoga Vidya[2] blows a trumpet crying out, "Yoga is self mesmerization, mesmerism is the *key* to it, and animal magnetism develops spirituality and is itself, God, Atman," deluding himself with the idea that he is assisting humanity and the cause of truth, unconscious of the fact that he is thus only degrading Yoga Vidya. The ignorant medium contends that her "control" is divine. There seems to be little difference between the claims of these two classes of dupes and the materialist who sets up a protoplasm in the place of God. Among the innumerable hosts of desecrated terms are *Trance, Yoga, Turya, initiation,* &c. It is therefore no wonder that Lytton, in a novel, has desecrated it and misapplied it to a mere

---

1 Divine science.
2 The knowledge of Yoga, which is, "joining with your higher self."

semi-cataleptic state. I, for one, prefer always to limit the term *Initiation* to its true sense, viz., those sacred ceremonies in which alone "Isis is unveiled."

Man's first initiation is *not* in trance, as Lytton means. Trance is an artificial, waking, somnambulistic state, in which one can learn nothing at all about the real nature of the elements of our physical consciousness, and much less any of any other. None of Lytton's admirers seems to have thought that he was chaffing at occultism, although he believed in it, and was not anxious to throw pearls before swine. Such a hierophant as Mejnour—not Lytton himself—could not have mistaken the tomfoolery of sommnambulism for even the first steps in Raja Yoga. This can be seen from the way in which Lytton gives out absolutely erroneous ideas about occultism, while at the same time he shows a knowledge which he could not have, did he believe himself in his own chaffing. It is pretty well recognized that he at last failed, after some progress in occultism as a high accepted disciple. His Glyndon might be Lytton, and Glyndon's sister Lady Lytton. The hieroglyphics of a book given him to decipher, and which he brought out as *Zanoni,* must be allegorical. The book is really the master's ideas which the pupil's highest consciousness endeavors to read. But they were only the mere commonplaces of the master's mind. The profane and the cowardly always say that the master descends to the plane of the pupil. Such can never happen. And precipitation of messages from the master is only possible when the pupil's highest ethical and intuitive faculties reach the level of the master's normal and objective state. In *Zanoni,* this is veiled by the assertion that he had to *read* the hieroglyphics—they did not *speak* to him. And he confesses in the preface that he is by no means sure that he has correctly deciphered them. "Enthusiasm," he says, "is when that part of the soul which is above intellect soars up to the Gods, and there derives the inspiration." Errors will therefore be due to wilful misstatements or to his difficulty in reading the cipher.

Such indefinite descriptions are worse than useless. The inward

> "In dreams I see a world so fair,
>   That life would love to linger there,
>   And pass from this to that bright sphere,
>   In dreams ecstatic, pure and free,
>   Strange forms my inward senses see,
>   While hands mysterious welcome me."

senses are psychic senses, and their perceiving strange forms and mere appearances in the astral world is not useful or instructive. Forms and appearances in the astral light are legion, and take their shape not only from the seer's mind unknown to himself, but are also, in many cases, reflections for other people's minds.

> "Oh, why should mine be ever less,
> And light ineffable bless
> Thee, in thy starry loneliness,"

seems to be utterly unethical. Here the seer is in the first place jealous of the light possessed by his guru, or he is groping in the dark, ignorant even of the *rationale* of himself being in lower states than his guru. However, Mr. Hellon has not erred about the existence of such a feeling. It does and should exist in the trance and dreaming state. In our ordinary waking state, attachments, desires, &c., are the very life of our physical senses, and in the same way the emotional energies manifest themselves on the astral plane in order to feed and fatten the seer's astral senses, sustaining them during his trance state. Unless thus animated, his astral nature would come to rest.

No proof is therefore needed for the proposition that any state which is sustained by desires and passions cannot be regarded as anything more than as a means for developing one part of the animal nature. Van Helmont is of the same opinion as Mr. Hellon.* We cannot, therefore, for a moment believe that in such a state the "I" of that state is *Atman*.[1] It is only the false "I"; the vehicle for the real one. It is *Ahankára*—lower self, or individuality of the waking state, for even in trance state the lower sixth principle plays no greater part and develops no more than in the wakeful state. The change is only in the field of action: from the waking one to the astral plane; the physical one remaining more or less at rest. Were it otherwise, we would find somnambules day by day exhibiting increase of intellect, whereas this does not occur.

Suppose that we induce the trance state in an illiterate man. He can then read from the astral counterpart of Herbert Spencer or Patanjali's books as many pages as we desire, or even the unpublished ideas of Spencer; but he can never make a comparison between the two systems, unless that has already been done by

---

* See *Zanoni*, Book IV, c. iii.
[1] Highest soul.

some other mind in no matter what language. Nor can any somnambule analyze and describe the complicated machinery of the astral faculties, much less of the emotional ones, or of the fifth principle. For in order to be analyzed they must be at rest so that the higher self may carry on the analysis. So when Mr. Hellon says:

> "A trance steals o'er my spirit now,"

he is undoubtedly wrong, as Atman, or spirit, cannot go into a trance. When a lower plane energy ascends to a higher plane, it becomes silent there for a while until by contract with the denizens of its new home its powers are animated. The somnambulic state has two conditions, (a) waking, which is psycho-physiological or astro-physical; (b) sleeping, which is psychical. In these two the trance steals partly or completely only over the physical consciousness and senses.

> "And from my forehead peers the sight," etc.

This, with much that follows is pure imagination or misconception. As for instance, "floating from sphere to sphere." In this state the seer is confined to but one sphere—the astral or psycho-physiological—; no higher one can he even comprehend.

Speaking of the period when the sixth sense shall be developed, he says:

> "No mystery then her sons shall find,
> Within the compass of mankind;
> The one shall read the other's mind."

In this the seer shows even a want of theoretical knowledge of the period spoken of. He has madly rushed into the astral world without a knowledge of the philosophy of the mystics. Even though the twelfth sense were developed—let alone the physical sixth—it shall ever remain as difficult as it is now, for people to read one another's mind. Such is the mystery of Manas.[1] He is evidently deluded by seeing the apparent triumphs during a transitional period of a race's mental development, of those minds abnormally developed which are able to look into the minds of others; and yet they do that only partially. If one with a highly developed sixth principle were to indulge for only six times in reading others' minds, he would surely drain that development down to fatten the mind and desires. Moreover, Mr. Hellon's seer seems to be totally unaware of the fact that the object of developing higher faculties

---

1 Fifth principle.

is not to peer into the minds of others, and that the economy of the occult world gives an important privilege to the mystic, in that the pages of his life and *manas* shall be carefully locked up against inquisitive prowlers, the key safely deposited with his guru, who never lends it to any one else. If with the occult world the laws of nature are so strict, how much more should they be with people in general. Otherwise, nothing would be safe. The sixth sense would then be as delusive and a curse to the ignorant as sight and learning are now. Nor shall this sixth sense man be "perfect." Truth for him shall be as difficult to attain through his "sense," as it is now. The horizon shall have only widened, and what we are now acquiring as truth will have passed into history, into literature, into axiom. "Sense" is always nothing else than a channel for desire to flow through and torment ourselves and others.

The whole poem is misleading, especially such expressions as: "His spirit views the world's turmoil; behold his body feed the soil.—A sixth sense race borne ages since, to God's own zone." Our higher self—Atman—can never "view the world's turmoil," nor behold the body. For supposing that it did view the body or the world's turmoil, it would be attracted to them, descending to the physical plane, where it would be converted more or less into physical nature. And the elevation of a sixth sense race unphilosophically supposes the raising up of that sense, which certainly has only to do with our physical nature, at most our astro-physical nature, to the sphere of God or Atman.

By merely training the psychical powers true progress is not gained, but only the enjoyment of those powers; a sort of alcohol on the astral plane, which results in unfavorable Karma. The true path to divine wisdom is in performing our duty unselfishly in the station in which we are placed, for thereby we convert lower nature into higher, following Dharma—our whole duty.

MURDHNA JOTI

Path, April-May, 1886

LIVING THE HIGHER LIFE

[In the early issues of the *Path* William Q. Judge published two articles by "Murdhna Joti"—"Seership" and "Living the Higher Life." It was often assumed that "Murdhna Joti" was one of several pseudonyms used by Mr. Judge. However, in 1961 the editors of *Theosophy* received evidence from a Theosophical student and correspondent which showed that "Murdhna Joti" was actually Bowaji, a Hindu member of the Society. In an unpublished letter to Judge, dated July 27, 1886, H.P.B. strongly objected to statements made in "Living the Higher Life" and expressed concern that the article might be interpreted as a canon of instruction regarding the ideal personal life of Theosophical students. She included with her letter an article of criticism by A.P. Sinnett entitled "Theosophic Morals," which Mr. Judge published in the *Path*, September, 1886, adding a note defending some of Murdhna Joti's ideas. Sinnett's article and Judge's note were reprinted in *Theosophy*, December, 1961, with details regarding this controversy presented in "On the Lookout."—Eds.]

I have no desire for any other line of life; but by the time I had awakened to a knowledge of this life, I found myself involved by circumstances against which I do not rebel, but out of and through which, I am *determined* to work, neglecting no known duty to others.

—Letter from a Friend

THE "Dweller of the Threshold" which stares even advanced occultists in the face and often threatens to overwhelm them, and the ordeals of Chelaship or of probation for Chelaship, differ from each other only in degree. It may not be unprofitable to analyze this Dweller and those ordeals. For our present purpose, it is enough to state, that they are of a triune nature and depend upon these three relations: (1) to our nationality; (2) to our family; and (3) to ourselves. And every one of these three relations is due to the assertion of a portion of our own past Karma, that is to say, to its effects.

Why should we be born in a particular nation and in a particular family? Because of the effect of a particular set of our Karmic attractions, which assert themselves in that manner. I mean that one set of our past Karmas exhaust themselves in throwing us in our present incarnation amidst a particular nation, another set introducing us into a particular family; and a third set serving to differentiate or individualize us from all the other members of the nation or of the family. One of our Eastern proverbs says: "the five children of a family differ like the five fingers of a hand." Unless we look at this difference from this standpoint, it must always appear to us a riddle, a problem too difficult to solve, a mystery, in short, why children born of one family, while they have some traits common to all, should still appear to differ vastly from one another. What applies to the family applies also to the nation, of which families are but units; and also to mankind as a whole, of whom nations are but families or units. The only way to decide the great question of the age, whether the laws of nature are blind and material, or spiritual, intelligent and divine, is, it seems to me, to point out in connection with every subject, the absolutely intelligent and divine manner in which these laws act, and how they force us to realize the economy of nature. This is the only way by which we could become spiritual; and I would, once for all, call upon my co-workers for the cause, to realize at every step of their study, as far as possible, the Divine Intelligence thus manifesting itself. Otherwise, how much soever you might believe or take it for granted, that the forces that govern the universe are spiritual, the belief, however deep rooted it might appear, would be of little use to you when you have to pass through the ordeals of Chelaship; and then you are sure to succumb and exclaim that the "Law is blind, unjust and cruel," especially when your selfishness and personality overwhelm you. When once a practical occultist and a learned philosopher met with, what seemed to him a "serious calamity and trial," in spite of himself he exclaimed to me frankly: "the law of Karma is surely blind, there is no God; what better proofs are needed?" So deep-rooted in human nature is infidelity and selfishness; no one need therefore to be sure of his own spiritual nature. No amount of lip learning will avail us in the hour of need. We have to study the law in all its aspects and assimilate to our highest consciousness,—that which is called by Du Prel super sensuous consciousness—all the data which go to prove and convince us that the Power is spiritual. Look around and see whether any two persons are absolutely identical, even for a time. How intelligent must be the power that ever strives to keep each and every one of us totally different *on the whole,* while if analyzed, we possess some traits in common, even with the Negro, with whom we are remotely allied.

In this connection I shall refer you to a passage in the article on "Chelas and Lay Chelas" (vide column 1, page 11 of "Supplement to the Theosophist" for July, 1883): "The Chela is not only called to face all latent evil propensities of his nature, but in addition, the whole volume of maleficent power accumulated by the community and nation to which he belongs . . . until the result is known." I shall only ask you to apply the same principle to your family relations affecting your present incarnation. Thus seven things are found to secure us a victory, or a sad, inglorious defeat in the mighty struggle known as the Dweller of the threshold and the ordeals of Chelaship: (1) The evil propensities common to ourselves and to our family; (2) those common to ourself and our nation; (3) those common to ourself and to mankind in general, or better known as the weakness of human nature, the fruits of Adam's first transgression; (4 to 6) the noble qualities common to us and to these three; (7) the peculiar way in which the 6 sets of our past Karmas choose or are allowed to influence us now, or their effects in producing in us the present tendency. The adept alone can take the seventh or last mentioned item completely into his own hands; and every mortal who would, as I have since recently begun to reiterate, direct all his energies to the highest plane possible for him ("Desire always to attain the unattainable"—says the author of "Light on the Path"),—such a mortal, too, could more or less do the same thing as the adept, insofar as he acts up to the rule. Every Chela, and also those who have a desire to be Chelas even, as they suppose secretly, have to do with the first six propensities or influences.

The world is inclined—at least in this Kali Yuga (the Dark Age)—always to begin at the wrong end of anything and direct all its faculties to the perception of effects and not of their causes. So the ideas of "renunciation," "asceticism" and of the "true feeling of universal Brotherhood" (or "mercy," as I call it, in accordance with South Indian Ethics), all of which are compatible with Gnanis, or the most exalted of Mahatmas, all these have come to be recognized by all our Theosophists, in general, as *the means* of progress for a beginner; while the real means of progress for us mortals—duties to our own families and to our own nation, or "kindness" and "patriotism" in the highest and ethical sense of the terms—are discarded. True, from the standpoint of a Jivanmukta, a true friend of humanity, these two Sadhanas are really "selfishness"; still, until we attain that exalted state, these two feelings should be made the ladders for raising ourselves, the means of not only getting ourselves rid of our family defects and natural idiosyncrasies, but also of strengthening in ourselves the noble qualities of our families and of our nation. Until we reach that ideal state where the blessed soul has to make neither good nor bad Karma, we must strive to be constantly doing "good" Karma, in order that we might become Karma-less (nish Karmis).

Let it not be understood at all, that I mean by "family duties" and "national duties," false attachments to the family or to the nation. Family duty consists not in sensuality or pleasure-hunting, but in cultivating and in elevating the emotional nature (the fourth principle), of ourselves and of our family, in being equally "kind," not only to the members of the family, but also to all creatures, and in enjoying all such pleasures of the family life as are consistent with the acquirement of "wealth" (all the means necessary for the performance of Dharma or whole duty) according to the teachings of Valluvar, and in utilizing such pleasures and means for the performance of our duty to our nation. Patriotism consists similarly in theosophising our own nation, in not only getting ourselves rid of our national defects, as well as other members of the nation rid of the same, but also in strengthening in ourselves and in our nation as a whole, all the noble qualities which belong to our nation; in the enjoyment of the privileges* of the nation and using them as a means for the performance of *Dharma*. If family duties are taken due care of, our duties to the nation and to humanity would, to a great extent, take care of themselves unimpeded. Our national duties, if strictly performed, serve to purify our fifth lower principle of its dross and to establish and develop the better part of it, while the performance of our duty to Humanity or the *realization of universal tolerance and mercy,* purifies the lower (human) stuff in the fifth higher principle and makes it divine, thus enabling us to free ourselves gradually from the bonds of ignorance common to all human beings.

The above assertions, might, at first sight, seem rather bold and untheosophical. But I should venture to state my conviction that

---

* I use this word "privilege" in its ethical sense; privileges are to the patriot what the "pleasures" are to the family life.

the whole edifice of Aryan religions and Aryan philosophy is based upon these principles, and that, on a careful consideration of the subject, the great importance attached to household life (Grihasta ashrama) in that philosophy, would be fully borne out. To my mind no ascetics, no teachers of mankind, however eminent and full of the highest knowledge, are really such good and practical benefactors of humanity as Valluvar, of ancient times, who incarnated on earth for the express purpose, among others, of setting an example of an ideal household life to mortals who were prematurely and madly rushing against the rocks of renunciation, and of proving the possibility of leading such a life in any age however degenerated; or as Ráma, who even after having become an *avatarpurusha,* came down amidst mortals and led a household life.

It has often been contended that the world has not progressed on *the path,* because *gnanis,* or Mahatmas, have dwindled in their number and greatness, and because it is Kali Yuga, or the dark age, now. Such arguments are due to our mistaking the effects for their causes. The only way to prepare the way for the advent of a favorable Yuga and for the increase of the number and greatness of Mahatmas, is to establish gradually the conditions for the leading of a true household life. I should unhesitatingly state, that that is the duty of earnest Theosophists and real philanthropists.

Is it not conceded by all philanthropists that unselfish labors for humanity can alone relieve us from the ocean of Sainsara (Rebirth), develop our highest potentialities and help us to alchemise our human weakness? Applying the same principle to unselfish discharge of our family and national duties, my position becomes tenable. A Mahatma has, it appears, declared that He has still "patriotism." But He has not said nor would say, that He has still family "attachments." This proves that He has got out of the defects of the family to which He belongs, while He is only striving to get out of national defects, some of which at any rate cling to Him. A Buddha would say, that He has "mercy," but no "patriotism."

The only effectual way to get out of family defects is to discharge all our duty to our family before leaving it, as ascetics, or before we die. Blessed is he* who, in each of his incarnations, *then and there,* gets rid of the defects of the family into which he is ushered,

____

* This is the man to be in the family and not of the family like the water on the lotus leaf, making only the good traits of the family the seat of his higher self.

thereby converts those defects in his parents, brothers and sisters, into noble qualities, thus strengthening and developing the good qualities both of himself and of his family, then strives to be born in the same family again and again, until he himself becomes a Buddha and assists his family to become a family fit for a Buddha to be born into, while he becomes the cream of all the noble qualities of the family without being tainted with its idiosyncrasies. A Dugpa (Black Magician) is frequently born in the same family and becomes the cream of all its evil propensities. Here again is the operation of the sublime and divinely intelligent law of universal and natural economy asserting itself. This is beautifully allegorized in the story of a Jivanmukta churning out of the ocean the elixir of life, and leaving the *visha* (the poison, all the evil propensities) for the Dugpas. This is one of the meanings of the allegory. Avoiding all personalities and questionable facts, I shall rely solely upon our Puranas and scriptures to prove that in every family where Adepts and Gnanis are (or choose to be) frequently born, often Dugpas are also born, as a matter of course. Krishna was the greatest of Gnanis and his uncle, Kansa (for our present purpose), was a terrible Dugpa. The five Pandavas had a hundred wicked cousins, the Kauravas. Devas and the whole brood of wicked Asuras were born of the same parent. *Vibhishana* had for his brother, *Ravana* the prince of Dugpas; so had the good Sugriva a brother like Vali. Prahlada had a monster for his father.

Take the case of one who has not done all his duty to his family, before he dies, or before he takes the vows of renunciation and becomes an ascetic. Such ascetics find themselves attracted by the family defects and selfishness of themselves (which hitherto perhaps lay more or less dormant and now become kindled and awakened by the selfishness of the relatives) and are disturbed in the performance of the duties of their new order or *Ashrama,* however unselfish their relatives might have been "unconsciously" or unintentionally. In spite of themselves these relatives arrest the progress of the ascetics in whom the family defects become thus strengthened and developed. Such is the mysterious law of attraction. This man must be born again (1) either in the same family, with the family defects strengthened, both in himself and in his family; (2) or in another family. In the first case, the noble qualities of the family are not strengthened and therefore gradually disappear both from him and from the family. In the second case, he becomes an undutiful son, brother or husband, in his new family, firstly because of the natural law of repetition, which, with the terrible Karmic interest, strengthens the tendency in him to disregard duty; secondly because of the "counter family attractions" (or repulsions). Let not this unfortunate wanderer from the post of his family duty console himself with the foolish idea that this tendency would confine its havoc to family traits (good and evil) and to family duties alone. It would extend itself in all directions, wherever it can; it would make him disregard his duties to his nation and to himself (or in other words, to humanity). He would suddenly be surprised to find himself apathetic to his nation and to his highest nature, or to mankind. Such are the mazes and unknown ramifications of our evil or good propensities. Any evil or noble element of human nature converts itself, under "favorable" conditions into any other element however apparently remote. The conditions are there ready wherever the element is strong; where there is a will there is a way. Performance of family duties therefore develops patriotism and mercy.

I do not at all mean to say that the effects of Karma *always* assert themselves in the same shape or form; but they often might and do. Nor do I mean that the affinities above stated, blossom and ripen in the incarnation immediately succeeding; they might develop ten or even one hundred incarnations after; but in such a case, the Karma only accumulates enormous interest. The affinities might not develop *at the same time* in both him and her, who was once his wife; if they did at the same time, the account could be easily settled,—otherwise, woe to him and her! Supposing that the attractions for him are developed in her, while the attachments for her are not developed in him at the same time; the result might be, that she pines and languishes for him, sends her poisonous darts consciously or "unconsciously" against him; if these arrows do not kindle the corresponding nature in him, for the time being they frustrate his achievements in other directions. Supposing by the time the affinities in him are developed, he becomes an initiate and she becomes, (let us suppose) his pupil (male or female). If at the time the pupil's affinities have become converted into devotion for the initiate, the latter becomes blinded in his philanthropic work and noble duties of a sage, and commits, through the infatuation of a love for the pupil, serious blunders, which result in a catastrophe to both of them and to humanity: and both the pupil and initiate fall down and have to mount their rugged pathway again with increased difficulties in their way.

Once, in an age and in a country, when and where household life continues to be ideal, one single wretch commits the first act of transgression by impetuously rushing into the circle of ascetics, or by dying before wholly discharging his duty to his family, the natural result is that both himself, his family, and his nation, become thereby seriously affected. The Akasa* becomes affected by the impulse to transgress in this direction; this impulse forces itself gradually (with accumulated interest, redoubled force) upon others; the ignoble example becomes a precedent; other cases of a like nature follow in quick succession. In course of time, (just when a sad descending cycle begins, such is the divine intelligence of the law that economizes energies and makes things fit it) the leading of the ideal family life becomes almost impossible and very rare; the whole community is thus ruined. Learned and great adepts retire to other spheres (where there then is an ascending cycle) and leave the nation to be swallowed by a cataclysm after ages of degradation and vice.

Let us now reverse this case, and suppose that in the most degenerate nation, in the darkest of cycles, one philanthropist becomes unselfish and intelligent enough to set a noble and intelligent example by fulfilling all family duties; then, as naturally as in the preceding case, the precedent gradually gains acceptance; the way is paved for the advent of an ascending cycle; Gnanis bless the noble man and come down from other unfavorable spheres, where descending cycles begin to dawn.

Now it may be easy to understand why Chelas and lay Chelas (who have not yet thrown off their family defects and thus become the cream of their family's good qualities) are told to be careful lest they become Dugpas (Black Magicians).

I will ask you to apply the same kinds of arguments to the necessity for performing (and the failure to perform) our duties to our nation and to mankind. You can see that the phenomena of heresy, downfall of religions, rise of new religions, the birth in Europe of a Max Müller, who expatiates upon the greatness of the Vedic philosophy, and Bradlaughs and other infidel sons of Christian parents—all these are due to the fact (and also to other causes), that the individuals concerned had not in some one or

---

* The Ether, the Astral Light.—[Ed.]

other of their past incarnations, done their duty to the nations (or religions), to which they respectively belonged. A study of the times when and in the manner in which the traits of these men are brought into play should be profitable in several ways. Extending the analogy, it may be said that heartlessness, murder, cannibalism, etc., are due to failure to discharge, in past incarnations, one's duty to humanity (that is to one's self).

In conclusion it might be added that the most important element in the "Dweller of the Threshold," and in the ordeals of Chelaship, is family defects, which ought to be *first* "conquered"; then in order come national defects and the "diseases of the flesh" in general. Though all these three have to be got rid of simultaneously as far as possible, and all the three kinds of duties performed, still beginners should pay more attention to the first than to the second, and more to the second than to the third, and none of these neglected.

In those happy Aryan ages, when Dharma was known and performed fully, those men and women who did not marry, remained in the family for performing their family duties and led a strictly ascetical and Vedantic life as Brahmacharis and Kannikas (or virgins). Those alone married, who were in every way qualified for leading a grihasta (household) life. Marriage was in those days a sacred and religious contract, and not at all a means of gratifying selfish desires and animal passions. These marriages were of two kinds: (1) Those who married for the express purpose of assisting each other (husband and wife) in their determination to lead a higher life, in fulfilling their family duties, in enjoying all pleasures enjoined for such a life and thereby acquiring the means for attaining the qualifications for higher ashrama of renunciation (Sannyása), and, above all, for giving the world the benefit of children, who would become gnanis and work for humanity. Such a husband and wife might be regarded as not having in their previous incarnations been able enough to become ripe for Chelaship. (2) Those who had, in their past incarnations already fitted themselves completely for entering the sanctuary of Occultism and gnana marga (path of wisdom). One of them, the Pati (the master or "husband") was the Guru who had advanced far higher than his Patin (co-worker or pupil or "wife"). As soon as the alliance between them was made, these retired into the forest to lead the life of celibacy and practical Occultism. But, before so retiring, they had invariably promised to their parents and other members of their family to assist and elevate them even from a distance and offered to periodically adjust* the inner life of all the relatives. I quote the language generally used in making such promises: "Whenever mother, father, sister and brothers, any of you think of me in your hour of need, wherever or whatever I may be, I solemnly promise to lend you a helping hand."

Needless to say, that such vows were conscientiously kept, and that those who were not really able to do so never made such promises nor retired from the side of their family, but chose to belong to the first class of married people. This second class of persons who thus retired into the forest and became hermits, were called Vanaprasthas. They always obtained the full consent† of their near relatives and renounced "pleasures" and material prosperity (money making, etc.).

The fourth highest order of life was complete renunciation (Sannyasis). These were the blessed few who had, then and there, in each incarnation, got out of family defects. Only those *were* admitted into this order whom the defects of no family could affect. Long before their admission into this order, they had, by fulfilling family duties, successively, incarnation after incarnation gone far beyond the reach of family defects. Brahmacharis and Kannikas could, after they had discharged family duties, become Sannyasis. All except those belonging to the second order of life, were called upon and did take a vow to give up one or more of their dearest and strongest defects.

Such, my friends, were the Laws of Manu. If any of you could establish a community on a better foundation, I should be happy to give up my allegiance to the great Sage, Saviour, and Legislator. As every Manu establishes the same Manava Dharma again and again, and as the Manus are higher than Buddha and other founders of religions, I should call upon you to pay all possible attention to this subject. Manu is higher, because he overshadows a Buddha.

I must request the readers, to study every word and the whole of this paper (if it deserves to be so called) and not tear it piece-meal or interpret passages and phrases in it, as they please. I must add, that by "family duties" I do not at all mean sacrificing your duty or

---

* I use the word in the peculiar sense which I have already attached to it.

† "Full consent" including the consent of all their various consciousnesses. If the Patin or Pati saw, and they ought to be able to see, that even in one of the consciousnesses of any of their near relatives there lurked a latent spark of hesitation to consent or of unwillingness, then the pair unselfishly gave up their determination to become Vanaprasthas and remained with the family until the proper time came.

conviction and Truth, to gratify the whims or selfish nature or sectarian views of any of your "relatives." But I use the expression "family duties" in a peculiar sense, namely, "that course and *only that course* of action, speech and thoughts by which you can not only get rid of your family defects in this very incarnation, but also strengthen in yourself all the noble qualities of your family, and which will at the same time enable your relatives (parents, brothers, sisters, wife, children, etc.,) also to get rid of *the same* defects and strengthen in themselves *the same* good qualities—so that you might be born again and again in the same family." "Patriotism" is used in a similar manner; and the article "Elixir of Life" (see *Theosophist*) should be read in the light of this paper.*

The question is asked, "Has the dweller of the threshold an objective form; upon what does its objective form depend; does it always appear to everyone in the same form as it did to Glyndon in Bulwer's story?"

It is objective to those who have gone very far.

It depends on (1) a certain thing I shall not here name; (2) the stage of development to which the chela or occultist has attained or is near attaining; (3) the mode of regarding elementals and the Dweller, peculiar to the chela or occultist, to his family and to his nation, or rather to the national and family legends or religion; (4) which form, more or less monstrous or incongruous, would be most frightful and overpowering to him at the critical period. Subject to the above four conditions, the Dweller assumes a form according to the manner in which the chela or occultist *has or has not fulfilled the threefold duties,* and according to the manner in which the sevenfold elements of the Dweller assert themselves upon him. The better he has fulfilled the threefold duties, the less does the Dweller affect him. Of course the form is not necessarily the same for everyone.

Why did the Dweller appear to Glyndon's sister, who was not undergoing probation, and why in the same form?

Because she was sympathetic and sensitive enough. The principle involved in this case is the same as in obsession.

The Dweller might either be but one elemental, or a group or several groups of elementals assuming one collective form. It is one elemental, when the crisis comes at the very commencement of the

---

* Reprinted in *Five Years of Theosophy.*—Eds.

chela's or occultist's attempt to elevate his lower nature. This is the case when he has the least (Karmic) stamina for the "uphill path." The later on his path is waylaid, the more numerous are the elementals of which the Dweller is composed.

It need not be imagined that this appearance or influence confronts the chela only once until he reaches the first initiation, and an initiate only once during the interval between two initiations. It appears as often as the stock of his Karmic stamina falls below the minimum limit.

By Karmic stamina is meant the *phala* (effect or fruit) of past unselfish, good Karma that has become ripened. Though the occultist might have an immense quantity of past unselfish good Karma stored up, still, if during his crisis there be not a sufficient number of present unselfish good thoughts to ripen a sufficient portion of that quantity, he finds himself destitute of the necessary stock of stamina. Few are they who have already laid up a good quantity of unselfish good Karma; and fewer still are they who have the requisite degree of unselfish and spiritual nature during the period of trial; and there are still fewer who would not rush for further Yoga development, without having all the requisite means.

When not qualified fully for it, we ought to and could go on developing ourselves in the ordinary way, and try to secure the necessary means by leading an unselfish life and setting an example to others, and this is the stage of nearly all ordinary Theosophists. They, in common with all their fellows, are influenced by a "Dweller," which is the effect upon them of their own, their family, and national defects; and although they may never, in this life, see objectively any such form, the influence is still there, and is commonly recognized as "bad inclinations and discouraging thoughts."

Seek then, to live the Higher life by beginning now to purify your thoughts by good deeds, and by right speech.

Murdhna Joti

Path, July-August, 1886

THE WORSHIP OF THE DEAD

SOME OF THE EVIL CONSEQUENCES OF MEDIUMSHIP
(Extracts From a Private Letter)

*Q*uestion—Is there any intermediate condition between the spiritual beatitude of Devachan and the forlorn shade-life of the only-half-conscious reliquae of human beings who have lost their sixth principle? Because, if so, that might give a *locus standi* in imagination to the "Ernests" and "Joeys" of the spiritual mediums,—the better sort of controlling spirits.

Ans.—Alas! no, my friend; not that I know of. From Sukhava down to the "Territory of Doubt" there is a variety of spiritual states, but I am not aware of any such intermediate condition. The "forlorn shadow" has to do the best it can. As soon as it has stepped outside the Kama-Loka,—crossed the "Golden Bridge" leading to the "Seven Golden Mountains"—the *Ego* can confabulate no more with easy-going mediums. No "Ernest" or "Joey" has ever returned from the Rupa-loka, let alone the Arupa-loka, to hold sweet intercourse with men. Of course there is a "better sort of reliquae"; and the "Shells" or "Earth-walkers," as they are here called, are not necessarily *all* bad. But even those who are good are made bad for the time being by mediums. The "Shells" may well not care, since they have nothing to lose anyhow. But there is another kind of "Spirits" we have lost sight of; the suicides and those *killed by accident.* Both kinds can communicate, and both have to pay dearly for such visits. And now to explain what I mean. Well, this class is the one which the French Spiritists call "les esprits souffrants." They are an exception to the rule, as they have to remain within the earth's attraction and in its atmosphere—the Kama-loka—till the very last moment of what would have been the natural duration of their lives. In other words, that particular wave of life-evolution must run on to its shore. But it is a sin and cruelty to revive their memory and intensify their suffering by giving them a chance of living an artificial life, a chance to overload their Karma, by tempting them into open doors, *viz.,* mediums and sensitives, for they will have to pay roundly for every such pleasure.

I will explain. The *Suicides,* who, foolishly hoping to escape life, find themselves still alive, have suffering enough in store for them from that very life. Their punishment is in the intensity of the latter. Having lost by the rash act their 7th and 6th principles, though not forever, as they can regain both, instead of accepting their punishment and taking their chances of redemption, they are often made *to regret life* and tempted to regain a hold upon it by sinful means. In the *Kama-loka,* the land of intense desires, they can gratify their earthly yearnings only through a *living* proxy; and by so doing, at the expiration of the natural term, they generally lose their monad forever. As to the victims of accident, these fare still worse. Unless they were so good and pure as to be drawn immediately within the Akasic Samadhi, *i.e.,* to fall into a state of quiet slumber, a sleep full of rosy dreams, during which they have no recollection of the accident, but move and live among their familiar friends and scenes until their natural life-term is finished, when they find themselves born in the Devachan, a gloomy fate is theirs. Unhappy shades, if sinful and sensual they wander about (not shells, for their connection with their two higher principles is not quite broken) until their *death*-hour comes. Cut off in the full flush of earthly passions which bind them to familiar scenes, they are enticed by the opportunities which mediums afford, to gratify them vicariously. They are the Pisachas, the Incubi and Succubi of mediaeval times; the demons of thirst, gluttony, lust, and avarice; Elementaries of intensified craft, wickedness, and cruelty; provoking their victims to horrid crimes, and revelling in their commission! They not only ruin their victims, but these psychic vampires, borne along by the torrent of their hellish impulses, at last— at the fixed close of their natural period of life—they are carried out of the earth's aura into regions where for ages they endure exquisite suffering and end with entire destruction.

Now the causes producing the "new being" and determining the nature of *Karma* are *Trishna* (or tanha)—thirst, desire for sentient existence, and *Upadana,* which is the realisation or consummation of *trishna* or that desire. And both of these the medium helps to develop *ne plus ultra* in an Elementary, be he a suicide or a victim, (alone the Shells and Elementals are left unhurt, tho' the morality of the sensitives can by no means be improved by the intercourse). The rule is that a person who dies a natural death will remain from "a few hours to several short years" within the earth's attraction, *i.e.,* the Kama-loka. But exceptions are the cases of suicides and those who die a violent death in general. Hence one of such Egos who was destined to live—say 80 or 90 years, but who either killed himself or was killed by some accident, let us suppose at the age of 20, would have to pass in the Kama-loka not a few years but, in his case, 60 or 70 years as an Elementary or rather an "earth-walker," since he is not, unfortunately for him, even a "Shell." Happy, thrice happy, in comparison, are those disembodied entities who sleep their long slumber and live in dream in the bosom of Space! And woe to those whose *trishna* may attract them to mediums, and woe to the latter who tempt them with such an easy *upadana.* For in grasping them and satisfying their thirst for life, the medium helps to develop in them—is in fact the cause of—a new set of *Skandhas,* a new body, with far worse tendencies and passions than the one they lost. All the future of this new body will be determined thus, not only by the Karma of demerit of the previous set or group, but also by that of the new set of the future being. Were the mediums and spiritualists but to know, as I said, that with every new "angel guide" they welcome with rapture, they entice the latter into an upadana which will be productive of untold evils for the Ego that will be reborn under its nefarious shadow; that with every seance, especially for materialisation, they multiply the causes for misery, causes that will make the unfortunate Ego fail in his spiritual birth or be reborn into a far worse existence than ever; they would perhaps be less lavish in their hospitality. . . . It is through this that the gross and pernicious doctrine of spirit brides and husbands arises. But one day it will return to curse those who now are guilty of thus attracting these wandering shades into the vehicle of a medium's body; it is now cursing many men who find themselves forever in a mental hell, at war with themselves and with their best thoughts, they know not why. And if some poor suicide, drawn thus down into vicarious existence, "misses his spiritual birth" and loses the monad—the God within, shall no Karma strike those who were the remote or proximate agents? It will.   * * *

Path, August, 1889

KAMA LOKA—SUICIDES—ACCIDENTAL DEATHS

(Extracts from a Private Letter upon Kama Loka and Suicides)

SUICIDES, although not wholly dissevered from their 6th and 7th "principles," and quite potent in the spiritualistic seance room, nevertheless, until the day when they would have died a natural death, are separated from their higher principles by a gulf.

The 6th and 7th "principles" remain passive and negative, whereas, in cases of accidental death, the higher and the lower groups actually attract each other. In cases of good and innocent egos, moreover, the latter gravitate irresistibly toward the 6th and 7th, and thus either slumber surrounded by happy dreams, or sleep a dreamless profound sleep until the hour strikes. With a little reflection and an eye to the eternal justice and fitness of things, you will see why.

The victim of accidental death, whether good or bad, is irresponsible for his death. Even if his death were due to some action of his in a previous life or an antecedent birth, was, in short, the working of the law of retribution, still it was not the *direct* result of an act deliberately committed by the *personal* Ego of that life during which he happened to be killed. Had he been allowed to live longer, he might have atoned for his antecedent still more effectually; and even now, the Ego having been made to pay off the debt of his maker (the personal Ego), is free from the blows of retributive justice. The Dhyan Chohans, who have no hand in the guidance of the living human Ego, protect the hapless victim when it is violently thrust out of its element into a new one before it is matured and made fit and ready for that new place. *We tell you what we know, for we are made to learn it through personal experience.* Yes, the victims, whether good or bad, sleep to the *hour of the last judgment,* which is that hour of the supreme struggle between the 6th and 7th, and the 5th and 4th "principles" at the threshold of the gestation state. And even after that, when the

6th and 7th principles, carrying with them a portion of the 5th, have gone into their Akasic Samadhi, even then it may happen that the "spiritual spoil" from the 5th "principle" will prove too weak to be reborn in Devachan; in which case it will then reclothe itself in a new body—the subjective "Being" created from the Karma of the victim (or no victim, as the case may be), and enter upon a new earth-existence—whether that be upon this or some other planet.

In no case, then,—with the exception of suicides and shells—is there a possibility for any other to be attracted to a seance room. And it is clear that this is not opposition to our former teaching; "that while shells will be many, spirits very few."

Referring now to men who fall victim to their vices, classed by some among "suicides."

In our humble opinion there is a great difference between suicides and those men who through excess of vicious indulgence fall into an early grave. We, who look at it from a standpoint which would not be acceptable to a Life Insurance Company, say that there are very few, if any, of the men who indulge in these vices, who feel perfectly sure that such a course of action will lead them eventually to premature death. Such is the penalty of illusion. They will not escape from the punishment for their "vices," but it is the causes of the vices, and not the effect, that will receive punishment, especially an unforseen though probable effect. As well call a man a "suicide" who meets his death in a storm at sea, as one who kills himself with overstudy. Water is liable to drown a man, or too much brain work to produce a softening of that organ which may carry him away. In such a case no one ought to cross the Kalapani, or even to take a bath for fear of getting faint in it and drowning. And there are such cases. If such a view prevailed no man would do his duty, least of all sacrifice himself for even a laudable and highly beneficial cause, as many of us do. Motive is everything, and man is punished in a case of direct responsibility and not otherwise.

In a victim's case the natural hour of death was anticipated *accidentally,* while in that of the "suicide" death is brought on voluntarily and with a full and deliberate knowledge of its immediate consequences. Thus a man who causes his death in a fit of temporary insanity is *not* a *felo de se* to the great grief and often trouble of Life Insurance Companies. Nor is he left a prey to the temptations which assail us in the state of Kama Loka, but falls asleep like my other victim.

A Guiteau will not remain in the earth's atmosphere with his higher principles over him—inactive and paralyzed—still there. Guiteau is gone into a state during the period of which *he will be ever firing at his president*—thereby tossing into confusion and shuffling the destinies of millions of persons—when he will be *ever tried and ever hung,* ever bathing in the reflection in the astral light of his deeds and thoughts, and especially those in which he indulged in his last hour upon the scaffold. And it is so with every murderer who is hung or otherwise despatched. Those who were vicious and not insane are only partly killed on execution. They live over their crime and their punishment in that plane of the astral light in which they are, and from there they affect all persons in any way sensitive whom they can get at. Especially at spiritualistic seances they surround the medium. And any one who is naturally gifted with the power to see their plane of the astral light, or has the power from training, can see and hear over and over again the scenes of blood and punishment continually repeated in the vicinity of these unfortunates. In cases of collective murder, such as where many men enter or storm a building and cruelly kill the inmates after a prolonged struggle with the latter, the whole scene will often be re-enacted several times a year so strongly that many can see it with all its horrible details, and nearly all can hear the sounds, the groans, cries, falls of bodies, and slashing of human flesh.

*

*   *

Path, November, 1889

NOTES ON DEVACHAN

By X

DEVACHAN is not, cannot be, monotonous; for this would be contrary to all analogies and antagonistic to the laws of effects, under which results are proportionate to antecedent energies.

There are two fields of causal manifestations; the objective and the subjective. The grosser energies find their outcome in the new personality of each birth in the cycle of evolving individuality. The moral and spiritual activities find their sphere of effects in Devachan.

The dream of Devachan lasts until Karma is satisfied in that direction, until the ripple of force reaches the edge of its cyclic basin and the being moves into the next area of causes.

That particular one *moment* which will be most intense and uppermost in the thoughts of the dying brain at the moment of dissolution, will regulate all subsequent moments. The moment thus selected becomes the key-note of the whole harmony, around which cluster in endless variety all the aspirations and desires which in connection with that moment had ever crossed the dreamer's brain during his lifetime, without being realized on earth,—the theme modelling itself on, and taking shape from, that group of desires which was most intense during life.

In Devachan there is no cognizance of time, of which the Devachanee loses all sense.

(To realize the bliss of Devachan or the woes of Avitchi you have to assimilate them as we do.)

The *a priori* ideas of space and time do not control his perceptions; for he absolutely creates and annihilates them at the same time. Physical existence has its cumulative intensity from infancy to prime, and its diminishing energy to dotage and death; so the dream-life of Devachan is lived correspondentially. Nature cheats no more the *devachanee* than she does the living physical man. Nature provides for him far more *real* bliss and happiness *there* than she does *here,* where all the conditions of evil and chance are against him.

To call the devachan existence a "dream" in any other sense than that of a conventional term, is to renounce forever the knowledge of the esoteric doctrine, the sole custodian of truth. As in actual earth life, so there is for the Ego in Devachan the first flutter of psychic life, the attainment of prime, the gradual exhaustion of force passing into semi-consciousness and lethargy, total oblivion, and—not death, but birth, birth into another personality, and the resumption of action which daily begets new congeries of causes that must be worked out in another term of Devachan and still another physical birth as a new personality. What the lives in Devachan and upon earth shall be respectively in each instance is determined by Karma, and this weary round of birth must be ever and ever run through until the being reaches the end of the seventh round, or attains in the interim the wisdom of an Arhat, then that of a Buddha, and thus gets relieved for a round or two, having learned how to burst through the vicious circle and to pass into Para-Nirvana.

A colorless, flavorless personality has a colorless, feeble devachanic state.

There is a change of occupation, a continual change in Devachan, just as much and far more than there is in the life of any man or woman who happens to follow in his or her whole life one sole occupation, whatever it may be, with this difference, that to the Devachanee this spiritual occupation is always pleasant and fills his life with rapture. Life in Devachan is the function of the aspirations of earth life; not the indefinite prolongation of that "single instant," but its infinite developments, the various incidents and events based upon and outflowing from that one "single moment" or moments. The dreams of the objective become the realities of the subjective existence. Two sympathetic souls will each work out their own devachanic sensations, making the other a sharer in its subjective bliss, yet each is dissociated from the other as regards actual mutual intercourse; for what companionship could there be between subjective entities which are not even as material as that Ethereal body—the Mayavi Rupa?

The stay in Devachan is proportionate to the unexhausted psychic impulses originating in earth life. Those whose attractions were preponderatingly material will sooner be drawn back into rebirth by the force of Tanha.

The reward provided by nature for men who are benevolent in a large, systematic way, and who have not focussed their affections on an individual or specialty, is that if pure they pass the quicker for that thro' the Kama and Rupa lokas into the higher sphere of Tribuvana, since it is one where the formulation of abstract ideas and the consideration of general principles fill the thought of its occupant.

The Devachan, or land of "Sukhavati," is allegorically described by our Lord Buddha himself. What he said may be found in the *Shan-aun-yi-tung*. Says Tathagato: ". . . Many thousand myriads of systems beyond this (ours) there is a region of bliss called Sukhavati. This region is encircled within *seven* rows of railings, *seven* rows of vast curtains, *seven* rows of waving trees; this holy abode of *Arhats* is governed by the Tathagatos (Dhyan Chohans) and is possessed by the Bodhisatwas. It hath *seven* precious lakes in the midst from which flow crystal waters, having 'seven and one' properties or distinctive qualities (the seven principles emanating from the One). This, O Saryambra, is the 'Devachan.' Its divine udambara flower casts a root *in* the shadow of *every earth,* and blossoms for all those who reach it. Those born in the blessed region are truly felicitous; there are no more griefs or sorrow *in that cycle* for them . . . myriads of Spirits resort there for rest, and then return to their own regions. Again in that land, O Saryambra, many who are born in it are Ardivartyas, etc."

Certainly the new Ego, once that it is reborn (in Devachan), retains for a certain time—proportionate to its earth life,—a complete recollection "of his life on earth"; but it can never visit the earth from Devachan except in reincarnation.

"Who goes to Devachan?" The personal Ego, of course; but beatified, purified, holy. Every Ego—the combination of the sixth and seventh principles—which after the period of unconscious gestation is reborn into the Devachan, is of necessity as innocent and pure as a new born babe. The fact of his being reborn at all shows the preponderance of good over evil in his old personality. And, while the Karma (of Evil) steps aside for the time being to follow him in his future earth re-incarnation, he brings along with him but the Karma of his good deeds, words, and thoughts into this Devachan. "Bad" is a relative term for us—as you were told more than once before—and the Law of Retribution is the only law that never errs. Hence all those who have not slipped down into the mire of unredeemable sin and bestiality go to the Devachan. They will have to pay for their sins, voluntary and involuntary, later on. Meanwhile they are rewarded; receive the *effects* of the causes produced by them.

Of course it is a *state,* so to say, of *intense selfishness,* during which an *Ego* reaps the reward of his unselfishness on earth. He is completely engrossed in the bliss of all his personal earthly affections, preferences, and thoughts, and gathers in the fruit of his meritorious actions. No pain, no grief, nor even the shadow of a sorrow comes to darken the bright horizon of his unalloyed happiness: for it is a *state of perpetual "Maya."* Since the conscious perception of one's *personality* on Earth is but an evanescent dream, that sense will be equally that of a dream in the Devachan—only a hundred-fold intensified. So much so, indeed, that the happy Ego is unable to see through the veil of evils, sorrows, and woes to which those it loved on earth may be subjected. It lives in that sweet dream with its loved—whether gone before or yet remaining on earth; it has them near itself, as happy, as blissful, and as innocent as the disembodied dreamer himself; and yet, apart from rare visions, the denizens of our gross planet feel it not. It is in this—during such a condition of complete Maya—that the souls or astral Egos of pure loving sensitives, laboring under the same delusion, think their loved ones come down to them on earth, while it is their own spirits that are raised towards those in the Devachan.

Yes, there are great varieties in the Devachan states, and all find their appropriate place. As many varieties of bliss as on Earth there are of perception and of capability to appreciate such reward. It is an ideal paradise; in each case of the Ego's own making, and by him filled with the scenery, crowded with the incidents, and thronged with the people he would expect to find in such a sphere of compensative bliss. And it is that variety which guides the temporary personal Ego into the current which will lead him to be reborn in a lower or higher condition in the next world of causes. Everything is so harmoniously arranged in nature—especially in the subjective world—that no mistake can be ever committed by the Tathagatos who guide the impulses.

Devachan is a "spiritual condition" only as contrasted with our own grossly material condition, and, as already stated, it is such degrees of spirituality that constitute and determine the great varieties of conditions within the limits of Devachan. A mother from a savage tribe is not less happy than a mother from a royal palace, with her lost child in her arms; and altho', as actual Egos, children prematurely dying before the perfection of their septenary entity do not find their way to Devachan, yet all the same, the mother's loving fancy finds her children there without one missing that her heart yearns for. Say it is but a dream, but, after all, what is objective life itself but a panorama of vivid unrealities? The pleasure realized by a Red Indian in his "happy hunting grounds" in that land of dreams is not less intense than the ecstacy felt by a connoisseur who passes aeons in the rapt delight of listening to divine symphonies by imaginary angelic choirs and orchestras. As it is no fault of the former if born a "savage" with an instinct to kill—tho' it caused the death of many an innocent animal—why, if with it all he was a loving father, son, husband, why should he not also enjoy *his* share of reward? The case would be quite different if the same cruel acts had been done by an educated and civilized person, from a mere love of sport. The savage in being reborn would simply take a low place in the scale, by reason of his imperfect moral development; while the *Karma* of the other would be tainted with moral delinquency. . . .

Remember, that we ourselves create our Devachan, as also our Avitchi, while yet on earth, and mostly during the latter days and even moments of our intellectual sentient lives. That feeling which is strongest in us at that supreme hour, when, as in a dream, the events of a long life to their minutest detail are marshalled in the greatest order in a few seconds in our vision,* that feeling will become the fashioner of our bliss or woe, the life-principle of our future existence. In the latter we have no substantial being, but only a present and momentary existence, whose duration has no bearing upon, no effect nor relation to its being, which, as every other effect of a transitory cause, will be as fleeting, and in its turn will vanish and cease to be. The real, full remembrance of our lives will come but at the end of the minor cycle,—not before. . . .

Unless a man *loves* well, or *hates* well, he need not trouble him-

---

* That vision takes place when a person is already proclaimed dead. The Brain is the last organ that dies.

self about Devachan; he will be neither in *Devachan* nor Avitchi. "Nature spews the lukewarm out of her mouth" means only that she annihilates their *personal* Egos (not the Shells, nor yet the sixth principle) in the Kama-loka and the Devachan. This does not prevent them from being immediately reborn, and if their lives were not very, *very* bad, there is no reason why the eternal Monad should not find the page of that life intact in the Book of Life.

Path, May-June, 1890

DEVACHAN

A CORRESPONDENT writes to say that there seems to be some confusion or contradiction in theosophical literature and among theosophical writers in respect to the length of time a person stays in Devachan, and cites the statement by Mr. Sinnett that the number of years is 1500, while I am quoted as giving a shorter time. Two things should be always remembered. First, that Mr. Sinnett in writing on Devachan in *Esoteric Buddhism* was repeating his own understanding of what Mme. Blavatsky's teachers had communicated through her to him—a copy of each letter being kept and now accessible, and he might very easily make an error in a subject with which he was not at all familiar; second, that only the Adepts who gave out the information could possibly know the exact number of years for which any course of life would compel one to remain in the Devachanic state; and as those Adepts have spoken in other places on this subject, the views of Mr. Sinnett must be read in connection with those superior utterances.

There is in reality no confusion save in the way different students have taken the theory, and always the mistakes that have arisen flow from hastiness as well as inaccuracy in dealing with the matter as a theory which involves a knowledge of the laws of mental action.

In *Key to Theosophy*, p. 143, 158, H.P.B. says, "The stay in Devachan depends on the degree of spirituality and the merit or demerit of the last incarnation. The *average* time is from 1000 to 1500 years. . . . Whether that interval lasts one year or a million."

Here the average time means "the time for the average person who has any devachanic tendencies," for many "average persons" have no such tendencies; and the remark on p. 158 gives a possible difference of 500 years. This is exactly in accord with the theory, because in a matter which depends on the subtle action of mind solely it would be very difficult—and for most of us impossible—to lay down exact figures.

But the Adept K. H., who wrote most of the letters on which Mr. Sinnett's treatment of Devachan was based, wrote other letters, two of which were published in THE PATH, in Vol. 5 in 1890, without signature. The authorship of those *Notes on Devachan* is now divulged. They were attributed to "X." He says:

"The 'dream of Devachan' lasts *until Karma* is satisfied in that direction. In Devachan there is a gradual exhaustion of force.

"The stay in Devachan is *proportionate to the unexhausted psychic impulses* originating in earth life. Those whose attractions were preponderatingly material *will be sooner brought back* into rebirth by the force of Tanha."

Very clearly in this, as was always taught, it is stated that the going into Devachan depends upon psychic (which here means spiritual and of the nature of the soul) thoughts of earth life. So he who has not originated many such impulses will have but little basis or force in him to throw his higher principles into the Devachanic state. And the second paragraph of his letter shows that the materialistic thinker, having laid down no spiritual or psychic basis of thought, is "sooner brought back to rebirth by the force of Tanha," which means the pulling or magnetic force of the thirst for life inherent in all beings and fixed in the depths of their essential nature. In such a case the average rule has no application, since the whole effect either way is due to a balancing of forces and is the outcome of action and reaction. And this sort of materialistic thinker might emerge to rebirth out of the Devachanic state in about a month, because we have to allow for the expending of certain psychic impulses generated in childhood before materialism obtained full sway. But as every one varies in his force and in respect to the impulses he may generate, some of this class might stay in the Devachanic state one, five, ten, twenty years, and so on, in accordance with the power of the forces generated in earth life.

For these reasons, and having had H.P.B.'s views ever since 1875 on the subject, I wrote in PATH, V., 1890, p. 190, "In the first place I have never believed that the period given by Mr. Sinnett in *Esoteric Buddhism* of 1500 years for the stay in that state was a fixed fact in nature. It might be fifteen minutes as well as 1500 years. But it is quite likely that for the majority of those who so constantly wish for a release and for an enjoyment of heaven, the period would be more than 1500 years." This contradicts nothing unless Mr. Sinnett shall be shown as saying positively that every man and woman is bound by an arbitrary inflexible rule to stay 1500 years—no more nor less—in the Devachanic state; and this it is quite unlikely he could say, since it would involve a contradiction of the whole philosophy of man's nature in which he has faith. And what was said in Vol. 5 of PATH accords with the views of those Adepts who have written on the subject, as well as with the very ancient teachings there-upon in the *Bhagavad-Gita* and elsewhere.

In everyday life many illustrations can be found of the operation upon living men of the same force which puts disembodied men into Devachan. The artist, poet, musician, and day-dreamer constantly show it. When rapt in melody, composition, color arrangement, and even foolish fancy, they are in a sort of living Devachanic state wherein they often lose consciousness of time and sense impressions. Their stay in that condition depends, as we well know, on the impulses toward it which they have amassed. If they were not subject to the body and its forces they might remain years in their "dream." The same laws, applied to the man divested of a body, will give us exactly the results for Devachan. But no one save a trained mathematical Adept could sum up the forces and give us the total number of years or minutes which might measure Devachan. On the Adepts, therefore, we have to depend for a specific time-statement, and they have declared 1000 to 1500 years to be a good general average.

This will therefore result in giving us what may be known as the general *Cycle of Reincarnation* for the average mass of units in any civilization. By means of this a very good approximation may be made toward forecasting the probable development of national thought, if we work back century by century, or by decades of this century, for fifteen hundred years in history.

WILLIAM Q. JUDGE

Path, March, 1893

NOTES ON "THE BHAGAVAD GITA"

WE assume, quite justifiably, I think, that the *Bhagavad-Gita* sets forth Aryan philosophy. The Aryan is white and noble in contradistinction to the black and ignoble. This book then, if Aryan, must give us a noble system of philosophy and ethics, useful not only for speculative minds but also in daily life. Whoever was the author, he, or they, compressed into a short conversation—that is, short for Indians—the essence of religion and philosophy.

The singular manner in which this conversation or lecturing or teaching came about should be first noted. It is after the very beginning of a battle, for the arrows had already begun to fly from side to side. A rain of arrows would first be thrown in before the hand-to-hand encounter began. Arjuna and Krishna are in Arjuna's great chariot. And there, between the two armies, Arjuna asks for advice and receives it through eighteen chapters. All of this has significance.

Arjuna is man or the soul struggling to the light, and while Krishna was one of the Avatars or manifestations of God among men, he is also the Higher Self. Arjuna as man in this world of sense and matter is of necessity either always in a battle or about to begin one, and is also ever in need of advice. This he can get only in a valuable way from his Higher Self. So the singular manner of placing the conversation where it is, and of beginning it as it begins, is the only way it ought to be done.

Arjuna is the man in the life his Karma has produced, and he must fight out the battle he himself invited. Arjuna's object was to regain a kingdom, and so each one of us may know that our fight is for a kingdom gainable only by individual effort and not by anyone's favour.

From the remarks by Arjuna to Krishna we can perceive that the kingdom he—like ourselves—wishes to regain is the one he had in some former age upon this planet or upon some far more ancient one. He has too much insight, too much evident soul-power and wisdom to be an Ego who only for the first, or second, or third time had visited this earth. We likewise are not new. We have been here so many times that we ought to be beginning to learn. And we have not only been here, but beyond doubt those of us who are inwardly and outwardly engaged in the Theosophical movement for the good of others, have been in a similar movement before this life.

This being so, and there being yet many more lives to come, what is the reason we should in any way be downcast? The first chapter of the Book is really not only the survey of the armies, but also the despondency of the principal person—Arjuna. He grows downcast after looking over all the regiments and seeing that he had, on both sides, friends, teachers, relatives, as well as enemies. He falters because want of knowledge prevents him from seeing that the conflict and many apparent deaths are inevitable. And Krishna then proceeds to give him the true philosophy of man and the universe so that he can either fight or refrain from fighting, whichever he sees at any time the best.

Krishna leads him gradually. He plays upon his pride by telling him that if he backs out all men will say he is the most ignoble of all cowards; then he plays upon his Hindu religious teaching, telling him that a warrior must obey the rules of his caste, and fight. He does not plunge at once into high metaphysical speculation or show him occult wonders. And herein it seems to me is a good lesson for all working Theosophists. Too many of us when trying to spread forth the theosophical teaching drag the poor Arjunas we have caught right into obscure realms where Theosophists themselves know nothing at all but terminology. Krishna's wise, practical and simple method should be followed, and much better results will be obtained. Our object is to spread theosophical philosophy as widely and quickly as possible. This cannot be done if we indulge in words and phrases far removed from daily life. What good does it do to talk about the Absolute, Parabrahm and Alaya, and to say *manas* when we mean mind, and *kama* when desire and passion are the English equivalents? It only puzzles the new enquirer, who feels that he has to learn a new language before he will be able to do anything with Theosophy. It is a good deal easier to show that the new terms can be learned afterwards.

The first chapter having introduced the practical question of life, the second is equally practical, for it directs attention at the outset to the larger and eternal life of which each incarnation is a day or a moment. For Krishna says:

> I myself never was not, nor thou, nor all the princes of the earth; nor shall we ever hereafter cease to be. As the Lord of this mortal frame experienceth therein infancy, youth and old age, so in future incarnations will it meet the same. One who is confirmed in this belief is not disturbed by anything that may come to pass.

Thus, continued *practical* existence as opposed to continued theoretical and so-called heavenly existence, and as opposed to materialistic annihilation, is declared at once. This is true immortality. The Christian Bible has no word in the original, teaching immortality such as this; and the preaching of the priests does not lean to an unselfish view of continued existence. And it is very certain that if one is fully confirmed in the knowledge of eternal life through reincarnation he is quite unlikely to be disturbed by things that disturb other people. So at the very outset the teachings of Krishna open up a tremendous vista of life, and confer a calmness most necessary for us in the fight.

The generality of men have many and widely branching objects for mental devotion. It is a devotion to sense, or to self, or to wrong belief or to improper practice. But the follower of the *Bhagavad-Gita* gradually comes to see that the true devotion is that which has but one object through all changes of scene, of thought, or of companionship. That object is the Self which is all in all. The Self, as object, is immovable, whereas the objects taken up by the unwise are movable and transitory.

Equal mindedness and skill in the right performance of duty are the true rules—this is yoga. This right performance of duty, means the mental state, for the mere performance of an act has no moral quality in it, since even a machine may be made to perform acts usually done by men. The moral quality resides in the person inside and in his presence or absence. If a human body, asleep or devoid of a soul, raised its hand and took the life of another, that would not be a crime. And oppositely the performance of a good act is no virtue unless the person within is in the right attitude of mind. Many an apparently good act is done from selfish, hypocritical, crafty or other wrong motives. These are only outwardly good. So we must attain to a proper state of mind, or mental devotion, in order to know how to skillfully perform our actions without doing so for the sake of the result; doing them because they ought to be done, because they are our duties.

Krishna warns Arjuna also against inactivity from a false view of the philosophy. This warning necessary then is so still. On hearing this teaching for the first time many say that it teaches inaction, sitting still, silence. And in India great numbers taking that view, retired from life and its duties, going into the caves and jungles away from men. Krishna says:—

"Firmly persisting in yoga perform thy duty."

To endeavour to follow these rules empirically, without understanding the philosophy and without making the fundamental doctrines a part of oneself, will lead to nothing but disgust and failure. Hence the philosophy must be understood. It is the philosophy of Oneness or Unity. The Supreme Self is one and includes all apparent others. We delude ourselves with the idea that we are separate. We must admit that we and every other person are the Self. From this we will begin to see that we may cease to be the actor although outwardly doing every act that is right. We can cease to be the actor when we know we can withdraw ourselves from the act. Attachment to the act arises from a self-interest in the result that is to follow. It is possible for us to do these things without that self-interest, and if we are trying to follow the rule of doing our actions because they ought to be done we will at last do only that which is right to be done.

A great deal of the unhappiness of life comes from having a number of interests in results which do not come out as expected. We find people pretending to believe in Providence and to rely on the Almighty but who are continually laying down plans for those powers to follow. They are not followed, and as the poor mortal fixed his mind and heart on the result, unhappiness follows.

But there is a greater unhappiness and misery caused by acting, as is the usual way, for the sake of results. It is this that causes rebirth over and over again unendingly. It is by this that the great humdrum mass of men and women are whirled around the wheel of rebirth for ages, always suffering, because they do not know what is happening to them, and only by an accident altering the poor character of births incessantly repeated.

The mind is the actor, the person who is attached. When it is deluded it is not able to throw off the subtle chains that bind it to reincarnation. Having spent an incarnation in looking after results it is full of earthly impressions, and has made the outer skandhas very powerful. So when its stay in Devachan is at its end the old images, impressions and the powerful skandhas drag it back to another life. At the time of bodily death the mind is temporarily almost altered into the image of the dominant thought of life, and so is beside itself or insane by comparison with the sage and with what ought to be its proper state. Being so it is impossible for it either to prevent rebirth or to select and take up an incarnation with a definite end and work in the world in view.

The bearing of the teaching upon ethics is in my opinion very important. It gives a vital system as opposed to a mechanical one. We are to do our duty with the thought that we are acting for and as the Supreme Being, because that Being acts only by and through the creatures. If this be our real rule it would in time be impossible for us to do wrong, for constantly thinking thus we grow careful as to what acts we commit and are always clearing up our view of duty as we proceed.

On the other hand a mechanical code of ethics leads to error. It is convenient because any fixed code is more convenient to follow than the application of broad principles in brotherly spirit. Mechanical codes are conventional and for that reason they lead to hypocrisy. They have led people to mistake etiquette for morality. They cause the follower of them to unrighteously judge his neighbour who does not come up to his conventional code which is part of his ethics. It was a mechanical system of ethics that permitted and encouraged the Inquisition, and similar ethics in our later days permit men professing the highest altruism to persecute their brothers in the same way in intention. If the law and liberty of the times were not opposed they would slay and torture too.

But I have only time to touch lightly upon some of the many valuable points found in the first two chapters. If but those two chapters were preserved and the others lost, we would still have enough.

The remaining chapters deal with universal cosmical truths as well as with philosophy and ethics. They all enforce the great doctrine of unity or non-separateness. In going over them we find such references as require us to know and to believe in the Wisdom-Religion. The rise and destruction of races is given, the obscurities and darkness between evolutionary periods, the universal great destructions and the minor ones are there. Through all these the Self sits calmly looking on as the spectator, the witness, the receptacle.

Where Arjuna the Archer is, he who was taught by Krishna, with him is glory, honour, fortune and success. He who knows Arjuna knows himself.

WILLIAM BREHON

Path, September, 1895

SOME VIEWS OF AN ASIATIC

YOU ask me what is my belief about "reincarnation." Well,
as it is a complicated question, I must give you a plain
statement of my full belief. To begin with, I am a Pantheist.
I believe that *the whole universe is God.* You must, however, well
understand that the word "God" does not convey to me any
meaning attached to that word by the Westerns. When I say "God"
I understand it to be nature or universe, and no more. Therefore
I might more appropriately be called a "naturalist." To my mind
there is no possibility of the existence of an extra-cosmical Deity.
For if there were, the harmony or equilibrium of nature could not
be preserved, and the whole, instead of being one harmonious
whole, would be a Tower of Babel. This harmony can be kept
only by the working of the immutable laws of Nature. And if the
laws of nature be immutable, they must be blind, and require no
guiding hand.[1] Hence the existence of an extra-cosmical Deity is
impossible. This is, as far as I can understand, the chief teaching
and principle of Aryan philosophy. As the position is logical, I
must accept it in preference to the Semitic theory, which rests on
blind faith alone.

Some of the Pantheists recognize the existence of two distinct
entities, viz, Matter and Spirit. But thinking deeply over the subject has lead me to the conclusion that their position is not quite
logical; for, as far as I can understand, there can be but one Infinite
entity and not two. Call it either matter or spirit, but it is one and
the same. Who can say that this is spirit and that matter? Take
an instance: Ice is a gross form of matter. If a little rarified it will
be water, which is still matter. Higher still it is vapor; still matter.
Higher, gas; it is still matter. Further it becomes ether, but it is still
matter; and then you may go on *ad infinitum.* Thus becoming more
and more sublimated, it will reach its climax by the way of spiritualization. But still it does not become nothing. For if it does, there

---

Note.—Portions of this letter by Damodar K. Mavalankar to Wm. Q. Judge
appeared in *The Platonist,* and later in *The Theosophist,* June, 1884, under the title
"Reincarnation." It is reprinted here from *The Path,* with Mr. Judge's footnotes.

1 Allowance must be made all through for a lack of complete knowledge of the
English language. What is here meant is that the inherent impulse acts according to its
own laws without any *extra-cosmic* power meddling with it as a guide.—EDITOR

must come a time when the whole universe will be nothing. If it is so, it is not infinite, as it has an end. If it has an end, it must have had a beginning; if it had a beginning, it must have been created; and thus we must assume the existence of an extra-cosmical Deity, which, as said above, is not logical. Then we thus logically find that this highest sublimated form of matter cannot be nothing. In this case matter has reached that climax of sublimation or spiritualization, when any further action would make it grosser, not finer. What is commonly understood by the word *spirit,* then, is nothing but that highly etherealized form of matter which we, with our finite senses, cannot comprehend. But it is still matter, inasmuch as it is still something and liable to be grosser.

There is then *only one* eternal infinite existence, call it either spirit or matter. I will, however, call it by the latter name, as that is most suited in its common understanding for what I am to state. Matter, as you know, we call *Maya.* Some say that this thing does not really exist; but I do not agree to that. In my opinion it is called Maya *simply on account of these transformations.* It is never steady. The process is ever working. The one infinite agglomeration of matter is in some of its modes becoming grosser, while in others becoming more sublimated. The circle is ever turning its round. Nothing goes out of that circle. Everything is kept within its bounds by the action of the centripetal and centrifugal forces. The *forms* are changing, but the *inner substance* remains the same.

You will ask: "What is the use of being good or bad; our souls in proper time will be etherealized?" But what is a soul? Is it material or immaterial? Well, it is material for me, and there is nothing immaterial, as we said above. As far as I can think, it is an agglomeration of all the attributes together with that something which gives us the consciousness that we *are.* But in the case of the ice, it was not sublimated until touched by heat. The centripetal force was strong in its action, and it required the centrifugal force to refine the ice. Just so with man. The action of the centripetal force keeps us to our gross forms, and if we have to etherealize ourselves, we must supply the centrifugal force, which is our *will.* And this is the first principle of Occultism. We must study and know the forces of nature. Every result must be in proportion to the cause producing it. We are every instant emitting and attracting atoms of matter. Now, a person who is not an occultist will have various desires, and unconsciously to himself he will produce a cause which will attract to him such atoms of matter as are not suited for his higher progress. The same way, when he is emitting others, he may give them such a tendency that they will mix with others evilly inclined; and thus other individualities, which are thus formed, will have to suffer for no fault of theirs. But an occultist directs both. He is the master of the situation. He guides them, and by knowing their action he produces such conditions as are favorable to his obtaining of "Nirvana."

But what is *Nirvana?* By Nirvana I mean a *state,* and not a locality. It is that condition in which we are so etherealized that instead of being merely a mode of the Infinite Existence, as at present, we are merged in totality, or we become the *whole.*[1] Another thing about the advanced occultist is that he is in a better position to benefit humanity.

The particles of which I am formed have always existed; yet I do not know in what form they existed before. Probably they have passed through billions of transformations.[2] Why do I not know these? Because I did not supply the force that would have prevented the disintegration of my individuality.[3] I will, if I attain Nirvana, remain there till the action of the force that put me there ceases; the effect being always in proportion to the cause. The law of Exhaustion must assert itself.[4]

In passing through this process of etherealization, you all along give a certain tendency to the particles of which you are composed. This tendency will always assert itself; and thus in every cycle, or reincarnation, you will have the same advantages which you can always utilize to soon be free, and by remaining longer in the Nirvana state than the generality of humanity, you are comparatively free.[5] So every consciousness, which has been once

---

1 It is said that Buddha attained to Nirvana before he left this earth, hence he was always free.—EDITOR.

2 That all the particles of the matter of our universe have passed through millions of transformations, and been in every sort of form, is an old assertion of the Adepts. H.P.B. in *Isis Unveiled,* and the *Secret Doctrine* points this out as showing how the Adept may use matter, and it will also bear upon the protean shapes the astral matter may assume.—EDITOR.

3 This word is used to mean the personalities; the person in any birth. Since the letter was written, *individuality* is much used to mean the indestructible part.—EDITOR.

4 If this be right—and I agree with it—Nirvana has to come to an end, just as Devachan must; and being ended, the individual must return to some manifested plane or world for further work.—EDITOR.

5 The comparison made is with the general run of men in all races. They are not free at any time. In the writer's opinion there is a certain amount of freedom in being in Nirvana, but he refers to other and secret doctrines which he does not explain.—EDITOR.

fully developed, must disintegrate, if not preserved by the purity of its successive Egos till the Nirvana state is attained. Now I believe that the full development of my consciousness as Krishna is possible only on this earth,[1] and therefore if I die before that is done I must be reborn here. If I reach the Nirvana state, even though I am in another body, I shall know myself as Krishna.

Now I suppose this is sufficient for you. It is difficult to put such ideas on paper. Such things are to be understood intuititionally.

* * *

Path, January, 1896

---

1 This has always been accepted, that only on earth could we unify the great potential trinity in each, so that we are conscious of the union, and that when that is done, and not before, we may triumph over all illusions, whether of name or form, place or time,

A FRIEND OF OLD TIME AND OF THE FUTURE

As such does William Q. Judge appear to me, as doubtless he does to many others in this and other lands.

The first Theosophical treatise that I read was his *Epitome of Theosophy;* my first meeting with him changed the whole current of my life. I trusted him then, as I trust him now and all those whom he trusted; to me it seems that "trust" is the bond that binds, makes the strength of the Movement, for it is of the heart. And this trust he called forth was not allowed to remain a blind trust, for as time went on, as the energy, steadfastness and devotion of the student became more marked, the "real W.Q.J." was more and more revealed, until the power that radiated through him became in each an ever present help in the work. As such it remains to-day, a living centre in each heart that trusted him, a focus for the Rays of the coming "great messenger."

Having been engaged in active T. S. work in Boston for over seven years, it has been my Karma to be brought in touch with him under many different circumstances, the various crises, local and general, through which the Society has safely passed. In all these, his was the voice that encouraged or admonished, this the hand that guided matters to a harmonious issue. Of his extraordinary power of organization, his marvellous insight into the character and capacity of individuals, his ability of turning seeming evils into powers for good, I have had many proofs.

That he was a "great occultist" many know by individual experience, but none have fathomed the depths of his power and knowledge. The future will reveal much in regard to him that is now hidden, will show the real scope of his life-work. We know that to us that life-work has been an inestimable boon, and that through us it must be bestowed on others. The lines have been laid down for us by H.P.B., W.Q.J., and Masters, and we can take again as our watchword, that which he gave us at the passing of H.P.B., "Work, watch, and wait." We will not have long to wait.

ROBERT CROSBIE

Path, May, 1896

OTHER SOURCES

THE DWELLERS ON HIGH MOUNTAINS

AN account of the dwellers upon high mountains would be incomplete without some reference to a widespread belief prevailing in Hindustan in regard to authorities and others, who are said to dwell in inaccessible places, and who are now and then seen by natives. It is true that all over India are to be found Fakirs of much or little sanctity, and of greater or less accumulation of dirt, but the natives all tell of Fakirs, as many of us would call them, who dwell alone in places remote from the habitation of man, and who are regarded with a feeling of veneration very different from that which is accorded to the ordinary traveling devotee.

The Hindu has an intense religious nature and says that devotion to religious contemplation is one of the highest walks in life. He therefore looks upon the traveling ascetic as one who by means of renunciation has gained a great degree of advancement toward final bliss, and he says that there are other men who are farther advanced in this line of practice. These others finding the magnetism or exhalations from ordinary people and from places where persons congregate to be inimical to further progress, have retired to spots difficult to find even when sought for, and not at all likely to be stumbled upon by accident. For that reason they select high mountains, because the path worn by man in going from place to place on earth are always by that route which is the shortest or most easy of travel, just as electricity by a law of its being will always follow the line of least resistance and quickest access.

And so English and French travelers tell of meeting from time to time with natives who repeat local traditions and lore relating to some very holy man who lives alone upon some neighboring mountain, where he devotes his time to contemplating the universe as a whole, and in trying to reach, if he may, final emancipation.

The name given to these men is "mahatma," meaning, in English, "great soul," because it is claimed that they could not renounce the world and its pleasures unless they possessed souls more noble and of greater dynamic force than the souls of the mere

---

NOTE.—Place and date of original publication of this article are unknown to us.—EDS.

ordinary man, who is content to live on through ages of reincarnations round the great wheel of the universe, awaiting a happy chanceful deliverance from the bond of matter some day.

The great traveler, the Abbé Huc, who went over a large part of Thibet and put his wonderful experiences, as a Catholic missionary there, into an interesting book of travels, refers often to these men with a different name. But he establishes the fact beyond dispute that they are believed to live as related, and to possess extraordinary power over the forces of nature, or as the learned and pious Abbé would say, an intimate and personal combination with the devil himself, who in return does great and miraculous works for them.

The French traveler Jacolliot also attests to the wide extent of the belief in these extraordinary men whose lesser disciples he claims to have seen and have had perform for him extraordinary and hair-raising feats of magic, which they said to him they were enabled to do by the power transmitted to them from their guru or teacher, one of the Mahatmas, a dweller on some high mountain.

It seems they assert that the air circulating around the tops of mountains of great altitude is very pure and untainted with the emanations from animals or man and that, therefore, the Mahatmas can see spiritually better and do more to advance their control over nature by living in such pure surroundings. There is indeed much to be said in favor of the sanitary virtue of such a residence. Upon a raw, moist day, down upon the level of our cities, one can easily see, made heavily and oppressively visible, the steamy exhalation from both human beings and quadrupeds. The fact that upon a fine day we do not see this is not proof that on those days the emanations are stopped. Science declares that they go on all the time, and are simply made palpable by the natural process of the settling of moisture upon cold and damp days.

Among Europeans in India all stories respecting the dwellers upon high mountains to whom we are referring are received in two ways. One is that which simply permits it to be asserted that such men exist, receiving the proposition with a shrug of either indifference or lack of faith. The other, that one which admits the truth of the proposition while wondering how it is to be proved. Many officers of the English army have testified to a belief in these traditions and many to not only belief, but also to have had ocular demonstrations of their wonderful powers. While the other side is simply represented by those who are unable to say that they ever had any proof at all.

The Hindu says that his ancient sages have always lived in these high places, safe from contamination and near the infinite. It is related that the pilgrims who annually do the round of pilgrimage through the sacred places of India, sometimes penetrate as far as a certain little temple on the sides of the sky-reaching Himalayas, and that in this is a brass tablet of great age stating that that is the highest point to which it is safe to go; and that from there one can now and then see, looking down at you from the cold and distant cliff still higher up, men of grave and venerable aspect. These are said by some to be the Mahatmas or great souls, dwelling up there alone and unsought. In Thibet the story can be heard any time of the Sacred Mountain where the great souls of the earth meet for converse and communion.

The Hindu early saw that his conquerors, the Dutch and English, were unable as well as incapable of appreciating his views of devotion and devotees, and therefore maintained a rather exasperating silence and claim of ignorance on such matters. But here and there when a listener, who was not also a scoffer, was found, he unbosomed himself, and it is now generally admitted by all well-informed Anglo-Indians and Indian scholars that there is a universal belief in these Mahatmas, or dwellers upon high mountains, extending from one end of India to the other throughout every caste.

For the Christian it ought to be significant here, that when Jehovah commanded Moses to attend him for instruction and to receive the law, he did not set the place of meeting in the plain, but designated Mount Sinai, a high place of awful ruggedness, and more or less inaccessible. Then in that high mountain he hid Moses in the cleft of the rock while he passed by, and from that high mountain, now roll and reverberate through Christendom the thunders of the Judaic law. All through the Semitic book, this peculiar connection of great events and men with high mountains is noticeable. Abraham, when he was ordered to sacrifice Isaac, received command to proceed to Mount Moriah. Sadly enough he set forth, not acquainting either the human victim or his family with his determination, and traveled some weary days to reach the appointed spot.

The thoughtful man will see the indicia of a unity of plan and action in nearly all these occurrences. The sacrifice of Isaac could with great ease and perfect propriety have been offered on the plain, but Abraham is made to go a long distance in order to reach the summit of a high mountain. And when he reached it, made his preparations, and piously lifted the fatal blade—he was restrained, and his son restored to him.

Passing rapidly through long centuries from the great patriarch down to Jesus of Nazareth, we find him preaching his most celebrated sermon not in the synagogue or at the corners of the streets, but from the mount, and from there also he distributes to the hungry multitude the loaves and fishes. Again, he is transfigured, but not in the city nor outside in view of all the people, but with two disciples he returns to the summit of a high mountain, and there the wonderful glory sat upon him. Or we watch him in the wilderness, only to see him again on a high mountain, where he resists the Arch temptation. And then, when the appointed hour for the veiling from human gaze of his earthly life is come, we have to follow him up the steep sides of the Mount Golgotha, where, in agony of body and woe of soul, with words of appealing anguish, his spirit flies to the father.

The story of Mohammed, that world-famed descendant of Ishmael, is closely associated with high mountains. He often sought the quiet and solitude of the hills to restore his health and increase his faith. It was while he was in the wilds of Mount Hira that the Angel Gabriel appeared to him, and told him he was Mohammed, the prophet of God, and to fear not. In his youth Mohammed had wandered much upon the sides and along the summits of high ranges of mountains. There the mighty trees waved their arms at him in appeal, while the sad, long traveling wind sighed pityingly through their branches, and the trembling leaves added to the force of the mighty cry of nature. Upon those mountains he was not oppressed by care nor by the adverse influences of his fellows, such as kept him down when he was one merely of a lot of camel drivers. So, then, when he returned to the mountain's clear and wide expansive view, his spiritual eyes and ears heard more than the simple moaning of the wind and saw greater meaning than unconscious motion in the beckoning of the trees. There he saw the vision of the different heavens, peopled by lovely houris, garlanded with flowers, and musical with the majestic tones of the universe; and then, too, he saw handed to him the sword with which he was to compel all people to bow to Allah and his prophet.

The countries of all the earth are full of similar traditions. In South America, Humboldt heard the story of the wonderful people who are said to dwell unfound among the inaccessible Cordilleras and, stern traveler that he was, he set out to find some trace of them. He went so far as to leave after him a fragment of testimony of his belief that somewhere in those awful wilds a people could easily live, and perhaps did.

It was from a high mountain where he had long lived, that Peter the Hermit rushed down upon Europe with his hordes of Crusaders, men, women and children, to wrest the holy land from the profaning hand of the Saracen; and the force and fury of the feelings that inspired William Tell were drawn in upon the tops of his native high mountain, to whom upon his return, he cried:

> Ye crags and peaks,
> I am with you once again.

Japan, the highly civilized country of Islands so long buried from European sight, and Corea, which has only just partly opened a door of communication, have always venerated a high mountain. This is called Fujiyama. They say that it can be seen from any part of the world and they regard it as extremely sacred. Its top is cold and covered with snow, while round its base the corn waves to the touch of the zephyr, and the flowers bloom.

The love for this mountain is so great that it is pictured on their china, in their paintings, and reproduced wherever possible, whether in mural decoration or elaborated carvings. Its sacredness is due to its being the residence, as they claim, of holy persons. And they also believe that there is, too, a spiritual Fujiyama, whose base is on earth and top in heaven.

WILLIAM Q. JUDGE

The Word, June, 1912

"THE SECRET DOCTRINE"
AND ITS STUDY

*Being extracts from the notes of personal teachings
given by H. P. Blavatsky to private pupils during
the years 1888 to 1891, included in a large manuscript volume left to me by my father, who was one
of the pupils.*

—P. G. BOWEN

H P. B. was specially interesting upon the matter of "The
Secret Doctrine" during the past week. I had better try to
sort it all out and get it safely down on paper while it is
fresh in my mind. As she said herself, it may be useful to someone
thirty or forty years hence. *The Secret Doctrine* is only quite a
small fragment of Esoteric Doctrine known to the higher members
of the Occult Brotherhoods. It contains, she says, just as much as
can be received by the world during this coming century. "The
World" (she explained) means Man living in the Personal Nature.
This "world" will find in the two volumes of the *S.D.* all its utmost
comprehension can grasp, but no more. But this is not to say that
the Disciple who is not living in "the world" cannot find any more
in the book than the "world" finds. Every form, no matter how
crude, contains the image of its "creator" concealed within it.
So likewise does an author's work, no matter how obscure, contain
the concealed image of the author's knowledge. . . . From this
saying, I take it that the *S.D.* must contain all that H.P.B. knows
herself, and a great deal more than that, seeing that much of it
comes from men whose knowledge is immensely wider than hers.
Furthermore, she implies unmistakably that another may well find
knowledge in it which she does not possess herself. It is a stimulat-
ing thought to consider that it is possible that I myself may find in
H.P.B.'s words knowledge of which she herself is unconscious.
She dwelt on this idea a good deal. X said afterwards: "H.P.B.
must be losing her grip," meaning, I suppose, confidence in her
own knowledge. But . . . and . . . and myself, also, see her meaning
better, I think. She is telling us without a doubt not to anchor ourselves to her as the final authority, nor to anyone else, but to de-

pend altogether upon our own widening perceptions.

(Later note on above: I was right. I put it to her direct and she nodded and smiled. It was worth something to get her approving smile!)

At last we have managed to get H.P.B. to put us right on the matter of the study of the *S.D.* Let me get it down while it is all fresh in mind. Reading the *S.D.* page by page as one reads any other book (she says) will only end us in confusion. The first thing to do, even if it takes years, is to get some grasp of the "Three Fundamental Principles" given in the Proem. Follow that up by study of the Recapitulation—the numbered items in the Summing Up to Volume I, Part I. Then take the Preliminary Notes (Vol. II) and the Conclusion (Vol. II) . . . .

H.P.B. seems pretty definite about the importance of the teaching (in the Conclusion) relating to the times of coming of the Races and Sub-Races. She put it more plainly than usual that there is really no such thing as a future "coming" of races. "There is neither COMING nor PASSING, but eternal BECOMING," she says. The Fourth Root-Race is still alive. So are the Third and Second and First— that is, their manifestations on our present plane of substance are present. I know what she means, I think, but it is beyond me to get it down in words. So likewise the Sixth Sub-Race is here, and the Sixth Root-Race, and the Seventh, and even people of the coming Rounds. After all, that's understandable. Disciples and Brothers and Adepts can't be people of the everyday Fifth Sub-Race, for the race is a state of evolution.

But she leaves no question but that, as far as humanity at large goes, we are hundreds of years (in time and space) from even the Sixth Sub-Race. I thought H.P.B. showed a peculiar anxiety in her insistence on this point. She hinted at "dangers and delusions" coming through ideas that the New Race had dawned definitely on the World. According to her the duration of a Sub-Race [Family-Race?—See *S.D.* II, 435] for humanity at large coincides with that of the Sidereal Year (the circle of the earth's axis—about 25,000 years). That puts the new race a long way off.

We have had a remarkable session on the study of the *S.D.* during the past three weeks. I must sort out my notes and get the result safely down before I lose them.

She talked a good deal about the "Fundamental Principles." She says: "If one imagines that one is going to get a satisfactory picture of the constitution of the Universe from the *S.D.* one will get only confusion from its study. It is not meant to give any such final verdict on existence, but to *lead towards the truth.*" She repeated this latter expression many times. It is worse than useless going to those whom we imagine to be advanced students (she said) and asking them to give us an "interpretation" of the *S.D.* They cannot do it. If they try, all they give are cut and dried exoteric renderings which do not remotely resemble the Truth. To accept such interpretation means anchoring ourselves to fixed ideas, whereas Truth lies beyond any ideas we can formulate or express. Exoteric interpretations are all very well, and she does not condemn them so long as they are taken as pointers for beginners, and are not accepted by them as anything more. Many persons who are in, or will in the future be in, the T.S. are of course potentially incapable of any advance beyond the range of a common exoteric conception. But there are, and will be others, and for them she sets out the following and true way of approach to the *S.D.*

Come to the *S.D.* (she says) without any hope of getting the final Truth of existence from it, or with any idea other than seeing how far it may lead *towards* the Truth. See in study a means of exercising and developing the mind never touched by other studies. Observe the following rules.

No matter what one may study in the *S.D.* let the mind hold fast, as the basis of its ideation to the following ideas:

a) *The fundamental unity of all existence.* This unity is a thing altogether different from the common notion of unity—as when we say that a nation or an army is united; or that this planet is united to that by lines of magnetic force or the like. The teaching is not that. It is that existence is *one thing,* not any collection of things linked together. Fundamentally, there is ONE BEING. This has two aspects, positive and negative. The positive is Spirit, or *consciousness.* The negative is substance, the *subject* of consciousness. This Being is the Absolute in its primary manifestation. Being absolute there is nothing outside it. It is ALL BEING. It is indivisible, else it would not be absolute. If a portion could be separated, that remaining could not be absolute, because there would at once arise the question of *comparison* between it and the separated part. Comparison is incompatible with any idea of absoluteness. Therefore it is clear that this fundamental One Existence, or Absolute Being, must be the Reality in every form there is. . . . (I said that though this was clear to me I did not think that many in the Lodges would grasp it. "Theosophy," she said, "is for those who can think, or for those who can drive themselves to think, not mental sluggards." H.P.B. has grown very mild of late, "Dumbskulls" used to be her name for the average student.)

The Atom, the Man, the God (she says) are each separately, as well as all collectively, Absolute Being in their last analysis, that is their *real individuality*. It is this idea which must be held always in the background of the mind to form the basis for every conception that arises from study of the *S.D.* The moment one lets it go (and it is most easy to do so when engaged in any of the many intricate aspects of the Esoteric Philosophy) the idea of separation supervenes, and the study loses its value.

b) The second idea to hold fast to is that *there is no dead matter*. Every last atom is alive. It cannot be otherwise, since every atom is itself fundamentally Absolute Being. Therefore there is no such thing as "spaces of ether," or Akasha, or call it what you like, in which angels and elementals disport themselves like trout in water. That's the common idea. The true idea shows every atom of substance, no matter of what plane, to be in itself a *life*.

c) The third basic idea to be held is that Man is the microcosm. As he is so, then all the Hierarchies of the Heavens exist within him. But in truth there is neither Macrocosm nor Microcosm but ONE EXISTENCE. Great and small are such only as viewed by a limited consciousness.

d) Fourth and last basic idea to be held is that expressed in the Great Hermetic Axiom. It really sums up and synthesizes all the others: "As is the inner, so is the outer; as is the great, so is the small; as it is above, so it is below; there is but One Life and Law: and he that worketh it is ONE. Nothing is inner, nothing is outer; nothing is great, nothing is small; nothing is high, nothing is low, in the Divine Economy."

No matter what one takes as study in the *S.D.* one must correlate it with those basic ideas.

I suggested that this is a kind of mental exercise which must be excessively fatiguing. H.P.B. smiled and nodded. One must not be a fool (she said) and drive oneself into the madhouse by attempting too much at first. The brain is the instrument of waking consciousness, and every conscious mental picture formed means change and destruction of the atoms of the brain. Ordinary intellectual activity moves on well-beaten paths in the brain, and does not compel sudden adjustments and destructions in its substance. But this new kind of mental effort calls for something very different—the carving out of new "brain paths," the ranking in different order of the little brain lives. If forced injudiciously it may do serious physical harm to the brain.

This mode of thinking (she says) is what the Indians call *Jnana Yoga*. As one progresses in *Jnana Yoga* one finds conceptions arising which, though one is conscious of them, one cannot express nor yet formulate into any sort of mental picture. As time goes on these conceptions will form into mental pictures. This is a time to be on guard and refuse to be deluded with the idea that the new-found and wonderful picture must represent reality. It does not. As one works on, one finds the once admired picture growing dull and unsatisfying and finally fading out or being thrown away. This is another danger point, because for the moment one is left in a void without any conception to support one, and one may be tempted to revive the cast-off picture for want of a better to cling to. The true student will, however, work on unconcerned, and presently further formless gleams come, which again in time give rise to a larger and more beautiful picture than the last. But the learner will now know that no picture will ever represent the truth. This last splendid picture will grow dull and fade like the others. And so the process goes on, until at last the mind and its pictures are transcended and the learner enters and dwells in the world of no-form, but of which all forms are narrowed reflections.

The true student of *The Secret Doctrine* is a *Jnana Yoga,* and this Path of Yoga is the True Path for the Western student. It is to provide him with sign-posts on that Path that *The Secret Doctrine* has been written.

Later note: I have read over this rendering of her teaching to H.P.B. asking if I have got her aright. She called me a silly dumb-skull to imagine anything can ever be put in words aright. But she smiled and nodded as well, and said I had really got it better than anyone else ever did, and better than she could do it herself.

I wonder why I am getting all this. It should be passed to the world, but I am too old ever to do it. I feel such a child to H.P.B. yet I am twenty years older than her in actual years.

She has changed much since I met her two years ago. It is marvelous how she holds up in the face of dire illness. If one knew nothing and believed nothing, H.P.B. would convince one that she is something away and beyond body and brain. I feel, especially during these last meetings since she has become so helpless bodily, that we are getting teachings from another and higher sphere. We seem to feel and know what she says rather than hear it with our bodily ears. X said much the same thing last night.

—ROBERT BOWEN
(Comdr.) R.N.

19th April, 1891

The Theosophical Forum, August, 1932

FROM "THE OCCULT WORLD"

[A.P. Sinnett's book, *The Occult World,* published in 1881, begins by contrasting occult and modern science, the author attempting to explain the policy of secrecy and retirement characteristic of advanced occultists. From his own experience, Sinnett assures his readers that, far from desiring to prove their powers or advertise their knowledge, the members of the Adept fraternity purposely avoid all publicity. It is *he*—not the Adepts—who is trying to convince the world of their existence and win a hearing for their philosophy. Determined to devise an infallible "proof" of Adept power, Sinnett proposed a test phenomenon be performed. The Mahatma's reply to this proposal and his comments on other matters are of value to students.

Since *The Occult World* has long been out of print, extracts from the Mahatma's correspondence are reprinted with some of Sinnett's accompanying narrative.—Eds]

ONE day, therefore, I asked Madame Blavatsky whether if I wrote a letter to one of the Brothers explaining my views, she could get it delivered for me. I hardly thought this was probable, as I knew how very unapproachable the Brothers generally are; but as she said that at any rate she would try, I wrote a letter, addressing it "to the Unknown Brother," and gave it to her to see if any result would ensue. . . . The idea I had specially in mind when I wrote the letter. . . , was that of all test phenomena one could wish for, the best would be the production in our presence in India of a copy of the London *Times* of that day's date. With such a piece of evidence in my hand, I argued, I would undertake to convert everybody in Simla who was capable of linking two ideas together, to a belief in the possibility of obtaining by occult agency physical results which were beyond the control of ordinary science. . . .

A day or two elapsed before I heard anything of the fate of my letter, but Madame Blavatsky then informed me that I was to have an answer. . . . Hearing this, I at once regretted that I had not written at greater length, arguing my view of the required concession more fully. I wrote again, therefore, without waiting for the actual receipt of the expected letter.

A day or two after, I found one evening on my writing table the first letter sent me by my new correspondent. I may here explain, what I learned afterwards, that he was a native of the Punjab who was attracted to occult studies from his earliest boyhood. He was sent to Europe while still a youth at the intervention of a relative—himself an occultist—to be educated in Western knowledge, and since then has been fully initiated in the greater knowledge of the East. From the self-complacent point of view of the ordinary European this will seem a strange reversal of the proper order of things, but I need not stop to examine that consideration now. My correspondent is known to me as the Mahatma Koot Hoomi. . . .

The letter I received began, *in medias res,* about the phenomena I had professed. "Precisely," the Mahatma wrote, "because the test of the London newspaper would close the mouths of the sceptics," it was inadmissable. "See it in what light you will, the world is yet in its first stage of disenthralment . . . hence unprepared. Very true we work by natural, not supernatural, means and laws. But as on the one hand science would find itself unable, in its present state, to account for the wonders given in its name, and on the other the ignorant masses would still be left to view the phenomenon in the light of a miracle, everyone who would thus be made a witness to the occurrence would be thrown off his balance, and the result would be deplorable. Believe me it would be so especially for yourself, who originated the idea, and for the devoted woman who so foolishly rushes into the wide, open door leading to notoriety. This door, though opened by so friendly a hand as yours, would prove very soon a trap—and a fatal one, indeed, for her. And such is not surely your object. . . .

"Were we to accede to your desires, know you really what consequences would follow in the trail of success? The inexorable shadow which follows all human innovations moves on, yet few are they who are ever conscious of its approach and dangers. What are, then, they to expect who would offer the world an innovation which, owing to human ignorance, if believed in, will surely be attributed to those dark agencies the two-thirds of humanity believe in and dread as yet? . . . The success of an attempt of such a kind as the one you propose must be calculated and based upon a thorough knowledge of the people around you. It depends entirely upon the social and moral conditions of the people in their bearing on these deepest and most mysterious questions which can stir the human mind—the deific powers in man and the possibilities contained in Nature. How many even of your best friends, of those who surround you, are more than superficially interested in these abstruse problems? You could count them upon the fingers of your right hand. Your race boasts of having liberated in their century the genius so long imprisoned in the narrow vase of dogmatism and intolerance—the genius of knowledge, wisdom, and free thought. It says that, in their turn, ignorant prejudice and religious bigotry, bottled up like the wicked *djin* of old, and sealed by the Solomons of science, rest at the bottom of the sea, and can never, escaping to the surface again, reign over the world as in the days of old: that the public mind is quite free, in short, and ready to accept any demonstrated truth.

"Ay, but is it verily so, my respected friend? Experimental knowledge does not quite date from 1662, when Bacon, Robert Boyle, and the Bishop of Chester transformed under the royal charter their 'invisible college' into a society for the promotion of experimental science. Ages before the Royal Society found itself becoming a reality upon the plan of the 'Prophetic Scheme,' an innate longing for the hidden, a passionate love for, and study of, Nature, had led men in every generation to try and fathom her secrets deeper than their neighbors did. *Roma ante Romulum fuit* [Rome was, before Romulus] is an axiom taught us in your English schools. . . . The *Vril* of the *Coming Race* was the common property of races now extinct. And as the very existence of those gigantic ancestors of ours is now questioned—though in the Himavats, on the very territory belonging to you, we have a cave full of the skeletons of these giants—and their huge frames, when found, are invariably regarded as isolated freaks of Nature—so the *vril,* or *akas* as we call it, is looked upon as an impossibility— a myth. And without a thorough knowledge of *akas*—its combinations and properties, how can science hope to account for such phenomena?

"We doubt not but the men of your science are open to conviction; yet facts must be first demonstrated to them; they must first have become their own property, have proved amenable to their modes of investigation, before you find them ready to admit them as facts. If you but look into the preface of the *Micrographia* you will find, in Hookes' suggestions, that the intimate relations of objects were of less account in his eyes than their external operation on the senses, and Newton's fine discoveries found in him their greatest opponent. The modern Hookeses are many. Like this learned but ignorant man of old, your modern men of science are less anxious to suggest a physical connection of facts which might unlock for them many an occult force in Nature, than to provide a convenient classification of scientific experiments, so that the most essential quality of a hypothesis is, not that it should be *true,* but only *plausible,* in their opinion.

"So far for science—as much as we know of it. As for human nature in general, it is the same now as it was a million years ago. Prejudice, based upon selfishness, a general unwillingness to give up an established order of things for new modes of life and thought—and occult study requires all that and much more— pride and stubborn resistance to truth, if it but upsets their previous notions of things—such are the characteristics of your age. . . . What, then, would be the results of the most astounding phenomena, supposing we consented to have them produced? However successful, danger would be growing proportionately with success. No choice would soon remain but to go on, ever *crescendo,* or to fall in this endless struggle with prejudice and ignorance, killed by your own weapons. Test after test would be required, and would have to be furnished; every subsequent phenomenon expected to be more marvellous than the preceding one. Your daily remark is, that one cannot be expected to believe unless he becomes an eye-witness. Would the lifetime of a man suffice to satisfy the whole world of sceptics?

"It may be an easy matter to increase the original number of believers at Simla to hundreds and thousands. But what of the hundreds of millions of those who could not be made eye-witness? The ignorant, unable to grapple with the invisible operators, might some day vent their rage on the visible agents at work; the higher and educated classes would go on disbelieving, as ever, tearing you to shreds as before. In common with many, you blame us for our great secrecy. Yet we know something of human nature, for the experience of long centuries—ay, ages, has taught us. And we know that so long as science has anything to learn, and a shadow of religious dogmatism lingers in the hearts of the multitudes, the world's prejudices have to be conquered step by step, not at a rush. As hoary antiquity had more than one Socrates, so the dim future will give birth to more than one martyr. Enfranchised Science contemptuously turned away her face from the Copernican opinion renewing the theories of Aristarchus Samius, who 'affirmeth that the earth moveth circularly about her own centre,' years before the Church sought to sacrifice Galileo as a *holocaust* to the Bible. The ablest mathematician at the Court of Edward VI., Robert Recorde, was left to starve in jail by his colleagues, who laughed at his *Castle of Knowledge,* declaring his discoveries vain phantasies. Wm. Gilbert of Colchester—Queen Elizabeth's physician—died poisoned, only because—this real founder of experimental science in England—has had the audacity of anticipating Galileo; of pointing out Copernicus' fallacy as to the 'third movement,' which was gravely alleged to account for the parallelism of the earth's axis of rotation! The enormous learning of the Paracelsi, of the Agrippas and the Deys was ever doubted. It was science which laid her sacrilegious hand upon the great work 'De Magnete'—'The Heavenly White Virgin' (*Akas*) and others. And it was the illustrious 'Chancellor of England and of Nature'—Lord Verulam-Bacon—who having won the name of the Father of Inductive Philosophy, permitted himself to speak of such men as the above-named as the 'Alchemicians of the Fantastic philosophy.'

"All this is old history, you will think. Verily so, but the chronicles of our modern days do not differ very essentially from their predecessors. And we have but to bear in mind the recent persecutions of mediums in England, the burning of supposed witches and sorcerers in South America, Russia, and the frontiers of Spain, to assure ourselves that the only salvation of the genuine proficient in occult sciences lies in the scepticism of the public: the charlatans and the jugglers are the natural shields of the adepts. The public safety is only ensured by our keeping secret the terrible weapons which might otherwise be used against it, and which, as you have been told, become deadly in the hands of the wicked and selfish."

I [Sinnett] replied to the letter above quoted at some length, arguing, if I remember rightly, that the European mind was less hopelessly intractable than Koot Hoomi represented it. His second letter was as follows:—

"We will be at cross purposes in our correspondence until it has been made entirely plain that occult science has its own methods of research, as fixed and arbitrary as the methods of its antithesis, physical science, are in their way. If the latter has its dicta, so also have the former; and he who would cross the boundary of the unseen world can no more prescribe how he will proceed, than the traveller who tries to penetrate to the inner subterranean recesses of L'Hassa the Blessed could show the way to his guide. The mysteries never were, never can be, put within the reach of the general public, not, at least, until that longed-for day when our religious philosophy becomes universal. At no time have more than a scarcely appreciable minority of men possessed Nature's secret, though multitudes have witnessed the practical evidences of the possibility of their possession. The adept is the rare efflorescence of a generation of inquirers; and to become one, he must obey the inward impulse of his soul, irrespective of the prudential considerations of worldly science or sagacity.

"Your desire is to be brought to communicate with one of us directly, without the agency of either Madame Blavatsky or any medium. Your idea would be, as I understand it, to obtain such communications, either by letters, as the present one, or by audible words, so as to be guided by one of us in the management, and principally in the instruction of the Society. You seek all this, and yet, as you say yourself, hitherto you have not found sufficient reasons to even give up your modes of life, directly hostile to such modes of communication. This is hardly reasonable. He who would lift up high the banner of mysticism and proclaim its reign near at hand must give the example to others. He must be the first to change his modes of life, and, regarding the study of the occult mysteries as the upper step in the ladder of knowledge, must loudly proclaim it such, despite exact science and the opposition of society. 'The kingdom of Heaven is obtained by force,' say the Christian mystics. It is but with armed hand, and ready to either conquer or perish, that the modern mystic can hope to achieve his object.

"My first answer covered, I believe, most of the questions contained in your second and even third letter. Having, then, expressed therein my opinion that the world in general was unripe for any too staggering proof of occult power, there but remains to deal with the isolated individuals who seek, like yourself, to penetrate behind the veil of matter into the world of primal causes—*i.e.*, we need only consider now the cases of yourself and Mr. Hume."

I [Sinnett] should explain that one of my friends at Simla,*

---

* A.O. Hume, who was a prominent Anglo-Indian official and a famous ornithologist.—Eds.

deeply interested with me in the progress of this investigation, had, on reading Koot Hoomi's first letter to me, addressed my correspondent himself. More favourably circumstanced than I, for such an enterprise, he had even proposed to make a complete sacrifice of his other pursuits, to pass away into any distant seclusion which might be appointed for the purpose, where he might, if accepted as a pupil in occultism, learn enough to return to the world armed with powers which would enable him to demonstrate the realities of spiritual development and the errors of modern materialism, and then devote his life to the task of combating modern incredulity and leading men to a practical comprehension of a better life. I resume the letter:—

"This gentleman also has done me the great honour to address me by name, offering to me a few questions, and stating the conditions upon which he would be willing to work for us seriously. But your motives and aspirations being of diametrically opposite character, and hence leading to different results, I must reply to each of you separately.

"The first and chief consideration in determining us to accept or reject your offer lies in the inner motive which propels you to seek our instruction and, in a certain sense, our guidance; the latter in all cases under reserve, as I understand it, and therefore remaining a question independent of aught else. Now, what are your motives? I may try to define them in their general aspects, leaving details for further consideration. They are—(1) the desire to see positive and unimpeachable proofs that there really are forces in Nature of which science knows nothing; (2) the hope to appropriate them some day—the sooner the better, for you do not like to wait—so as to enable yourself (*a*) to demonstrate their existence to a few chosen Western minds, (*b*) to contemplate future life as an objective reality built upon the rock of knowledge, not of faith, and (*c*) to finally learn—most important this, among all your motives, perhaps, though the most occult and the best guarded—the whole truth about our lodges and ourselves; to get, in short, the positive assurance that the 'Brothers,' of whom everyone hears so much and sees so little, are real entities, not fictions of a disordered, hallucinated brain. Such, viewed in their best light, appear to us your motives for addressing me. And in the same spirit do I answer them, hoping that my sincerity will not be interpreted in a wrong way, or attributed to anything like an unfriendly spirit.

"To our minds, then, these motives, sincere and worthy of every serious consideration from the worldly standpoint, appear *selfish*. (You have to pardon me what you might view as crudeness of language, if your desire is that which you really profess—to learn truth and get instruction from us who belong to quite a different world from the one you move in.) They are selfish, because you must be aware that the chief object of the Theosophical Society is not so much to gratify individual aspirations as to serve our fellow-men, and the real value of this term 'selfish,' which may jar upon your ear, has a peculiar significance with us which it cannot have with you: therefore, to begin with, you must not accept it otherwise than in the former sense. Perhaps you will better appreciate our meaning when told that in our view the highest aspirations for the welfare of humanity become tainted with selfishness, if, in the mind of the philanthropist, there lurks the shadow of a desire for self-benefit, or a tendency to do injustice, even where these exist unconsciously to himself. Yet you have ever discussed, but to put down, the idea of a Universal Brotherhood, questioned its usefulness, and advised to remodel the Theosophical Society on the principle of a college for the special study of occultism. This, my respected and esteemed friend and brother—will never do!

"Having disposed of personal motives, let us analyze your terms for helping us to do public good. Broadly stated, these terms are— first, that an independent Anglo-Indian Theosophical Society shall be founded through your kind services, in the management of which neither of our present representatives shall have any voice, and second, that one of us shall take the new body 'under his patronage,' be 'in free and direct communication with its leaders,' and afford them 'direct proof that he really possessed that superior knowledge of the forces of Nature and the attributes of the human soul which would inspire them with proper confidence in his leadership.' I have copied your own words so as to avoid inaccuracy in defining the position.

"From your point of view, therefore, those terms may seem so very reasonable as to provoke no dissent, and, indeed, a majority of your countrymen—if not of Europeans—might share that opinion. What, will you say, can be more reasonable than to ask that that teacher anxious to disseminate his knowledge, and pupil offering him to do so, should be brought face to face, and the one give the experimental proof to the other that his instructions were correct? Man of the world, living in, and in full sympathy with it, you are undoubtedly right. But the men of this other world of ours, untutored in your modes of thought, and who find it very hard at times to follow and appreciate the latter, can hardly be blamed for not responding as heartily to your suggestions as in your opinion they deserve. The first and most important of our objections is to be found in our *rules*. True, we have our schools and teachers, our neophytes and 'shaberons' (superior adepts) and the door is always opened to the right man who knocks. And we invariably welcome the new comer; only, instead of going over to him, he has to come to us. More than that, unless he has reached that point in the path of occultism from which return is impossible by his having irrevocably pledged himself to our Association, we never—except in cases of utmost moment—visit him or even cross the threshold of his door in visible appearance.

"Is any of you so eager for knowledge and the beneficent powers it confers, as to be ready to leave your world and come into ours? Then let him come, but he must not think to return until the seal of the mysteries has locked his lips even against the chances of his own weakness or indiscretion. Let him come by all means as a pupil to the master, and without conditions, or let him wait, as so many others have, and be satisfied with such crumbs of knowledge as may fall in his way. And supposing you were thus to come, as two of your own countrymen have already—as Madame B. [H. P. Blavatsky] did and Mr. O. [H. S. Olcott] will—supposing you were to abandon all for the truth; to toil wearily for years up the hard, steep road, not daunted by obstacles, firm under every temptation; were to faithfully keep within your heart the secrets entrusted to you as a trial; had worked with all your energies and unselfishly to spread the truth and provoke men to correct thinking and a correct life—would you consider it just, if, after all your efforts, we were to grant to Madame B., or Mr. O. as 'outsiders' the terms you now ask for yourselves? Of these two persons, one has already given three-fourths of a life, the other six years of manhood's prime to us, and both will so labour to the close of their days; though ever working for their merited reward, yet never demanding it, nor murmuring when disappointed. Even though they respectively could accomplish far less than they do, would it not be a palpable injustice to ignore them in an important field of Theosophical effort? Ingratitude is not among our vices, nor do we imagine you would wish to advise it.

"Neither of them has the least inclination to interfere with the management of the contemplated Anglo-Indian Branch, nor dictate its officers. But the new Society, if formed at all, must, though bearing a distinctive title of its own, be, in fact, a branch of the parent body, as is the British Theosophical Society at London, and contribute to its vitality and usefulness by promoting its leading idea of a Universal Brotherhood,* and in other practicable ways.

"Badly as the phenomena may have been shown, there have still been, as yourself admit, certain ones that are unimpeachable. The 'raps on the table when no one touches it,' and the 'bell sounds in the air,' have, you say, always been regarded as satisfactory, &c, &c. From this, you reason that good test phenomena 'may easily be multiplied *ad infinitum.*' So they can—in any place where our magnetic and other conditions are constantly offered, and where we do not have to act with and through an enfeebled female body, in which, as we might say, a vital cyclone is raging much of the time. But imperfect as may be our visible agent, yet she is the best available at present, and her phenomena have for about half a century astonished and baffled some of the cleverest minds of the age. . . ."

Madame Blavatsky [Mr. Sinnett writes] had been deeply hurt by the behaviour of some incredulous persons at Simla whom she had met at our house and elsewhere, who, being unable to assimilate the experience they had had of her phenomena, got by degrees into that hostile frame of mind which is one of the phases of feeling I am now used to seeing developed. Perfectly unable to show how the phenomena can be the result of fraud, but thinking that, because they do not understand them, they must be fraudulent, people of a certain temperament become possessed with the spirit which animated persecution by religious authorities in the infancy of physical science. And, by a piece of bad luck, a gentleman who was thus affected was annoyed at a trifling indiscretion on the part of Colonel Olcott, who, in a letter to one of the Bombay papers, quoted some expressions he had made use of in praise of the Theosophical Society and its good influence on the natives. All the irritation thus set up, worked on Madame Blavatsky's excitable temperament to an extent which only those who know her will be

---

* "The term 'Universal Brotherhood'," the Adept writes in another letter, "is no idle phrase. Humanity in the mass has a paramount claim upon us, as I try to explain in my letter to Mr. Hume, which you had better ask the loan of. It is the only secure foundation for universal morality. If it be a dream, it is at least a noble one for mankind; and it is the aspiration of the *true adept.*"—EDS.

able to imagine. The allusions in Koot Hoomi's letter will now be understood. After some reference to important business with which he had been concerned since writing to me last, Koot Hoomi went on:—

"You see, then, that we have weightier matters than small societies to think about; yet the Theosophical Society must not be neglected. The affair has taken an impulse which, if not well guided, might beget very evil issues. Recall to mind the avalanches of your admired Alps, and remember that at first their mass is small, and their momentum little. A trite comparison, you may say, but I cannot think of a better illustration when viewing the gradual aggregation of trifling events growing into a menacing destiny for the Theosophical Society. It came quite forcibly upon me the other day as I was coming down the defiles of Konenlun—Karakorum you call them—and saw an avalanche tumble. I had gone personally to our chief. . . . and was crossing over to Lhadak on my way home. What other speculations might have followed I cannot say. But just as I was taking advantage of the awful stillness which usually follows such cataclysms, to get a clearer view of the present situation, and the disposition of the 'mystics' at Simla, I was rudely recalled to my senses. A familiar voice, as shrill as one attributed to Saraswati's peacock—which, if we may credit tradition, frightened off the King of the Nagas—shouted along the current —'. . . Koot Hoomi come quicker and help me!' and in her excitement, forgot she was speaking English. I must say that the 'Old Lady's' telegrams do strike one like stones from a catapult.

"What could I do but come? Argument through space with one who was in cold despair and in a state of moral chaos, was useless. So I determined to emerge from a seclusion of many years, and spend some time with her to comfort her as well as I could. But our friend is not one to cause her mind to reflect the philosophical resignation of Marcus Aurelius. The Fates never wrote that she could say:—'It is a royal thing when one is doing good to hear evil spoken of himself,' I had come for a few days, but now find that I myself cannot endure for any length of time the stifling magnetism even of my own countrymen. I have seen some of our proud old Sikhs drunk and staggering over the marble pavement of their sacred temple. I have heard an English-speaking Vakil declaim against Yog Vidya and Theosophy as a delusion and a lie, declaring that English science had emancipated them from such degrading superstitions, and saying that it was an insult to India to maintain that the dirty Yogees and Sannyasis knew anything about the mysteries of Nature, or that any living man can, or ever could, perform any phenomena. I turn my face homeward tomorrow.

". . . I have telegraphed you my thanks for your obliging compliance with my wishes in the matter you allude to in your letter of the 24th. . . . Received at Amritsur, on the 27th, at 2 P.M. I got your letter about thirty miles beyond Rawul Pinder, five minutes later, and had an acknowledgement wired to you from Jhelum at 4 P.M. on the same afternoon. Our modes of accelerated delivery and quick communication* are not, then, as you will see, to be despised by the Western world, or even the Aryan English-speaking and skeptical vakils.

" I could not ask a more judicial frame of mind in an ally than that in which you are beginning to find yourself. My brother, you have already changed your attitude toward us in a distinct degree. What is to prevent a perfect mutual understanding one day? . . . It is not possible that there should be much more at best than a benevolent neutrality shown by your people toward ours. There is so very minute a point of contact between the two civilizations they respectively represent, that one might almost say they could not touch at all. Nor would they, but for the few—shall I say eccentrics?—who, like you, dream better and bolder dreams than the rest, and, provoking thought, bring the two together by their own admirable audacity."

The letter before me at present [writes Sinnett] is occupied so much with matters personal to myself, that I can only make quotations here and there; but these are specially interesting, as investing with an air of reality subjects which are generally treated in vague and pompous language. Koot Hoomi was anxious to guard me from idealizing the Brothers too much on the strength of my admiration for their marvellous powers.

"Are you certain," he writes, "that the pleasant impression you now may have from our correspondence would not instantly be destroyed upon seeing me? And which of our holy *shaberons* has had the benefit of even the little university education and inkling of

---

*Many old Indians, and some books about the Indian Mutiny, take note of the perfectly incomprehensible way news of events transpiring at a distance would sometimes be found to have penetrated the native bazaars before it had reached the Europeans at such places by the quickest means of communication at their disposal. . . . (A.P.S.)

European manners that has fallen to my share? An instance: I desired Madame Blavatsky to select, among the two or three Aryan Punjabees who study Yog Vidya and are natural mystics, one whom, without disclosing myself to him too much, I could designate as an agent between yourself and us, and whom I was anxious to dispatch to you with a letter of introduction, and have him to speak to you of Yoga and its practical effects. This young gentleman, who is as pure as purity itself, whose aspirations and thoughts are of the most spiritual, ennobling kind, and who, merely through self-exertion, is able to penetrate into the regions of the formless world—this young man is not fit for a drawing-room. Having explained to him that the greatest good might result for his country if he helped you to organize a branch of English mystics, by proving to them practically to what wonderful results led the study of Yog, Madame Blavatsky asked him, in guarded and very delicate terms, to change his dress and turban before starting for Allahabad; for—though she did not give him this reason—they were very dirty and slovenly. You are to tell Mr. Sinnett, she said, that you bring him a letter from the Brother, with whom he corresponds; but if he asks you anything either of him or the other Brothers, answer him simply and truthfully that you are not allowed to expatiate upon the subject. Speak of Yog, and prove to him what powers you have attained. This young man who had consented, wrote later on the following curious letter:—'Madame,' he said, 'you who preach the highest standard of morality, or truthfulness, &c., you would have me play the part of an imposter. You ask me to change my clothes at the risk of giving a false idea of my personality and mystifying the gentleman you send me to. . . .' Here is an illustration of the difficulties under which we have to labour. Powerless to send you a neophyte before you have pledged yourself to us, we have to either keep back or despatch to you one who, at best, would shock, if not inspire you at once with disgust." . . . In a guarded way Koot Hoomi said that as often as it was practicable to communicate with me, "whether by dreams, waking impressions, letters (in or out of pillows) or personal visits in astral form, it will be done. But remember," he added, "that Simla is 7,000 feet higher than Allahabad, and the difficulties to be surmounted at the latter are tremendous." To the ordinary mind, feats of "magic" are hardly distinguishable by degrees of difficulty, and the little hint contained in the last sentence may thus help to show that, magical as the phenomena of the Brothers appear (as soon as the dull-witted hypothesis of fraud is abandoned), they are magic of a kind which is amenable to its own laws.

I am here enabled [Sinnett writes] to insert the greater part of a letter addressed by Koot Hoomi to the friend referred to in a former passage,* as having opened up a correspondence with him in reference to the idea which he contemplated under certain conditions, of devoting himself entirely to the pursuit of occultism. This letter throws a great deal of light upon some of the metaphysical conceptions of the occultists, and their metaphysics, be it remembered, are a great deal more than abstract speculation.

"Dear Sir—Availing of the first moments of leisure to formally answer your letter of the 17th ultimo, I will now report the result of my conference with our chiefs upon the proposition therein contained, trying at the same time to answer all your questions.

"I am first to thank you on behalf of the whole section of our fraternity that is especially interested in the welfare of India for an offer of help whose importance and sincerity no one can doubt. Tracing our lineage through the vicissitudes of Indian civilization from a remote past, we have a love for our mother-land so deep and passionate that it has survived even the broadening and cosmopolitanizing (pardon me if that is not an English word) effect of our studies in the laws of Nature. And so I, and every other Indian patriot, feel the strongest gratitude for every kind word or deed that is given in her behalf.

"Imagine, then, that since we are all convinced that the degradation of India is largely due to the suffocation of her ancient spirituality, and that whatever helps to restore that higher standard of thought and morals, must be regenerating in national force, every one of us would naturally and without urging, be disposed to push forward a society untainted by selfish motive, and whose object is the revival of ancient science, and tendency, to rehabilitate our country in the world's estimation. Take this for granted without further asseverations. But you know, as any man who has read history, that patriots may burst their hearts in vain if circumstances are against them. Sometimes it has happened that no human power, not even the fury and force of the loftiest patriotism, has been able to bend an iron destiny aside from its fixed course, and nations have gone out like torches dropped into the water in the engulfing blackness of ruin. Thus, we who have the sense of our country's

---

* A. O. Hume, Sinnett's associate in the proposed new "branch" of the T.S.—EDS.

fall, though not the power to lift her up at once, cannot do as we would either as to general affairs or this particular one. And with the readiness, but not the right to meet your advances more than half way, we are forced to say that the idea entertained by Mr. Sinnett and yourself is impracticable in part. It is, in a word, impossible for myself or any Brother, or even an advanced neophyte, to be specially assigned and set apart as the guiding spirit or chief of the Anglo-Indian branch. We know it would be a good thing to have you and a few of your colleagues regularly instructed and shown the phenomena and their rationale. For though none but you few would be convinced, still it would be a decided gain to have even a few Englishmen, of first-class ability, enlisted as students of Asiatic Psychology. We are aware of all this, and much more; hence we do not refuse to correspond with, and otherwise help you in various ways. But what we do refuse is, to take any other responsibility upon ourselves than this periodical correspondence and assistance with our advice, and, as occasion favours, such tangible, possibly visible proofs, as would satisfy you of our presence and interest. To 'guide' you we will not consent. However much we may be able to do, yet we can promise only to give you the full measure of your deserts. Deserve much, and we will prove honest debtors; little, and you need only expect a compensating return.

"This is not a mere text taken from a schoolboy's copybook, though it sounds so, but only the clumsy statement of the law of our order, and we cannot transcend it. Utterly unacquainted with Western, especially English, modes of thought and action, were we to meddle in an organization of such a kind, you would find all your fixed habits and traditions incessantly clashing, if not with the new aspirations themselves, at least with their modes of realization as suggested by us. You could not get unanimous consent to go even the length you might yourself.

"I have asked Mr. Sinnett to draft a plan embodying your joint ideas for submission to our chiefs, this seeming the shortest way to a mutual agreement. Under our 'guidance' your branch could not live, you not being men to be guided at all in that sense. Hence the society would be a premature birth and a failure, looking as incongruous as a Paris Daumont drawn by a team of Indian yaks or camels. You ask us to teach you true science—the occult aspect of the known side of Nature; and this you think can be as easily done as asked. You do not seem to realize the tremendous difficulties in the way of imparting even the rudiments of *our* science to those who have been trained in the familiar methods of yours. You do not see that the more you have of the one the less capable you are of instinctively comprehending the other, for a man can only think in his worn grooves, and unless he has the courage to fill up these, and make new ones for himself, he must perforce travel on the old lines.

"Allow me a few instances. In conformity with exact science you would define but one cosmic energy, and see no difference between the energy expended by the traveller who pushes aside the bush that obstructs his path, and the scientific experimenter who expends an equal amount of energy in setting a pendulum in motion. We do; for we know there is a world of difference between the two. The one uselessly dissipates and scatters force, the other concentrates and stores it. And here please understand that I do not refer to the relative utility of the two, as one might imagine, but only to the fact that in the one case there is but brute force flung out without any transmutation of that brute energy into the higher potential form of spiritual dynamics, and in the other there is just that.

"Please do not consider me vaguely metaphysical. The idea I wish to convey is that the result of the highest intellection in the scientifically occupied brain is the evolution of a sublimated form of spiritual energy, which, in the cosmic action, is productive of illimitable results; while the automatically acting brain holds, or stores up in itself, only a certain quantum of brute force that is unfruitful of benefit for the individual or humanity. The human brain is an exhaustless generator of the most refined quality of cosmic force out of the low, brute energy of Nature; and the complete adept has made himself a centre from which irradiate potentialities that beget correlations upon correlations through Æons of time to come. This is the key to the mystery of his being able to project into and materialize in the visible world the forms that his imagination has constructed out of inert cosmic matter in the invisible world. The adept does not create anything new, but only utilizes and manipulates materials which Nature has in store around him, and material which, throughout eternities, has passed through all the forms. He has but to choose the one he wants, and recall it into objective existence. Would not this sound to one of your 'learned' biologists like a madman's dream?

"You say there are few branches of science with which you do not possess more or less acquaintance, and that you believe you are doing a certain amount of good, having acquired the position to do this by long years of study. Doubtless you do; but will you permit me to sketch for you still more clearly the difference between the modes of physical (called 'exact' often out of mere compliment) and metaphysical sciences? The latter, as you know, being incapable of verification before mixed audiences, is classed by Mr. Tyndall with the fictions of poetry. The realistic science of fact, on the other hand, is utterly prosaic. Now, for us, poor unknown philanthropists, no fact of either of these sciences is interesting except in the degree of its potentiality of moral results, and in the ratio of its usefulness to mankind. And what, in its proud isolation, can be more utterly indifferent to everyone and everything, or more bound to nothing but the selfish requisites for its advancement, than this materialistic science of fact?

"May I ask then, . . . what have the laws of Faraday, Tyndall, or others to do with philanthropy in their abstract relations with humanity, viewed as an intelligent whole? What care they for *Man* as an isolated atom of this great and harmonious whole, even though they may be sometimes of practical use to him? Cosmic energy is something eternal and incessant; matter is indestructible: and there stand the scientific facts. Doubt them, and you are an ignoramus; deny them, a dangerous lunatic, a bigot; pretend to improve upon the theories—an impertinent charlatan. And yet even these scientific facts never suggested any proof to the world of experimenters that Nature consciously prefers that matter should be indestructible under organic rather than inorganic forms, and that she works slowly but incessantly towards the realization of this object—the evolution of conscious life out of inert material. Hence, their ignorance about the scattering and concretion of cosmic energy in its metaphysical aspects, their division about Darwin's theories, their uncertainty about the degree of conscious life in separate elements, and, as a necessity, the scornful rejection of every phenomenon outside their own stated conditions, and the very idea of worlds of semi-intelligent if not intellectual forces at work in hidden corners of Nature.

"To give you another practical illustration—we see a vast difference between the two qualities of two equal amounts of energy expended by two men, of whom one, let us suppose, is on his way to his daily quiet work, and another on his way to denounce a fellow-creature at the police station, while the men of science see none; and we—not they—see a specific difference between the energy in the motion of the wind and that of a revolving wheel. And why? Because every thought of man upon being evolved passes into the inner world, and becomes an active entity by associating itself, coalescing we might term it, with an elemental—that is to say, with one of the semi-intelligent forces of the kingdoms. It survives as an active intelligence—a creature of the mind's begetting—for a longer or shorter period proportionate with the original intensity of the cerebral action which generated it. Thus, a good thought is perpetuated as an active, beneficient power, an evil one as a maleficent demon. And so man is continually peopling his current in space with a world of his own, crowded with the offsprings of his fancies, desires, impulses, and passions; a current which re-acts upon any sensitive or nervous organization which comes in contact with it, in proportion to its dynamic intensity.

"The Buddhist calls this his 'Skandha'; the Hindu gives it the name of 'Karma.' The adept evolves these shapes consciously; other men throw them off unconsciously. The adept, to be successful and preserve his power, must dwell in solitude, and more or less within his own soul. Still less does exact science perceive that while the building ant, the busy bee, the nidificant bird, accumulates each in its own humble way as much cosmic energy in its potential form as a Haydn, a Plato, or a ploughman turning his furrow, in theirs; the hunter who kills game for his pleasure or profit, or the positivist who applies his intellect to proving that $+ \times + =$ —, are wasting and scattering energy no less than the tiger which springs upon its prey. They all rob Nature instead of enriching her, and will all, in the degree of their intelligence, find themselves accountable.

"Exact experimental science has nothing to do with morality, virtue, philanthropy—therefore, can make no claim upon our help until it blends itself with metaphysics. Being but a cold classification of facts outside man, and existing before and after him, her domain of usefulness ceases for us at the outer boundary of these facts; and whatever the inferences and results for humanity from the materials acquired by her method, she little cares. Therefore, as our sphere lies entirely outside hers—as far as the path of *Uranus* is outside the Earth's—we distinctly refuse to be broken on any wheel of her construction. Heat is but a mode of motion to her, and motion develops heat, but why the mechanical motion of the revolving wheel should be metaphysically of a higher value than the heat into which it is gradually transformed she has yet to discover.

"The philosophical and transcendental (hence absurd) notion of the mediæval Theosophists that the final progress of human labour, aided by the incessant discoveries of man, must one day culminate in a process which, in imitation of the Sun's energy—in its capacity as a direct motor—shall result in the evolution of nutritious food out of inorganic matter, is unthinkable for men of science. Were the sun, the great nourishing father of our planetary system, to hatch granite chickens out of a boulder 'under test conditions' to-morrow, they (the men of science) would accept it as a scientific fact without wasting a regret that the fowls were not alive so as to feed the hungry and the starving. But let a *shaberon* cross the Himalayas in a time of famine and multiply sacks of rice for the perishing multitudes—as he could—and your magistrates and collectors would probably lodge him in jail to make him confess what granary he had robbed. This is exact science and your realistic world. And though, as you say, you are impressed by the vast extent of the world's ignorance on every subject, which you pertinently designate as a 'few palpable facts collected and roughly generalized, and a technical jargon invented to hide man's ignorance of all that lies behind these facts,' and though you speak of your faith in the infinite possibilities of Nature, yet you are content to spend your life in a work which aids only that same exact science. . . .

———————•———————

"Of your several questions we will first discuss, if you please, the one relating to the presumed failure of the 'Fraternity' to 'leave any mark upon the history of the world.'* They ought, you think, to have been able, with their extraordinary advantages, to have 'gathered into their schools a considerable portion of the more enlightened minds of every race.' How do you know they have made no such mark? Are you acquainted with their efforts, successes, and failures? Have you any dock upon which to arraign them? How could your world collect proofs of the doings of men who have sedulously kept closed every possible door of approach by which the inquisitive could spy upon them? The prime condition of their success was that they should never be supervised or obstructed. What they have done they know; all that those outside their circle could perceive was results, the causes of which were

---

* This Mahatma letter is repeatedly drawn upon by Wm. Q. Judge in his writings. This particular passage appears in the first chapter of *The Ocean of Theosophy.*—Eds.

masked from view. To account for these results, men have, in different ages, invented theories of the interposition of gods, special providences, fates, the benign or hostile influence of the stars. There never was a time, within or before the so-called historical period, when our predecessors were not moulding events and 'making history,' the facts of which were subsquently and invariably distorted by historians to suit contemporary prejudices. Are you quite sure that the visible heroic figures in the successive dramas were not often but their puppets? We never pretended to be able to draw nations in the mass to this or that crisis in spite of the general drift of the world's cosmic relations. The cycles must run their rounds. Periods of mental and moral light and darkness succeed each other as day does night. The major and minor yugas must be accomplished according to the established order of things. And we, borne along on the mighty tide, can only modify and direct some of its minor currents. If we had the powers of the imaginary Personal God, and the universal and immutable laws were but toys to play with, then, indeed, might we have created conditions that would have turned this earth into an arcadia for lofty souls. But having to deal with an immutable law, being ourselves its creatures, we have had to do what we could, and rest thankful.

"There have been times when 'a considerable portion of enlightened minds' were taught in our schools. Such times there were in India, Persia, Egypt, Greece, and Rome. But, as I remarked in a letter to Mr. Sinnett, the adept is the efflorescence of his age, and comparatively few ever appear in a single century. Earth is the battle-ground of moral no less than of physical forces, and the boisterousness of animal passion, under the stimulus of the rude energies of the lower group of etheric agents, always tends to quench spirituality. What else could one expect of men so nearly related to the lower kingdom from which they evolved? True, also, our numbers are just now diminishing, but this is because, as I have said, we are of the human race, subject to its cyclic impulse, and powerless to turn that back upon itself. Can you turn the Gunga of the Brahmaputra back to its source; can you even dam it so that its piled-up waters will not overflow the banks? No; but you may draw the stream partly into canals, and utilize its hydraulic power for the good of mankind. So we, who cannot stop the world from going in its destined direction, are yet able to divert some part of its energy into useful channels. Think of us as demi-gods, and my explanation will not satisfy you; view us as simple men—perhaps a little wiser as the result of special study—and it ought to answer your objection.

" 'What good,' you say, 'is to be attained for my fellows and myself (the two are inseparable) by these occult sciences?' When the natives see that an interest is taken by the English, and even by some high officials in India, in their ancestral science and philosophies, they will themselves take openly to their study. And when they come to realize that the old 'divine' phenomena were not miracles, but scientific effects, superstition will abate. Thus, the greatest evil that now oppresses and retards the revival of Indian civilization will in time disappear. The present tendency of education is to make them materialistic and root out spirituality. With a proper understanding of what their ancestors meant by their writings and teachings, education would become a blessing, whereas now it is often a curse. At present the non-educated, as much as the learned natives, regard the English as too prejudiced, because of their Christian religion and modern science, to care to understand them or their traditions. They mutually hate and mistrust each other. This changed attitude towards the older philosophy, would influence the native princes and wealthy men to endow normal schools for the education of the pundits; and old MSS., hitherto buried out of reach of the Europeans, would again come to light, and with them the key to much of that which was hidden for ages from the popular understanding, for which your skeptical Sanscritists do not care, which your religious missionaries do not *dare,* to understand. Science would gain much, humanity everything. Under the stimulus of the Anglo-Indian Theosophical Society, we might in time see another golden age of Sanscrit literature. . . .

"If we look at Ceylon we shall see the most scholarly priests combining, under the lead of the Theosophical Society, in a new exegesis of Buddhistic philosophy; and at Galle, on the 15th of September, a secular Theosophical School for the teaching of the Singhalese youth opened with an attendance of over three hundred scholars; an example about to be imitated at three other points in that island. If the Theosophical Society, 'as at present constituted,' has indeed no 'real vitality,' and yet in its modest way has done so much practical good, how much greater results might not be anticipated from a body organized upon the better plan you could suggest?

"These same causes that are materializing the Hindu mind are equally affecting all Western thought. Education enthrones skepticism, but imprisons spirituality. You can do immense good by helping to give the Western nations a secure basis upon which to reconstruct their crumbling faith. And what they need is the evidence that Asiatic psychology alone supplies. Give this, and you will confer happiness of mind on thousands. The era of blind faith is gone; that of inquiry is here. Inquiry that only unmasks errors, without discovering anything upon which the soul can build, will but make iconoclasts. Iconoclasm, from its very destructiveness, can give nothing; it can only raze. But man cannot rest satisfied with bare negation. Agnosticism is but a temporary halt. This is the moment to guide the recurrent impulse which must soon come, and which will push the age towards extreme atheism, or drag it back to extreme sacerdotalism, if it is not led to the primitive soul-satisfying philosophy of the Aryans.

"He who observes what is going on to-day, on the one hand among the Catholics, who are breeding miracles as fast as the white ants do their young, on the other among the free-thinkers, who are converting, by masses, into Agnostics—will see the drift of things. The age is revelling at a debauch of phenomena. The same marvels that the spiritualists quote in opposition to the dogmas of eternal perdition and atonement, the Catholics swarm to witness as proof of their faith in miracles. The skeptics make game of both. All are blind and there is no one to lead them. You and your colleagues may help to furnish the materials for a needed universal religious philosophy—one impregnable to scientific assault, because itself the finality of absolute science; and a religion that is indeed worthy of the name, since it includes the relations of man physical to man psychical, and of the two to all that is above and below them. Is not this worth a slight sacrifice? And if, after reflection, you should decide to enter this new career, let it be known that your society is no miracle-mongering or banqueting club, nor specially given to the study of phenomenalism. Its chief aim is to extirpate current superstitions and skepticism, and from long-sealed ancient fountains to draw the proof that man may shape his own future destiny, and know for a certainty that he can live hereafter, if he only wills, and that all 'phenomena' are but manifestations of natural law, to try to comprehend which is the duty of every intelligent being."

NOTES "FROM MADAME"

[A clue to one of the more obscure of Theosophical subjects
—the meanings of Avatar and Jivanmukta—was found in the
manuscript notebooks left by Countess Constance Wachmeister,
who served H.P.B. devotedly during her stay in Europe, while
writing the *Secret Doctrine*. In one of these notebooks, hand-
written in ink, is an item labeled "From Madame"—indicating
that the words are H.P.B.'s although whether a copy of something written or the record of a conversation is not disclosed.
The material is headed "The Meaning of Jivanmukta" and is reprinted with a minimum of editing. Another of the notes "From
Madame" of value to students is also included here with a few
minor corrections.—Eds.]

THE MEANING OF JIVANMUKTA

A distinction has to be made between an "Incarnation" and an
"Avatar." Krishna, Sita (perhaps Rama, Tsong-kha-pa too) and
Sankaracharya are Avatars, not Incarnations. Gautama Buddha
was an incarnation, not an Avatar. The term *Jivanmukta* is to be
applied only to *Avatar purushas* who are not born of flesh, of no
Mother's womb. But Buddha and other Saviors as well as Mahatmas, Occultists and ordinary men incarnate; that is to say, they
are born of flesh, of a Mother's womb. Those who pass through the
womb must all, in a comparatively short time, say 10 or 7 months
rather, pass through the whole course of evolution, even physically
from mineral to vegetable to animal, and animal to man. Then,
after being born on earth as a child, they must go through school
training, learn grammar, language, philosophy, and even go
through chelaship, various initiations, etc. All these are accomplished by a Buddha far more easily, far sooner, and to far greater
perfection than others. Such is the secret of the grand universal
law of repetition.

An *Avatar purusha* has not to go through any of these things;
he has not to pass through the ten days' ordeal that Buddha went
through. An *Avatari* just begins from where he left off. An *Avatari*
had become a *Jivanmukta* at the last incarnation in which he had
to be born of a Mother. For such an *Avatari* there is no more in-

carnation at all, though according to the requirements of cyclic laws and of humanity's welfare, he might become several times, again and again, an *Avatar purusha*. The Avatars are not to be regarded as incarnations. In the same way, an Initiate or a Mahatma (like Mah-ji of Benares and others) who enters the body of another and lives in it has not on that occasion or on that account to pass through the Vikaras or awful changes in the womb, nor through the ordeals of chelaship and initiations which he had before gone through. But if afterwards that Initiate or Mahatma has to be born and to incarnate, then he must pass through the whole course of his past progress in a nutshell again. This is why I said that a Jivanmukta in any of his Avatars has to repeat no past training whatsoever. If an Avatar chooses for the sake of humanity to incarnate again, then he has to pass through the whole path once trodden, for he allows himself to fall into the ocean of incarnation, and it is not soon that he can again become an avatar.

———————•———————

How is it that our eyes see a thousand things every hour and still impress our "consciousness" with only a few of these things? How is it that every hour a thousand thoughts pass through our lower mind, while only a few of them we say are "unconscious?" What does this "consciousness" mean? This "consciousness" is simply our emotional nature, our fourth principle.

Suppose I have *now* a certain set of emotions, a certain portion of my fourth principle is more active than the remaining portion. If at that time my eyes mechanically look at certain things, and if these things do not contain at that time the same set of emotions that are agitating me—that is, if those things that my eyes are set upon are not animated or agitated powerfully by elementals or forces or gods corresponding to my present emotions—then I am said to be not impressed by those things thus seen. I say I am not conscious of them, I am not interested in them, I paid no attention to them. But if those things, on the other hand, be agitated more or less powerfully by some or all of the same emotions, then I more or less become conscious or impressed by what the eyes saw. You see a tree, and yet you say you did not take notice of many things about it. I say I saw you, but did not observe something in or about you. This is the secret of the matter. This is the law of attraction.

Similarly a number of thoughts *pass now* through my lower mind. If those thoughts have not in them the same emotions that agitate at present in my fourth principle, then I am said not to have cognized these thoughts. How remarkable that the fourth principle, which is just the center of all our nature, the very middle of all our seven principles, three above and three below, should be the keynote to all attractions, pleasures and pain.

INDEX
ALPHABETICAL

after 241   vision at time of 246 (and fn)

Deity
impersonal and absolute principle 62-4 a Unity 89   the unknown, abstract, and its phenomenal vehicle 196-97 extra-cosmical is impossible 257-58

Demiurgus
corresponds to Dhyan Chohans and Iswara 55

Desire
essential to get rid of inward 42-3   in relation to occultism 137-42   as opposed to will 194

Destiny
defined 57-8

Devachan (see Devachanee)
delusion of individuality 21   not a place but monads diffused through space 22 26fn   monad has tone of personal essence and only one state of consciousness in 24-5   what it is and its necessity 26-7   Western ideas of post mortem contrasted with 27 ridiculousness of post mortem corporeal or astral association 31   degrees in rupa and arupa states 32-3   elaboration of knowledge begun in life, never dull 98-9   personal consciousness purified before merging with monad in 100 lasts generally 1500 years 170 248-50 Karana Sarira assimilates spiritual essence of previous life during 205   no soul returns to earthlife during 236 moral and spiritual activities in 242 described and discussed 242-47

Devachanee(s)
thoughts and feelings of, can be learned by adept 18   intercourse between two, an illusion 21   does not descend to earth but may be linked by spiritual love 22-3 25-6 33 ignorant of suffering of loved one in Avitchi 26   experiences rupa and arupa states 32-3   personal ties and relationships may be exhausted 33-4   thoughts of, never dull 98-9 spirit of living may in dream reach 100

Devotion
the Self is object of true 253

Dharma (see Duty)
vehicle of seventh principle 54

Dhyan Chohan(s)
aggregate cosmic intelligence resulting from evolution 55   assist victims of accidental death but not living ego 239

Dogma
use of phrases without idea creates 131

Dreams
occultist's and scientist's concepts of 19-21   states of sleep and 213-16 219

Duty
to family and country in Vision of Scipio 176-83   path to divine wisdom is in 223   real means of progress 226-34   importance of mental state in performing 253-55

Dweller of Threshold
seven things secure victory in struggle with 226-27   family defects most important element in 232   form assumed by, dependent on four conditions 234-35

Earth
trinity within can be unified only on 260fn

Education
lack of aim in modern 156   modern, enthrones skepticism and imprisons spirituality 296-97

Ego
instruments of 154-55   method of, in establishing relation with external objects 155-56   to recognize true, must eliminate false 191   ray of Universal Mind 208   and personal ego in accidental deaths 239-40   personal experiences of, in Devachan 244   no devachan when death is premature 246

Elementals
half-blind forces of nature 87-88   active forces and correlations of fire, water, earth and air 108   "temperament" and immunity to burns indicate abnormal amount of fire-elementals 109-10   guard avenues of ideal world from trespass 214   every thought coalesces with an 293